CRITICAL APPROACHES TO DEATH, DYING AND BEREAVEMENT

This book is the first of its kind to examine key topics in death, dying, and bereavement through a critical lens, highlighting how the understanding and experience of death can vary considerably based on social, cultural, historical, political, and medical contexts. It looks at the complex ways in which death and dying are managed, from the political level down to end-of-life care, and the inequalities that surround and impact experiences of death, dying, and bereavement.

Readers are introduced to key theories, such as medicalisation, as well as contemporary issues, such as social movements, pandemics, and assisted dying. The book stresses how death is not only a biological process or event but rather shaped by a range of intersecting factors. Issues of inequalities in health, inequities in support, and intersectional analyses are brought to the fore, and each chapter is dedicated to an issue that has interdisciplinary resonance, thus showcasing the wider socio-cultural and political factors that impact this time of life.

This book is valuable reading for scholars in thanatology and death studies, and for those in related fields such as sociology of health, medical and social anthropology, and interdisciplinary social science courses.

Erica Borgstrom is Professor of Medical Anthropology at The Open University in the United Kingdom. She leads Open Thanatology, The Open University's interdisciplinary research group for the study and education of death, dying, loss, and grief across the life course, and is co-editor-in-chief for the interdisciplinary journal *Mortality* and Bristol University Press book series *Death and Culture*.

Renske Visser is a post-doctoral researcher at the University of Oulu in Finland. She runs the blog *Dead Good Reading* (www.deadgoodreading.com) featuring books about death, dying, and loss. She also co-hosts *The Death Studies Podcast*. She was previously the administrator for the Association for the Study of Death and Society (ASDS).

Critical Approaches to Health

The Routledge *Critical Approaches to Health* series aims to present critical, inter-disciplinary books around psychological, social and cultural issues related to health. Each volume in the series provides a critical approach to a particular issue or important topic, and is of interest and relevance to students and practitioners across the social sciences. The series is produced in association with the International Society of Critical Health Psychology (ISCHP).

Series Editors: Kerry Chamberlain & Antonia Lyons

Titles in the series:

Migration and Health
Critical Perspectives
Heide Castañeda

Rethinking Global Health
Frameworks of Power
Rochelle A. Burgess

Medical Humanities
Ethics, Aesthetics, Politics
Alan Bleakley

Making Mental Health
A Global History
Elizabeth Roberts-Pedersen

Critical Approaches to Death, Dying and Bereavement
Erica Borgstrom and Renske Visser

For more information about this series, please visit: www.routledge.com/Critical-Approaches-to-Health/book-series/CRITHEA

CRITICAL APPROACHES TO DEATH, DYING AND BEREAVEMENT

Erica Borgstrom and Renske Visser

Routledge
Taylor & Francis Group

LONDON AND NEW YORK

Designed cover image: Getty Images @ Tara Moore

First published 2025
by Routledge
4 Park Square, Milton Park, Abingdon, Oxon OX14 4RN

and by Routledge
605 Third Avenue, New York, NY 10158

Routledge is an imprint of the Taylor & Francis Group, an informa business

British Library Cataloguing-in-Publication Data
A catalogue record for this book is available from the British Library

Library of Congress Cataloging-in-Publication Data
Names: Borgstrom, Erica, author. | Visser, Renske, author.
Title: Critical approaches to death, dying and bereavement / Erica Borgstrom and Renske Visser.
Description: Abingdon, Oxon ; New York : Routledge, 2025. |
Series: Critical approaches to health series | Includes bibliographical references and index.
Identifiers: LCCN 2024019816 (print) | LCCN 2024019817 (ebook) |
ISBN 9781032330617 (hardback) | ISBN 9781032330624 (paperback) |
ISBN 9781003318002 (ebook)
Subjects: LCSH: Death–Social aspects. | Bereavement. | Terminal care.
Classification: LCC HQ1073 .B68 2025 (print) | LCC HQ1073 (ebook) |
DDC 306.9–dc23/eng/20240522
LC record available at https://lccn.loc.gov/2024019816
LC ebook record available at https://lccn.loc.gov/2024019817

ISBN: 9781032330617 (hbk)
ISBN: 9781032330624 (pbk)
ISBN: 9781003318002 (ebk)

DOI: 10.4324/9781003318002

Typeset in Times New Roman
by Newgen Publishing UK

CONTENTS

TABLES

SERIES EDITORS' PREFACE

Critical Approaches to Health

Health is a major issue for people all around the world, and is fundamental to individual well-being, personal achievement and satisfaction, as well as to families, communities, and societies. It is also embedded in social notions of participation and citizenship. Much has been written about health, from a variety of perspectives and disciplines, but a lot of this writing takes a biomedical and positivist approach to health matters, neglecting the historical, social, and cultural contexts and environments within which health is experienced, understood, and practiced. We developed this series of books to offer critical social science perspectives on important, relevant, and timely health topics.

The *Critical Approaches to Health* series provides new writing on health by presenting books that offer critical, interdisciplinary, and theoretical writing about health, where matters of health are framed quite broadly. The series seeks to include books ranging across important health matters, including general health-related issues (such as gender and media), major social issues for health (such as medicalisation, obesity, and palliative care), particular health concerns (such as pain, doctor–patient interaction, health services, and health technologies), particular health problems (such as diabetes, autoimmune disease, and medically unexplained illness), or health for specific groups of people (such as the health of migrants, the homeless, and the aged), or combinations of these.

The series seeks above all to promote critical thought about health matters. By critical, we mean going beyond the critique of the topic and work in the field, to more general considerations of power and benefit, and in particular, to addressing concerns about whose understandings and interests are upheld and whose are marginalised by the approaches, findings, and practices in these various domains of health. Such critical agendas involve reflections on what constitutes knowledge, how it is created, and how it is used. Accordingly, critical approaches consider epistemological and theoretical positioning, as well as issues of methodology and practice, and seek to examine how health is enmeshed within broader social relations and structures. Books within this series take up this challenge and seek to provide new insights and understandings by applying a critical agenda to their topics. Explore the previous 17 books in the series at www.routledge.com/Critical-Approaches-to-Health/book-series/CRITHEA.

In this book, *Critical Approaches to Death, Dying and Bereavement*, Erica Borgstrom and Renske Visser discuss a comprehensive range of matters surrounding death and processes around dying, taking a critical perspective throughout. Their discussions are shaped by theoretical considerations of power, governmentality, biopolitics, necropolitics, grievability, and disenfranchisement. The book successfully covers a wide range of death and dying topics from many angles and in many contexts, delivering insightful overviews and critical considerations.

Mortality statistics, and the history of counting deaths, show how these practices have shaped, and continue to shape, understandings of death and responses to it. The interests of governments and states in death, and the power dynamics implicated through the policies they construct around death, are discussed to show how these are implicated in our understandings of death, dying, and afterlife. The social and political responses to death and dying in mass death events – epidemics, pandemics, and disasters – are considered, and the authors engagingly argue how these responses shape the treatment of the dying, the dead, and the mourning. The ways in which death is socially and culturally managed is further illustrated by contrasting specific social movements, including Black Lives Matter and the Death Positive Movement. This shows dissatisfactions with how death occurs and is treated, and how social movements have challenged the power that others have over lives. The authors also examine and critically consider the increasing medicalisation of death and end-of-life care, illustrating how people have sought to resist, adapt to, or complement medical involvement in processes of dying, and how this can foster inequality and inequity.

A critical consideration of palliative care and the hospice movement documents the rise of professionalisation in care for the dying and an increased focus on dying well, but also highlights variability and inequality in access to hospice care. The ethical, moral, and social implications of death are examined through the ongoing debates about assisted dying in contexts where it is and is not legalised and how these shape inequalities in access. Using case studies of maternal mortality and dying in prison, the authors document disenfranchised dying and show how people who are marginalised in life can also be marginalised in death. The authors then discuss the dead body and explore how it raises social and cultural issues around practices of body disposal, and how such practices are shaped by changing technologies and socio-cultural understandings. In the final section of the book, normative understandings and practices of grieving are examined to show how grief is a social rather than an individual issue. The authors critique the ways in which the psy-disciplines have come to dominate cultural and popular understanding of grieving. Death by suicide is discussed, and the authors critique the utility of suicide risk factors and research into suicide that fails to consider the complexity and multi-factored issues underlying the phenomenon.

This book therefore provides a wide-ranging and inclusive treatment of major issues that surround death, dying, and bereavement, offering an in-depth discussion on each within separate chapters. The book takes a critical perspective on these matters throughout, drawing on key theoretical concepts, to show how our understandings of death, dying, and grieving are shaped in ways that advantage some and marginalise others. The book draws together, amplifies and challenges scholarship on death and dying. It offers an engaging, compelling read, and makes a great addition to the *Critical Approaches to Health* series.

Kerry Chamberlain and Antonia Lyons

ACKNOWLEDGEMENTS

Whilst books are written by authors, their creation involves a vital network of support. We would like to thank the series editors – Kerry Chamberlain and Antonia Lyons – and the publisher's editor, Lucy Kennedy, for their ongoing encouragement, feedback, and guidance. We are also grateful for our partners, families, and colleagues who have enabled us to write this book over the past few years, supplying tea, advice, or proof-reading, or relaxation when needed. Erica would also like to thank the singer Anthony Ramos, whose album 'Love and Lies' was the soundtrack to many of her writing sessions. We would also like to acknowledge the contributions we each brought to this project, from ideas to patience and guidance, as well as shared laughter and mutual understanding.

PROLOGUE

This book fits within the *Critical Approaches to Health* series by positioning death, dying, and bereavement as something that can be understood as 'health matters' whilst also showcasing the wider socio-cultural and political factors that impact this time of life and indeed may impact when and how a person dies. This does not mean that we see death (and grief) as inherently medical or health matters, but that they can be and are made to be in different contexts. Many of the chapter topics have been selected to bring issues of inequalities in health, inequities in support/ care, and intersectional analyses to the fore. Much like the social determinants of health (WHO, 2008), the social determinants of death are worthy of consideration (Sallnow et al., 2022a).

Every book is influenced by the time it was written and the people who wrote it. This prologue provides some information about the context surrounding this book. Ideas for this book were formulated in 2021, with writing occurring predominately in 2022 and 2023 and editing in 2024.

Many global events preceding and during this time influenced the choice of topics and the writing processes. We felt that these events signified a need for a critical approach to death, dying, and grief – not just to help people understand such events but to recognise the centrality of death and grief and the frequent inequalities that are present within such events. One of the primary contexts of this book has been the COVID-19 pandemic, which, for many, brought mortality and grief to the fore; Erica Borgstrom has researched and written several pieces about death and COVID-19 (Borgstrom, Sowden, and Sellman, 2024; Driessen, Borgstrom, and Cohn, 2021b; Selman, Sowden, and Borgstrom, 2021; Sowden, Borgstrom, and Selman, 2021; Borgstrom and Mallon, 2021; Jones, Schnitzler, and

Borgstrom, 2022). Other significant events include the death of George Floyd and the resurgence of the Black Lives Matter movement; the death of Queen Elizabeth II in the United Kingdom; wars in Ukraine and Gaza, as well as civil wars in several African countries (including in Sudan and the Congo); multiple earthquakes and other disasters with significant death tolls. Political strategies often not identified directly with death also changed. For example, in the United Kingdom, political stances limiting the right to protest, anti-immigration, and reductions in welfare and support for unhoused people all impact how people can live and die.

Both authors are trained anthropologists, identifying themselves within broader social sciences and death studies. This training has attuned us to question the supposed 'givenness' of such events and policies, and our often interdisciplinary work has led us to draw on a range of literature in this book to help make sense of the topics at hand. Of course, this book is only one example of how such topics can be approached, but we hope that the book will encourage readers to think critically. We have not sought to specify what people should think but rather to give examples of how one can think about death and its aftermath and the contexts that shape these.

The book has been influenced by our work and life outside of writing this manuscript, including the academic environments we are in and our positionality. For Renske Visser, this includes postdoctoral research on prisons, reviewing books about death for her blog (www.deadgoodreading.com/), and interviewing a wide range of people as part of the Death Studies Podcast (co-hosted with Beth Michael-Fox; https://thedeathstudiespodcast.com/). During some of the writing period, Visser has been an independent scholar but she has recently returned to academia part time at the University of Oulu, and holds part-time non-academic jobs. Erica Borgstrom is employed within The Open University in the United Kingdom. Her primary teaching and research focuses on end-of-life care issues. In particular, she works on policy and organisation of care and how these impact how people experience the end of life and bereavement. Borgstrom is also a journal and book series editor and research group lead, exposing her to various international perspectives in death studies and related fields. Both Visser and Borgstrom are white women in their 30s; Borgstrom is a mother to two young children. Both Visser and Borgstrom are multilingual and living in countries they were not born in. Visser has links to the Netherlands, the United Kingdom, and Finland; Borgstrom has links to the United States, the United Kingdom, and Germany. These elements of life have influenced the writing of the book in different ways, including what topics we have individually focused on and, at times, the selection of case examples.

In this preface, we also wanted to note how events in our personal lives have impacted the crafting of this book. We have both experienced significant 'life events' summed up here as a collection rather than individually attributable: bereavements, job changes, house moves, and new medical diagnoses. At times, this has meant we needed to disengage with the topics enclosed in this book. At other times, the personal events provided another perspective to think with. We have more in the introduction about the self and engaging with these topics to share some of our practices and to reflect on how it may be for readers as they engage with the different topics within the book.

1

INTRODUCTION

Introduction

Whilst death is often cited as being a universal human experience, how death is understood, managed, and indeed experienced varies incredibly based on social, cultural, historical, political, and medical contexts. This book provides an insight into some of the complex ways in which death and dying are managed (from the political level down to end-of-life care) and the inequalities that surround and impact experiences of death, dying, and bereavement in a range of contexts. It does this by applying a critical lens to key topics in the field of death studies, covering the spectrum of dying, death, bereavement, and the wider aftermath of a death.

Death studies (also known as thanatology) is an interdisciplinary field which has grown since the 1950s, with particular growth as an international field since the 1990s. Whilst it is beyond the scope of this introduction to provide an extensive history and synthesis of the field, there are several aspects that are useful to highlight as they have informed the development of the book.[1] Death and dying are social processes, and how they have occurred and been made sense of over time and space differs (Thompson and Cox, 2017; Kellehear, 2008). Some have focused on the social practices, particularly rituals and the role of religion (Davies, 2017) or biomedicine and capitalism (e.g. Kaufman, 2005, 2015; Timmermans, 2013) that shape death experiences. Others have focused on media (Seale, 2004) or politics and normalised violence (Haritaworn, Kuntsman, and Posocco, 2014), noting the different cultural scripts and death worlds available and imposed on people. Importantly, within the field, there is a never-ending curiosity and questioning about death, what leads up to it and its aftermath: it and responses to death are not assumed to be value-neutral or without consequence. This book adds to the field of death studies by bringing together a unique range of topics not typically

DOI: 10.4324/9781003318002-1

collectively covered in monographs and rooting them in questions of power, inequity, and social context.

Critical Approaches to Death, Dying, and Bereavement

There are several ways to critically approach topics linked to death; here, we outline the key ways in which we have done this within the book. Critical theory 'refers to a family of theories that aim at a critique and transformation of society by integrating normative perspectives with empirically informed analysis of society's conflicts, contradictions, and tendencies' (Celikates and Flynn, 2023), and there are many strands of critical theory. For us, we have engaged critically with the topics under study by attending to several crucial elements and questioning: structure, power, and social norms. Much of death studies, and indeed theories within the field, are often concerned with the deaths and experiences of those in Western countries or risk exoticising practices in the Global South. We appreciate that many of the readers of this book are likely to reside in North America, Europe, and Australasia. As such, we have included examples from these places and reflect how policies and cultural movements from these countries have influenced other geographical areas. As part of our critical approach, we interrogate the examples to consider the impact of how death is experienced and the potential (un)intended consequences of policies, medicine, and even therapy for how people live, die, and grieve. Below is an introduction to the key concepts that are used throughout the book that inform our critical approach.

Power: Governmentality, Biopolitics, and Necropolitics

The concepts discussed here arise from and/or are inspired by the work of Michel Foucault, a French philosopher who wrote in the latter half of the 20th century. In his work, he sought to articulate how European rulers in the early modern period (1400–1700s) began to turn their attention to the well-being of the people living within their territories as a way to make the population more docile and productive rather than focus solely on preservation of their sovereignty (Foucault, 2003). Others, such as Agamben, have argued that this political interest in people's lives and well-being can be traced to ancient civilisations (Prozorov, 2022). Meloni, for example, challenges Foucault's historical framing and argues that one should view Foucault's ideas as hypotheses rather than actual accounts of how history unfolded (Meloni, 2023).[2] Consequently, for this chapter, it is less important to focus on when this shift started and more important to attend to the ways in which the concepts can help understand the contemporary world.

   Foucault coined the term biopolitics to refer to a style of government that regulated people through a particular form of power, which he referred to as 'biopower'. He used these terms to 'draw attention to a mode of power, which operates through the administration of life itself – meaning bodies (both individually and collectively), their health, sanitation, procreation, mental and physical capacities, and so forth' (Mckee, 2009). Foucault notes that this was made possible partly through advances in understanding and practising medicine, which enabled specific ways of knowing the body and acting upon it. For some, biopolitics and biopower are interpreted as 'good' or 'positive' by attending to improving health and living conditions in an effort to 'make live' or foster life (Prozorov, 2013).

Biopower is exercised through governmentality, another word developed by Foucault. He uses it to describe the wide range of techniques used to govern people's conduct. Foucault described two primary forms of governmentality: disciplinary power and control mechanisms (Prozorov, 2013). These forms of governmentality can include policy or law which seeks to change people's behaviour and punish certain behaviours, such as financial fines for not wearing a seat belt in a car. Control mechanisms may be more subtle and seek to shape what people can and cannot do, encouraging people to adopt particular 'desirable' behaviours, such as healthy eating guidance with messaging about reducing one's mortality risk. Both of these techniques ultimately exert a form of power over individuals and collectives in a way that shapes life and death.

Drawing on these concepts but bringing death more to the fore, Achille Mbembe coined the terms necropower and necropolitics to emphasise 'how life in a biopolitical frame is always already subjugated to and determined by the power of death' (Mbembe 2003 and 2019 cited in Quinan and Thiele, 2020). Key in this shift is a focus on 'who must live and who is let or must die', showcasing how certain lives are invested in through necropolitics, and others are 'systematically marked for death' (Quinan and Thiele, 2020, 3). Importantly, biopolitics and necropolitics are not opposites – one does not exclusively focus on life and the other on death. Braidotti (2013, 122) notes that they are 'two sides of the same coin'; they both point to how power shapes lives, dying, and death and enable an analysis of the politics of life and death both within a state and on a global or planetary scale.

Mbembe also focuses on the role of racism and colonialism in necropolitics and the racialised manifestation of an unequal world (Mbembe, 2019; Sumba, 2021). For example, Mbembe (2019, 38) notes that there are deaths to which 'nobody feels any obligation to respond', as certain groups of people (referred to in his text as 'the Other') are consistently dehumanised. An example of this is demonstrated in the queer necropolitics literature, which demonstrate that deaths un-responded to (e.g. those that are 'ignored') can alert one to other forms of discrimination that influence who is 'let [to] die' as a consequence of politics and governmentality, such as trans people (see later). Authors who use the concept of necropolitics often attend to issues of colonisation, globalisation, and discrimination (DeBoom, 2022; Banerjee, 2006; Afeworki Abay and Wechuli, 2022), including how governmentality in one state could be influenced by the policies of other countries, either through force (e.g. through colonial rule) or through the management and performance politics of international relations. Consequently, it is not only Global North countries that exercise necropower but rather it is a form of power possible within all states.

Marginalised Loss: Grievability and Disenfranchised Grief

Whilst loss may be thought of as universal, what kinds of losses can be grieved within a particular time and place is not. Instead, social norms and social discourses, for example, can influence what kinds of losses are deemed to be legitimate. They can also inform what kinds of behaviours, practices, and rituals are considered acceptable. It is, therefore, important to attend to the power, relationships, and structures that underlie such norms.

Butler uses the term grievability to point out that whose life is considered mournable – or something that can and should be grieved – is not to be assumed but is culturally and socially contextual (Butler, 2009). As Judith Butler (2004, x–xi) notes

> Some lives are grievable, and others are not; the differential allocation of grievability that decides what kind of subject must be grieved, and which kind of subject must not, operates to produce and maintain certain exclusionary conceptions of who is normatively human: what counts as a livable life and a grievable death?

Their work demonstrates that media portrayals can reshape what lives and deaths are considered worthy, including casting some groups of people as an existential threat rather than seeing them as people in need of support. Necropolitics and grievablity are useful to consider together, as we do in several chapters in this book.

If a particular type of death or group of people is deemed ungrievable, this can lead to people feeling their grief is disenfranchised. Doka defines disenfranchised grief 'as grief that results when a person experiences a significant loss and the resultant grief is not openly acknowledged, socially validated, or publicly mourned' (Doka, 2014). This means that even if they are feeling grief (or emotions in the aftermath of a death or loss), this is not recognised by others around them. Therefore, they may receive no sympathy, social support, and/or care from professionals linked to their grief. Several chapters in the book engage with the concept of disenfranchised grief and Chapter 9 extends this concept to consider disenfranchised dying.

Tending to the Self

As death studies scholars, we are aware of how working and engaging with this field of work can impact us personally. We have both written about our emotional experiences (Visser, 2017) as well as how there can be a blur between personal and professional boundaries when encountering death in our social lives and through work (Borgstrom and Ellis, 2021). We have used this knowledge about our past experiences of working in death studies to inform the book writing and share some insights to enable readers to reflect on how they engage with the text.

Before embarking on writing this book, we discussed these issues and what topics we felt we could work on in a way that would not unduly impact our overall well-being. For example, for Erica, engaging extensively with literature on suicide is something that she knows can be emotionally difficult for her; Renske was able to lead on the chapter, although she had to pace the writing of this as she found it harrowing experiencing a disconnect between quantitative research and very intense personal narratives. We also devised strategies that could support us as we did the work for this book: how to keep ourselves well when researching, reading, drafting, and editing. This included taking breaks (sometimes extended) from the material, crafting writing environments that felt comfortable and supportive (including plenty of tea, music, and chocolate), and ensuring we had outlets for how the topics were whirling around in our heads. This included talking to others, moving our bodies, and engaging in art practices. Sometimes, life and death 'got in the way' or complicated our relationship with the book; for instance, we both experienced bereavement during the project. We, therefore, also had to practice self-compassion, aiming for the ultimate continuity of the project rather than focusing on consistent productivity. We believe that rendering these experiences and practices visible is important, especially in books like this that seek to adopt a critical lens and where positionality is paramount for understanding how this is done.

We encourage readers to think about how they will tend to themselves when engaging with the materials of the book and how it may impact how they relate with others, their communities, and society. This does not mean that we automatically assume the entire book is difficult or that the materials are specifically sensitive. Rather, we acknowledge that there can be a wide range of things for anyone that may make reading about death, dying, loss, grief, and bereavement – as well as disease, war, and imprisonment – upsetting, challenging, perplexing, and maybe even motivating. For some readers, this may mean choosing which chapters to read and we have aimed for chapters to be able to be read independently, noting links between chapters where applicable. Individual chapters do not have content warnings; we have highlighted the topic level content below. For others, it could be about pacing the reading, taking regular breaks, or ensuring a space between engaging with the text and one's next activity to enable some processing time. It may mean devising a set of actions – to turn reading into applied change. It may also mean finding a 'reading spot' that works for you – maybe it needs to be cosy or busy or have a space to draw or move as you read. The book covers a range of topics, and how you engage with each may also differ; you may find yourself re-evaluating personal experiences or world events. This may be the first time you've encountered a book where the authors ask you to think about how you may look after yourself as and after you read. We do not intend this to be patronising; we see it as an extension of an awareness that knowledge production is not neutral and, therefore, one's engagement with knowledge is also influenced by the self, social and environmental contexts, historical events, and can later impact one and their experiences.

Structure of the Book

The book has 11 chapters that are divided into three sections, plus introductory pieces and a conclusion. This introduction sets out the approach to the book and key concepts used throughout the book. The preface provides contextual information on what has influenced and impacted the crafting of this book. As book co-authors, we have each taken a lead in individual chapters, with Erica Borgstrom leading the chapters in approximately the first half of the book and Renske Visser leading the writing of the last five chapters.

Section I (Population, Politics, and Society) has four chapters. These chapters tend to macro-level factors that shape understandings, practices, and experiences of death, dying, and loss. The first of the chapters in this section is about mortality statistics (Chapter 2), critically examining these statistics and how they shape knowledge and policy about death. The next chapter (Chapter 3) examines policy more specifically, considering how policies directly and indirectly shape people's deaths and mortality risks using several examples, including end-of-life care and migration. Chapter 4 then turns to examine mass death events (including pandemics, natural disasters, and war), reflecting on how social worlds are confronted by and remade by such events. This is evidenced through the reshaping of practices around caring for the dead and post-death rituals, including memorialisation. The last chapter in this section (Chapter 5) turns to another way such practices can be reshaped by exploring social movements (Black Lives Matter and the Death Positive Movement), which seek to actively change social contexts, discourses, and practices around dying, death and grief. This chapter looks at how grief can be a motivating and/or central factor for social movements, attending to social injustices that impact who dies and how their deaths are treated.

Section II (Dying) has four chapters concentrating on understanding dying as a situated social process. Whilst the chapters do not focus on micro-practices, they illustrate how there are different forms of dying, each influenced by social, political, medical, and legal frameworks and contexts. The first chapter in this section explores the concept of medicalisation (Chapter 6). The following chapter focuses specifically on the Modern Hospice Movement (Chapter 7), with links to palliative and end-of-life care. This chapter also covers the concept of good death as an idealised form of dying. Chapter 8 discusses assisted dying, providing a discussion of the terminology and variance in practices, as well as different legal, moral, and social stances on these. The last chapter in this section (Chapter 9) looks at examples of disenfranchised dying, which contrasts the kinds of dying outlined in the previous chapters. The focus of this chapter is deaths in prison and maternal mortality. Whilst the concept of disenfranchised grief is more common in the literature, we show that it is possible to think about how people can be deprived of the ideals of good death and choice through structural violence and indifference.

The book's final section has three chapters concerned with the aftermath of death. The first chapter provides examples of disposal practices, including burial and cremation, and considers issues around space limitations and sustainability (Chapter 10). The next chapter is dedicated to grief theories and therapies (Chapter 11). It outlines the notion of grief and how, in the academic literature, approaches to grief have been rooted in psychological theories and therapies of the individual self. The final chapter continues with the theme of grief, examining it in the context of suicide (Chapter 12). It demonstrates how particular kinds of death may mean those who are bereaved experience stigma and/or disenfranchised grief and how the bereaved may become a site for intervention to prevent further death.

Notes

1 Readers of this book may also be interested in the collated reference list provided by The Collective for Radical Death Studies: www.radicaldeathstudies.com/genre.
2 Within different disciplines, there is also pushback on the dominance of Foucault and his theorisations for thinking about power. Part of this is a critique of his behaviour (Valls et al., 2022) and part acknowledges a wider range of scholars who have theorised state power (Lukes, 2005; Gunew, 2013). Since this chapter discusses necropolitics, it was necessary to refer to the linage of Foucault's thinking that influenced the concept.

SECTION I

Populations, Politics, and Society

2

THINKING WITH AND BEYOND
MORTALITY STATISTICS

Introduction

Counting deaths – how many people have died and from what – has been a
mechanism for understanding the health of society for hundreds of years. Along
with counting births, marriages, and other 'life events', such measurements
are referred to as vital statistics. Specifically, mortality statistics are a way of
numerically representing information about death in relation to populations. There
are different kinds of mortality statistics that researchers, public health officials,
and policymakers use. Mortality statistics can include the frequency of death,
measures of specific causes of death, and average life expectancy. This chapter
provides an overview of the history of mortality statistics, examples of several
types of mortality statistics, information about practices of collecting this data,
and a reflection on how counting death shapes understandings of death and the
relationship between death and human action.

Mortality statistics can have many uses. This can include governmental social
planning, comparing and determining healthcare services and in epidemiological
studies to understand disease. For example, within the United Kingdom, the Office
for National Statistics regularly uses mortality statistics to produce estimates
and population projections. Similar actions are taken by many countries and
can complement census activities. The United Nations Statistics Division has a
database of country profiles and links to their national offices, demonstrating that
collecting, managing, and monitoring a wide range of statistics is not limited to
high-income countries (United Nations Statistics Division, n.d.).

National and local government agencies, in turn, use these estimates and
projections to plan infrastructure such as schools and care provision. Crowcroft
and Majeed (2001) summarised the significant uses of mortality statistics from

DOI: 10.4324/9781003318002-3

a healthcare perspective as: monitoring the health of the population, making international comparisons of health and healthcare services, determining health service priorities, allocating healthcare resources, performing health needs assessment, assessing the effect of health service interventions, and monitoring the quality of clinical care in clinical governance programmes. These multiple uses signify that mortality statistics can be used to influence a range of economic, political and social actions. It is, therefore, important to understand how they are created and used, which will be the focus of this chapter.

History of Mortality Statistics

Mortality statistics are related to the broader field of epidemiology, which is the study of the distribution and determinants of health-related events in populations. Epidemiology is considered the 'basic science of public health' (Savitz, Poole, and Miller, 1999; Jackson, 2003). The 'birth' of epidemiology is often attributed to John Snow, who reportedly figured out that a cholera outbreak in 1854 in London was linked to a shared communal water pump. On the one hand, the history of epidemiology is remembered as detailed data collection within an area that led to an act that stops the spread of disease. Alternatively, there is a more layered way of understanding this field, which acknowledges that it rests on particular ways of knowing and othering.

John Graunt is accredited to analysing causes of death as early as 1662 (Lancaster, 1990). He used weekly records of deaths and burials to determine cause of death in London, mainly focusing on plagues and the irregularity of deaths attributed to plague compared with diseases such as tuberculosis, which led him to believe there were environmental causes (Morabia, 2013). One of the significant elements about what Graunt did was that his analysis required aggregating people into populations for group comparisons. The notion of population is central to mortality statistics. It requires that individuals are aggregated into groups based on specific characteristics – such as age, sex, race, or geographical location. While these characteristics are often treated as 'facts', sociologically, they are social constructs, and how a person is categorised into one or another cannot be automatically assumed. How epidemiologists categorise people reflects 'social constructions of identity and biases that exist in broader society' (Morabia, 2013), which can cause people to be misrepresented and overlook people's lived experiences. Social constructions have important implications for inclusivity in data collection and can negatively impact how meaningful epidemiological analysis can be in various contexts. Moreover, there is a power that is exerted when someone is determining what a population is – who is in or out – especially when considering how epidemiology can be used to invest resources in different populations.

The question of 'who' is counted also extends to how epidemiological data has been created over the past centuries. This is less about how populations are defined and shifts the focus to what knowledge can be gained from individual bodies. Downs has illustrated that before Snow's research about cholera in London, medical men involved in colonialism during the 17th and 18th centuries were noticing patterns of disease and death within slave ships, prisons, and port towns (Downs, 2021) and that such observations influenced actions like increased ventilation in slave quarters to ensure more would survive the journey (thereby increasing profits).

Within philosophy, history, and social sciences, academics have drawn attention to how governments exert power over life and death, often noting how this links to notions of control and governance. Foucault argued that since the 7th century, the state became 'managers of life and survival' (Foucault, 1978, 1:137), where they intervened on both individual and population levels. He argued that part of their ability to do this is through counting, monitoring, and intervening on vital characteristics and life events, such as birth, sexuality, and illness. Rabinow and Rose (2006, 195) take this further and argue that in contemporary states, biopower 'entails a relation between "letting die" ... and making live', noting the political decisions that influence what aspects of life are intervened upon and the technologies used to do this. This is relevant to the issue of mortality statistics in that one can examine how governments create, use, or reject the data to inform action that may prevent certain types of death.

Creating and Understanding Mortality Statistics

Mortality statistics are a range of numerical ways of describing how many people are dying, with the potential to describe this by cause, age, gender, location, or other attribution. This section first outlines some of the more commonly used mortality statistics and how they are calculated. It then gives examples of how people make sense of such statistics, including using non-numerical ways to represent data.

Types of Mortality Statistics

Crude death rates – typically referred to as just 'death rate' or 'mortality rate' – reflect the total number of deaths counted in the specified time interval per either typically 1,000 or 100,000 people. An example of how it is calculated is

$$\frac{\text{Total number of deaths with a population}}{\text{Total size of the population}} \times 1,000$$

For example, if there were a city with 675 deaths in one year when the population was 198,430, the equation would look like the one below, and the crude death rate would be 3.40 for the city:

$$\frac{675}{198,430} \times 1,000 = 3.40$$

TABLE 2.1 Mortality Rates in Different Countries

Country	Crude death rate (deaths per 1,000 population)
Bulgaria	15.382
Lesotho	14.327
Serbia	13.172
Italy	10.474
Democratic People's Republic of Korea	9.057
Angola	8.332
Myanmar	8.19
Papua New Guinea	7.451
Pakistan	6.983
Iceland	6.699
Ethiopia	6.662
Honduras	4.437
Saudi Arabia	3.47
Qatar	1.191

Source: Collated using United Nations Data provided by UNData for 2015–2020.[1]

This is the type of data used by organisations, like the World Health Organization (WHO) and the United Nations, to compare the general health of populations internationally, such as in Table 2.1. This table includes some countries with the highest and lowest crude death rates between 2015 and 2020. Note how Lesotho has a mortality rate of 14.327, whilst Qatar has a mortality rate of 1.191. This means that there is a higher frequency of death within the general population in Lesotho than in Qatar; however, such rates do not tell us why there are differences, what people are dying from or if death is equally distributed amongst the population. Some countries like Serbia may be expected to have a higher death rate due to having a population that proportionally has more older people in it. However, age distribution within a population does not clarify all differences between countries when considering death rates.

Cause-specific death rates are calculated in a similar manner as crude death rates but only focusing on the number of deaths that are attributed to a specific cause, such as cancer or road traffic accidents. Within a country, these rates can be used to understand the 'leading causes of death'. This is typically represented per 100,000. The way cause-specific death rates are presented differs from 'leading causes of death' lists, which may provide the total number of deaths attributed to a specific cause, so caution should be used when evaluating and comparing data. A more critical discussion about the cause of death is given in the later sections. Table 2.2 provides cause-specific death rates for the Bahamas using 2019 data for all ages and all sexes. In this country, there is a mixture of communicable, non-communicable, and injury-related incidents that cause the most deaths. If this data is separated by sex, the top ten causes are distributed differently, with the rate of

TABLE 2.2 Cause-Specific Death Rates for Top Eight Causes of Death in the Bahamas for Both Sexes and All Ages

Cause of death	Classification of cause	Deaths per 1,000,000 population
Ischaemic heart disease	Non-communicable disease	85.79
Stroke	Non-communicable disease	57.53
Diabetes mellitus	Non-communicable disease	39.43
Interpersonal violence	Injuries	38.12
HIV/AIDS	Communicable, maternal, perinatal and nutritional conditions	34.47
Kidney disease	Non-communicable disease	30.75
Lower respiratory infections	Communicable, maternal, perinatal and nutritional conditions	25.05
Breast cancer	Non-communicable disease	17.69

Source: Collated using data from WHO (2019).[2]

interpersonal violence rising to 68.26 for males and not featuring on the top ten list for cause of death for females.

Several kinds of mortality statistics seek to understand death rates amongst different groups within a population; the examples discussed here are not exhaustive but are given for illustrative purposes. For example, age-specific mortality rates refer to the number of deaths in that age group calculated in proportion to the total number of people in that age group. An example of this is the infant mortality rate, which measures the number of deaths among children who are under one year old in relation to the number of live births reported during the same period, typically represented per 1,000; neonatal mortality rates only cover up to 28 days instead of year. Infant mortality rates are considered to reflect the health of the mother and infant during pregnancy and the first year thereafter; their health is typically impacted by access to prenatal and postnatal care, the prevalence of certain health behaviours during pregnancy (e.g. smoking), early childhood immunisation, sanitation and infection control within society (Lesson 3: Measures of Risk, CDC Archive, n.d.). Maternal mortality ratio (MMR) – the number of deaths attributed to pregnancy-related causes in relation to live births – is used to understand the risk of maternal death relative to the number of live births, and according to the WHO,[3] 'essentially captures the risk of death in a single pregnancy or a single live birth'. Mortality rates can also be calculated in ways that are specific to sex, race, or combinations of cause, age, sex and/or race.

Life expectancy is another form of statistics that relates to death – it is used to reflect the average period that a person may expect to live, or in other words, the average age of death in a population. Life expectancies, like death rates, are used

TABLE 2.3 Life Expectancy in Senegal Between 1960 and 2020

Year	Life expectancy (in years)
1960	38
1970	39
1980	49
1990	57
2000	58
2010	64
2020	68

Source: Compiled from data available via the World Bank.[4]

TABLE 2.4 Life Expectancy Across Countries in 2020

Country	Life expectancy (in years)
Hong Kong	85
Austria	81
Costa Rica	80
Egypt	72
India	70
Burkina Faso	62
South Sudan	58
World average	73

Source: Compiled from data available via the World Bank.[5]

for assessing population health; there is a correlation between life expectancy and national income, with wealthier countries typically having a higher life expectancy (Miladinov, 2020). Table 2.3 illustrates how life expectancy has changed in Senegal over seven decades; Table 2.4 shows life expectancy in several different countries based on 2020 data to demonstrate the variability in life expectancy. Globally, the average life expectancy has more than doubled since 1900 ('Life Expectancy – Our World in Data', n.d.), although since the COVID-19 pandemic, life expectancy has decreased in over 25 countries considered as upper-middle and high-income countries which typically have higher life expectancies, including Russia, the United States, Bulgaria, and Spain (Islam et al., 2021).

The phrase 'excess mortality' has been in the popular press since 2020 to provide an understanding of the impact of coronavirus and social interventions during the pandemic (Edouard et al., 2020). Excess mortality is an analysis that examines the number of deaths during a set period and compares this to the estimated number of deaths expected based on models of previous years' death rates during that period. Excess mortality is used to calculate death from all causes above what would be expected under 'normal' circumstances.

Making Sense of the Numbers

As outlined previously, mortality statistics are based on mathematical equations. Research has found that people find it easier to understand statistics in the form of 1 per 10 (known as natural frequency format), for example, rather than 10% (presented as a probability; Frontiers, 2018). Mortality statistics are often presented in natural frequency format, such as 1 in 1,000. However, it can be difficult for people to make sense of this, visualising groupings of 1,000.

Some people find it useful to compare statistics to put the numbers into perspective. For example, during the COVID-19 pandemic, a Twitter/X account (@Covid_scale)[6] regularly compared the contemporary death total in the United States with other events that resulted in mass deaths, such as hurricanes, mass shootings, and aircraft accidents. For example, on 1 September 2022, the account compared the to-date death record in the United Sates (1,071,420 people had to that date had deaths attributed to COVID) with the equivalence of 583 Hurricane Katrinas (in which over 1,800 died). The reason this can be helpful is that it provides a sense of scale – it is something smaller or larger than something else. The strategic use of 'tragic events' by this social media account was deliberate to entice people to recognise the death rates from COVID-19 as significant and on a scale with or beyond previous events deemed to be 'tragic' within the country. Another example is when two different causes of death are compared with one another to imply relative risk (i.e. one is more likely to happen than another). For example, within the United States, the National Safety Council has a lifetime odds of death comparison chart[7](: this is the likelihood that someone may die from this cause throughout their entire lifetime. They produce this table to help people understand the relative risk to inform their behaviours: for example, someone is more likely to die from an opioid overdose (1 in 67) than from fire or smoke (1 in 1,450). It is important to note that these are not individualised odds, and one's likelihood of dying one way or another is influenced by the activities the person partakes in and the contexts of their living.

Data visualisation is the use of images to represent the abstracted numerical information visually, and there are entire books dedicated to the topic (e.g. *Visualizing Mortality Dynamics in the Lexis Diagram* by Rau et al., 2018). This could be through graphs or diagrams, including infographics. Data visualisation has become increasingly available with greater access to computers to create graphics. However, the practice of using visuals to represent abstract information is older than the practice of generating mortality statistics (Few, 2007). Yet, whilst images may help people communicate about data, visual communication still requires understanding how to use and make sense of the visuals. Moreover, when these visuals are embedded in texts – such as online news platforms – unless they have a reliable alternative description, they are not fully accessible to readers who may rely on screen-reading software (Marriott et al., 2021). Lastly, research has shown that how people receive data and visualisations depends on their emotional engagements with data, including trust and frustration (Kennedy and Hill, 2018). Therefore, it is important to remember when creating and interpreting visual representations that one considers how the information is being conveyed and the social context in which it is consumed.

To add visualisation of death rates, artists have also engaged with a range of means to make the scale of death tangible. A famous example of this is 'The Shoes on the Danube Promenade', created by Can Togay and Gyula Pauer in Budapest: 60 pairs of old-fashioned shoes sculpted to the ground to represent the Hungarian Jews who were forced to remove their shoes before being shot and discarded in a river during 1944–1945. Artists may use large spaces to help viewers appreciate the scale of an event, such as the use of 650,000 white flags in front of the National Mall in the United States in 2021 by Suzanne Brennan Fistenberg to represent those who had died from COVID-19. Another example is the UK AIDS Memorial Quilt, which was inspired by an American quilt made in the late 1980s and measures over 430 m^2 to memorialise over 350 people who died during the 1980s from HIV/AIDS (Heath, n.d.). Such projects not only help creators remember the individuals who have died but also connect with viewers in emotional and empathetic ways.

However, there are some critiques about whether data visualisation can convey or increase empathy when it comes to death, including mass death events (Zer-Aviv, 2015). Some types of data visualisation or art may be seen to trivialise the death(s) by further abstracting the information or turning death data into an economic commodity. Research on the combination of storytelling and visual communication indicated that whilst storytelling may foster understanding of data, empathy may not be effectively elicited through these methods (Zer-Aviv, 2015).

Lastly, people are not necessarily good at understanding the link between mortality statistics and their own personal risk. For example, research done in the United States has shown that although more people die from heart disease than cancer, more people believe cancer is more common and that their personal risk of cancer is higher (Scheideler et al., 2017). One explanation for such mismatches is the framing effect. This is where how information is presented influences the importance people place on it. In the case of the risk of cancer, long-standing societal reactions to cancer as a 'death sentence' and the public knowledge about there being multiple types of cancer can influence people's perception of their individual likelihood of dying from cancer compared with other causes (Martin, 1994). Therefore, it is essential to consider how information is presented, as this can influence how people make sense of it.

Sources and Quality of Data

'Public health experts say that what counts is what you count' (Wendland, 2018). The data used by countries and international organisations, like the WHO, to create mortality statistics come from a range of sources. Typically, they are understood to be estimates or provisional, as there are new births and deaths every minute. Sources of data include but are not limited to national vital (birth and death) registration data, United Nations partners and projects, and scientific studies. While the preferred measure for epidemiologists and policymakers for creating mortality data is through death registration systems, in many countries such registers do not exist. So, mortality data is collected through retrospective measurement in household surveys (Mathers and Boerma, 2010). To meet the targets of the Sustainable Development Goals, countries are expected to regularly report on 'child mortality, maternal mortality and mortality due to non-communicable diseases, suicide, pollution, road traffic injuries, homicide, natural disasters and conflict' (WHO, 2020, 4).

Within the United Kingdom, the Office for National Statistics (ONS) collects data in adherence with a Code of Practice for Statistics aimed at improving the standard of data and being free from political interference (UK Statistics Authority, 2018). It focuses on the trustworthiness, quality, and value of the statistics and the processes involved in their collection and dissemination. Similarly, the WHO states that mortality estimates used in their report are documented by following the Guidelines for Accurate and Transparent Health Estimates Reporting (WHO, 2020). For the creation of WHO reports, for data up to 2020, only 67 out of 183 Member States had data that met WHO inclusion criteria from vital registration systems (WHO, 2020, 7). That these organisations must declare that they adhere to this standard illustrates that historically and internationally, one could not reliably presume that those who produce and promote mortality statistics were doing so in a way that is transparent and of benefit to the populations measured.

Researchers in Australia have developed a ten-step guide for assessing the quality of mortality data AbouZahr et al. (2010).The ten steps begin with preparing tabulations of deaths by age, sex, and cause (step 1) before reviewing crude deaths rates (step 2). Steps 3–5 involve reviewing age and sex-specific death rates, age distribution, and child mortality rates. Steps 6–10 involve reviewing a range of aspects linked to major causes of death and ill-defined causes; steps 6–10 are not recommended for data sets that do not use the International Statistical Classification of Disease and Related Health Problems (ICD) standards. The ten-step guide is aimed at data collectors and practitioners to help them self-diagnose issues with data consistency and plausibility. Completing the steps enables one to analyse mortality data's internal validity and coherence.

The maternal mortality ratio (MMR) is the measure of the number of women dying of pregnancy-related causes per 100,000 live births, indicating the population-level risk of maternal death. Despite known persistent measurement challenges, it is used internationally as a key measure, including as part of the Sustainable Development Goals. Storeng and Béhague (2014) noted that one expert in this field claims that maternal mortality data are widely presumed 'guilty until proven innocent' (Storeng and Béhague, 2014). This is because most countries with high levels of maternal mortality lack robust registration systems, and other methods, such as surveys, produce imprecise measures (Storeng and Béhague,

2017). Reflecting on how maternal mortality measurements have been deployed politically, by philanthropic donors, and within research communities, Storeng and Béhague critique the money spent on developing techniques of estimation instead of investing in local infrastructure, most notably in Africa.

Cause of Death and Issues of Categorisation

First, whilst international guidelines are designed to enable standardisation about how to count deaths and generate mortality statistics, what is considered a cause of death needs to be determined. How this is determined varies across time and place. In some countries, where the cause of death is unclear, a specialist doctor – such as a medical examiner or coroner – undertakes a post-mortem examination (e.g. autopsy) of the body to look for signs of disease and injury. Here, they are looking for biological causes of death. One study in Norway found that over 60% of listed causes of death were changed on death certificates following autopsy findings, with over 30% of cases needing to be given a different ICD code (Alfsen and Maehlen, 2012). Another study using data from Australia about 'natural deaths' found that the presumed cause of death, as initially noted on the death certificate, was completely wrong following autopsy results (Seuc et al., 2018). This indicates that what is initially listed on a death certificate, including what people may presume to be the most likely cause of death, given someone's history and means of death, can be contested, and changed. Cause of death may also not be listed on death certificates in circumstances where populations are relatively underserved by medical services and/or someone has died at home. Because of this, the One Million Death Study was set up in India since the cause of approximately 10 million annual deaths in the country was unknown before 2002. They have subsequently used verbal autopsies with family members to understand circumstances before death to ascertain likely causes of death (Gomes et al., 2017).

Moreover, on some death certificates, there may be multiple causes listed. Listing multiple causes is considered to be important due to ageing populations and multimorbidity (Moreno-Betancur et al., 2017), and analysis can be done to understand links between causes of death on a population level (Seuc et al., 2018). There is a distinction made between contributing cause – what is presumed to be the most immediate cause directly leading to death – and underlying causes, which are the diseases or injuries considered to have initiated the train of events leading directly to death or the circumstances of the accident or violence that created the fatal injury (WHO definition)[8]. In this way, the forms encourage a hierarchical listing of causes.

There have been debates about what can be legitimately listed as the direct cause; for example, 'old age' can only be listed in very limited circumstances and doing so may risk unrecording morbidities (Adhiyaman and Chattopadhyay, 2021). Another contested cause has been COVID-19, where the distinction of 'dying from' or 'dying with' evoked political debate and memes mocking how the cause of death is attributed (R.C. Keller, 2022). It is important to realise how the cause of death can be mobilised outside of medical and epidemiological studies, as it shows us how different lives and deaths are valued.

Lastly, the ICD codes and ways of talking about causes of death are biomedical. They do not account for other ways of understanding and knowing how people can die. Across the world, different cultures attribute death to spirits and supernatural intervention. For example, Evans-Pritchard tells of how among the Azande of Central Africa, a collapsing granary resulting in the death of a person is attributed to witchcraft (Evans-Pritchard, 1976); the cause of death is linked to spirits rather than being framed as a biological event or accident. More recently, one study in Australia took the ICD codes for the top causes of death for Aboriginal people in the 1980s and worked with local communities to reclassify these as being of land, body, or spirit (Weeramanthri and Plummer, 1994). The focus of this was to understand death from an Aboriginal worldview perspective and to put focus on intersectoral understanding and what the community wanted to do to address causes. Another example is of Hmong refugees in the United States who experience what doctors have considered stress and trauma but are understood within their cultural group to be suffering from spiritual possession and die suddenly in their sleep (Tobin and Friedman, 1983). This indicates that there are differing categorisations by which people understand the world and death within and that these different worldviews may not be readily captured or comparable to biomedical and technical ways of categorising death.

International Statistical Classification of Disease and Related Health Problems

Vital registration systems can record a range of data about the individual and their death. This can include their age, sex, race, and cause of death. The WHO has an International Statistical Classification of Disease and Related Health Problems (known as ICD) to standardise how the cause of disease and death is reported, including being used on death certificates. It was first developed in the 19th century and is now in its 11th version (ICD-11), which has been a legally mandated health data standard in use since 2022 (Harrison, Chang, and Fan, 2021). Previous versions of the ICD had over 14,000 different codes, and WHO Member States could modify the list of codes to suit their needs better as new diseases emerge; ICD-11 has 17,000 diagnostic categories and has been designed to reduce local variants (Harrison, Chang, and Fan, 2021). Although all Member States have committed to using ICD-11, WHO reports that it is not yet fully implemented globally, with no data about implementation available for large parts of Western and Central Africa (Harrison, Chang, and Fan, 2021). Some of the limitations to implementation are around training in using the coding system and suitable technology to store the data (e.g. computers with internet connections). The ICD, therefore, is an example of an infrastructure for health (and death) information to enable certain ways of collecting and comparing mortality statistics; however, its ability to fully standardise reporting of deaths is not universal.

The ICD codes have a biomedical ontology – which means it is concerned with names and structures of items that are considered within the domain of biological and medical understandings of the body and the relationships between these items (Harrison, Chang, and Fan, 2021). As new diseases are identified and studied, new codes can be created for ICD, as was done for COVID-19 and related variants. However, inputting the data into information systems relies heavily on humans making sense of an event and recording it in line with these codes. It can be challenging to use the classification when there is little or no information about an individual (Kurbasic et al., 2008). Cause of death may not be immediately apparent, which may result in a post-mortem examination where available or deaths being classified with 'causes not known' (Rukmini, 2021). When it comes to 'mental disorders', clinicians may differ in terms of their preference to code using ICD, which is considered by some to allow for more clinical discretion with diagnosis, or the Diagnostic and Statistical Manual of Mental Disorders (DSM), because of its links with research-oriented classifications (Tyrer, 2014). These examples illustrate that even when there are 'agreed' international standards for understanding human conditions, how they are deployed can vary, affecting the data used in mortality statistics and comparisons.

Relationship Between Mortality Statistics and Action

Mortality statistics may be used in media and public health campaigns to promote specific behaviours. For example, statistics about lung cancer or skin cancer are used in campaigns in several countries to encourage the reduction of smoking and increase sunscreen use, respectively. Whilst these statistics may be about cancer rates rather than death rates, they are circulating in societies where cancer is often associated with death (even if rates of surviving cancer have increased due to medical intervention; e.g. Clarke and Everest, 2006). Moreover, these messages – like 'smoking causes 9 out of 10 lung cancers' – on plain packaging of cigarettes are coupled with messaging about death, such as 'smoking kills'. In Ireland, public health messaging about smoking states that '1 in every two smokers will die from a tobacco-related disease' ('Smoking Facts and Figures – HSE.Ie', n.d.). The statistics are often aggregated so that it is easier for the average consumer to relate the statement to themselves (i.e. 'I could be the one in the two people'). These campaigns and messaging intend to use the statistics to encourage people to change their behaviours. However, various evaluations of the effectiveness of such messaging have shown mixed results, with current evidence suggesting that the use of pictorial messaging and immediate information on how to create behaviour change is more effective than information about harm alone ('Smoking Facts and Figures – HSE.Ie', n.d.).

Information on the cause of death can be useful for epidemiological studies. For example, the links between asbestos exposure and lung cancer helped identify workplace risks. In 2018, a global report noted that asbestos causes an estimated 255,000 deaths annually, with work-related exposure responsible for 233,000 of those deaths; it is a leading cause of lung cancer (Furuya et al., 2018). Despite the links being made between asbestos and cancer back in the 1930s, just over 50 countries currently ban the substance (Furuya et al., 2018). Where asbestos bans have been implemented, like in Sweden and the Netherlands, there is some indication that rates of specific types of lung cancer are going down (Furuya et al., 2018). This is an example of where mortality statistics can be used to encourage political action and how ongoing monitoring of mortality statistics can be used to indicate if such interventions are having the intended effect.

Importantly, it should not be assumed that media and governments align their focus on the causes of death based on frequency. While one may assume that what causes the most deaths should relatively receive the most attention and funding, this is not necessarily the case. Researchers focusing on the United States have demonstrated a mismatch between the top ten causes of death and what is focused on in the media, government legislation, and funding (Pilar et al., 2020). This is summarised in Table 2.5. The authors note that the largest misalignment is related to tobacco: it causes many deaths but receives relatively less media and policy attention. They suggest that this may be due to several reasons, such as established knowledge about tobacco's health effects. In contrast, other causes of death are less well understood, such as the political influence of the tobacco industry and the lack of awareness-raising events which focus attention on specific issues. This is useful to critically examine as a range of factors are at play, which are not always under the sole purview of politics, media, and/or medical practice.

TABLE 2.5 Top Ten Causes of Death: what are the topc causes according to different perspectives

Rank	Actual cause of death	Media presence: media cloud	Policy: bills passed	Government funding
1	Poor diet	Poor diet	Physical inactivity	Sexual behaviour
2	Tobacco	Motor vehicles	Poor diet	Illicit drug use
3	Toxic agents	Firearms	Illicit drug use	Microbial agents
4	Microbial agents	Illicit drug use	Toxic agents	Poor diet
5	Illicit drug use	Physical inactivity	Microbial agents	Alcohol
6	Alcohol	Microbial agents	Motor vehicles	Tobacco
7	Physical inactivity	Toxic agents	Sexual behaviour	Toxic agents
8	Firearms	Alcohol	Firearms	Physical inactivity
9	Motor vehicles	Sexual behaviour	Alcohol	Motor vehicles
10	Sexual behaviour	Tobacco	Tobacco	Firearms

Source: Adapted from Pilar et al. (2020) based on data from the United States from 2010 to 2019.

Using mortality statistics in public messaging, however, is not without unintended consequences. One concern is that the focus on numbers can desensitise people, providing a separation between the individuals who have died and those who consume the statistics (Kirby, Borgstrom, and MacArtney, 2020). Research in 2020 demonstrated that whilst death rates were widely reported in media during the early months of the COVID-19 pandemic, as death rates rose, people's anxiety decreased (Stevens, Oh, and Taylor, 2021). Desensitisation – a diminished emotional response to something after repeated exposure – can explain this; it is also a typical human response to the ongoing disaster (Easthope, 2022; Lowe, 2016). Zavattaro and colleagues (2021) have argued that how death rates for specific groups of people during the pandemic in the United States are discussed in the media and by politicians can also desensitise people, privileging a focus on deaths that impact economic value more than others and implying that some people are 'worthy' of death. In these ways, discussions about mortality statistics, whilst, on one hand, may be used to generate fear and concern, may also minimise the experiences of some groups of people.

Conclusion

Mortality statistics are frequently used in various contexts, for example, to compare death rates from different diseases or as a metric to compare countries. Yet counting deaths in this way is a relatively new practice, and processes have been designed to standardise how these statistics are collated both within and between countries. Whilst the United Nations notes that most countries have a national office of statistics (United Nations Statistics Division, n.d.), there is a disparity in terms of the financial investment provided to these offices, the impact of national politics on what topics are covered, and the relative volume of work the office can undertake. Whilst there are standardised practices, it is useful to remember that how the data is collected and managed can vary and thus complicate aggregated and comparing data from different countries.

The standardised practices can privilege a medical way of viewing the cause of death and can seem like they reduce human lives to a number. Mortality statistics, however, can be useful for epidemiological studies, to help identify policy intervention areas, and to raise public awareness to encourage behaviour change. Countries that are able to undertake analyses of mortality statistics are able to identify areas of public life to target for interventions and policy changes, and to generate measures to evaluate such interventions. Since national systems are not always adequate to enable such actions, there are calls to involve donors, non-governmental agencies, academic institutions and the private sector to further develop vital statistic systems internationally with the intention of improving health (AbouZahr et al., 2015).

As demonstrated in this chapter, a critical approach to mortality statistics considers the history of them and how they are generated. The capturing and use of mortality statistics is ultimately a practice that considers the creation of knowledge. Critical approaches therefore capture both what this knowledge is and examine the (un)intended consequence of using such information.

Notes

1 See www.who.int/data/gho/data/themes/mortality-and-global-health-estimates/ghe-leading-causes-of-death
2 See https://data.worldbank.org/indicator/SP.DYN.LE00.IN?locations=SN
3 www.who.int/data/gho/indicator-metadata-registry/imr-details/26
4 See https://data.worldbank.org/indicator/SP.DYN.LE00.IN?locations=SN
5 See https://twitter.com/COVID_Scale
6 For raw data, see https://data.un.org/Data.aspx?d=PopDiv&f=variableID%3A65.
7 See https://injuryfacts.nsc.org/all-injuries/preventable-death-overview/odds-of-dying/
8 See www.who.int/standards/classifications/classification-of-diseases/cause-of-death

3

POLICY AND DEATH

Introduction

Death is a matter that is of interest to states and the governments that provide the bureaucracy within states. That is because death impacts a wide range of issues that states seek to have some form of control or influence over, such as economic productivity, health, national security, and reproduction for population growth. Governments seek to either directly or indirectly shape how people live as well as when, how, and where people die.

One way governments do this is through creating and implementing policies. The term policy can be defined in many ways, but for this chapter, it is a set of guidelines or principles that define a set of decisions and/or actions. This means that policies do not always need to be formal laws to have an influence; this is particularly important when looking at policies that impact death and dying. For example, governments can propose policies that are predominantly about other areas of political oversight, such as income distribution and taxation, land access, and policing, that nevertheless influence people's mortality risk and impact how they live and die. Some policies are directly about death, such as China's policies about accidental deaths aimed to encourage local bureaucrats to reduce such deaths (Fisman and Wang, 2017) or manage mortality risks through behaviours, such as laws in many countries about the use of seat belts in cars to reduce risk of death in road traffic collisions. Some countries also have policies focusing on dying and end-of-life care, which is explored more later in this chapter. Lastly, as discussed later, state policies and (in)action can also adopt a stance that perceives certain groups of people as having lives that are less worthy of protection, such as anti-immigration policies that seek to reduce asylum-seeking. Therefore, when studying death and dying, policy should not be ignored.

DOI: 10.4324/9781003318002-4

Studying and making sense of policies is a multi-disciplinary field and can include, but is not limited to, political studies, law, gender studies, sociology, and anthropology. There are many different ways one can examine policy and the consequences, intended or unintended, of such policies. As a brief overview, here are three ways to think about policy in the context of death studies. First, one can examine policy documents and what is written in them. These tend to be the formal statements produced by governments or other organisations (such as medical organisations) with power over the issues they seek to influence with the policy. This can include law, policy statements, and guidelines. Studies of these documents may focus on the language, noting what and who is included or excluded, what values are promoted, and the intended impact (Javanparast, Anaf, and Tieman, 2022; Greenwood, 2023; Borgstrom, 2020). Second, research may seek to understand or improve policy implementation (Kinney et al., 2021; Byron and Hoskins, 2013; Adams, Scarneo, and Casa, 2017). Policy implementation is the process of people and organisations adopting, enacting, and implementing the guidelines, values, and behaviours outlined in a policy. It is not uncommon for there to be a 'policy–practice gap', and studies may seek to understand why this is so (Zolala et al., 2011; Borgstrom, Jordan, and Henry, 2022; Michel, 2020). Lastly, researchers can examine the impacts of policy and the effects policies may have on different people and their lives. This can include documenting the unintended consequences of a policy and/or measuring the impact of policy (e.g. see Cornelius, 2001; Chang, Chang, and Fan, 2020). There is, therefore, a wide range of ways in which policy and its impacts can be researched. Notably, a critical approach can be adopted in all of the ways outlined previously by attending to issues of power, questioning unequal impacts, and considering what kinds of living, dying, and death are promoted within them.

This chapter adopts a critical lens when examining policy. This is done by using several key concepts to understand how states and policies influence and seek to control issues of life and death. This includes governmentality, biopolitics, and necropolitics. The definitions of these are covered in Chapter 1. Using these concepts highlights where and how states are talking about or putting into practice things that determine who can live life in specific ways that promote their well-being, how policies can impact how people live and die, and how such power can be both explicit and implicit. To illustrate this, several examples are used. The chapter examines end-of-life care policies and considers how dying has been crafted as something with a specific policy focus. There are then two sections that discuss how policies not explicitly about death can impact how and when people die, including considering what lives are deemed worthy of being liveable and grievable. By attending to this range of topics, the chapter illustrates why politics – and policy specifically – matters in death studies and how adopting a critical lens when reviewing policies and their impacts enables one to appreciate this.

End-of-Life Care Policy: Crafting Dying as a Specific Policy Focus

Within the United Kingdom, the government has released several policies that focus on end-of-life care (EOLC), including stressing the importance of the provision of palliative and end-of-life care in law (Health and Care Act 2022, n.d.). The national End of Life Care Strategy (Department of Health, 2008) has been identified as the first of its kind internationally to focus explicitly on the care of dying persons (Economist Intelligence Unit, 2010). This section will illustrate how this UK policy creates dying as something that should be politically considered and the specific types of death and dying that are rendered within these policies. Moreover, it will consider how the values and practices promoted in the policy have 'travelled' to other contexts and the applicability of the policy in other countries.

First, how does the strategy discuss death and dying? The language used in the document refers to death predominately through the concept of 'end-of-life care' (EOLC). It describes EOLC as the holistic care of people, irrespective of diagnosis or age, as they approach the end of their lives (Department of Health, 2008). EOLC is informed by the history of palliative and hospice care within the United Kingdom (Seymour, 2012); the difference between these is discussed in Chapter 7. Consequently, drawing on values and practices in contemporary EOLC, the strategy has three underlying assumptions about death and dying within EOLC policy: (1) that as people die, they have needs; (2) that dying, and therefore these needs, can be anticipated and planned for; and (3) if these needs are not met, people cannot experience a 'good death'. Dying and death within EOLC are presumed to be something that can be foreseen and managed. The intention of the policy was that people identified as being near the end of life would receive supportive and clinically appropriate care that is in line with their personal preferences, irrespective of where they are being cared for or the time that needs arise (Borgstrom, 2016a).

But why has EOLC – and therefore dying – become something governments want to influence? Analysis of the policy documents and surrounding promotion and implementation can provide insight into this question (see Borgstrom, 2016a, 2015b for more details). For example, the strategy outlines several issues which are used to legitimise the need for the policy. First, it describes how demographic changes mean there is not only an ageing population which is likely to experience death after a period of chronic illness (which means dying is more likely to be foreseen) but also more people who are likely to die each year. Second, it outlines how people have unequal access to existing EOLC services. Therefore, there is a need for a national strategy to increase the availability of services and increase the quality of care people receive. The focus on people's health, well-being, and quality of life can be interpreted as a form of biopolitics.

Issues of governmentality are visible in terms of what changes the policy sought to achieve and the mechanisms – or techniques to use Foucault's term – outlined for this. Whilst there are many changes the policy wanted to create, this chapter focuses on the location of death. The strategy sought to change where people died – promoting deaths in a person's home as the most preferred and hospital as 'inappropriate' for most people at the end of life, even if statistically, most people die in them (Department of Health, 2008). In other words, it seeks to change structures and behaviours to enable more people to have a managed dying phase supported by care professionals but for this to be located in the home (Visser, 2017; Borgstrom, 2016a; Driessen, Borgstrom, and Cohn, 2021a). In the policy accounts, the place of death is entwined with assumed different types of care that people receive based on location, perceived personal autonomy of the dying person, and the impact on those around the dying person, especially their family. Therefore, the rationale within the strategy is that by focusing on location, several wider factors can be impacted and improved. Ultimately, the policy conflates 'home death' with 'good death' (Borgstrom, 2020).

In order to enable more people to die at home, the strategy promotes processes that encourage people to declare a preference for where they want to die (presumed within the policy to likely be home). The statement of preference enables certain actions within the healthcare system that can, in theory, reduce the use of hospitals. This is a form of control mechanism aimed to alter both the behaviour of individuals – documenting preferences through advance care planning – and systems. Coupled with this, implementing the strategy employed disciplinary power in the form of financial incentives to local healthcare systems based on metrics and uptake of practices linked to policy. Both of these techniques have been criticised (Wrigley, 2015; Borgstrom and Dekker, 2022; Borgstrom and Walter, 2015), and subsequent policy has adopted an approach that devolves power to local governing bodies rather than national ones (National Palliative and End of Life Care Partnership, 2021).

Nevertheless, the United Kingdom's EOLC policies and techniques supporting them have 'travelled' to other countries, both within Europe and beyond. Several reports have promoted the United Kingdom's policies by ranking EOLC internationally (Economist Intelligence Unit, 2010, 2015), which fuels an adoption of its way of framing death and dying in other contexts. Certain practices for managing the last few days of life – such as the Liverpool Care Pathway,[1] featured in the EOLC strategy – have been implemented in other contexts, including the Netherlands (Borgstrom and Dekker, 2022). Scholars and practitioners have begun to question the legitimacy of the wholesale adoption of EOLC policies internationally (Zaman et al., 2016), noting that doing so rarely considers local understandings of death and dying or local healthcare systems. Consequently, this raises questions about the dominance and power of particular (e.g. British or English) ways of 'doing dying' that can obfuscate a more pluralistic understanding of how dying can be experienced, supported, and/or managed through policy.

Lastly, whilst the End of Life Care Strategy is a clear example of how dying can be a policy issue, it is essential to note that only specific forms of dying and death are covered by the assumptions operating within EOLC. For example, assisted dying is explicitly not covered within the strategy and is deemed to be a separate policy issue, currently illegal in the United Kingdom, raising moral questions for society (Richards, 2016; see also Chapter 8). The EOLC strategy promotes a view that people who are dying after a period of chronic and/or identifiable life-limiting illness should receive high-quality care and achieve a 'good death'. In contrast, other known causes of death, such as from opioid addiction and overdose, are politically framed as moral issues of individual responsibility. So, whilst some forms of death and dying are facilitated, others are restricted or demonised by the same states and governments.

Necropolitics: Migration, Queerness, and War

As described earlier, necropolitics builds on the concept of biopolitics to emphasise how states, through their policies and actions, deem some lives as less worthy and 'let [people] die'. This generates contexts in which certain groups of people are subjugated to processes that exacerbate the potentiality for death. These consequences may not always be direct or intended, although, as illustrated in the examples mentioned later, this does not diminish their impact on people's lives, deaths, and even grief. Necropolitics can affect a wide and often intersectional range of people, and this chapter will focus on three examples to illustrate this: migration, war, and politics around queerness.

Migration – both historic and contemporary – is a topic that can be understood through necropolitics in terms of who is able to move, where, when, and how they move. Mbembe (2019, 10) discusses colonisation as a technology for regulating migratory practices from the early 16th century onwards. He describes how within the slave trade, colonialists viewed it as good for both the country people came from and where they arrived, as promoters of the slave trade conceived it as (forcibly) moving 'idle men and women' from African countries and training them to be more productive in their new locations (Antoine de Montchrestien cited by Mbembe, 2019, 10–11). This extraction of people, however, places them in regular danger of death – through undernourished sea voyages to physical punishment within plantations. It also created a way of thinking that promoted Othering – seeing the enslaved people as other than human – by treating them as a resource to be managed.

Contemporary migration policies are also Othering, and necropower is embedded in the structures of immigration and asylum apparatuses (Wilson et al., 2023). Australia, the United States, the United Kingdom, and countries in Europe have consistently promoted policies deemed to regulate who can immigrate into the state and increasingly openly adopt 'hostile' policies to deter asylum seekers (York, 2018; Goodfellow, 2019). Amnesty International (n.d.) define an asylum seeker as someone who 'has left their country and is seeking protection from persecution and serious human rights violations in another country, but who hasn't yet been legally recognised as a refugee and is waiting to receive a decision on their asylum claim. Seeking asylum is a human right'. In their ethnographic account of asylum seekers within the United States, Wilson et al. (2023) note that this form of migration brings multiple risks of injury and fatality, especially under hostile policies, that make border crossing less safe by diverting them through rough terrain, arming border patrol, under-providing healthcare in immigration detention centres, and deporting people to unsafe locations. The governmentality here is through techniques that seek to control how people access the border, which may, in turn, cause them to turn to 'illegal' methods of crossing and disciplinary punishment for not accessing formal routes or meeting strict asylum criteria. Politicians have even recognised the deadliness of their policy ('Radiolab Presents: Border Trilogy', 2018; US Border Patrol, 1994, cited in Wilson et al., 2023) showing a recognition of both the intended and 'unintended' deaths that arise from such policies. Despite attempts to reduce the 'flow' of migrants, there are questions about such policies' ability to deter or prevent such migration (Cornelius, 2004). Researchers have also noted similar issues with migration policies in Europe, with increasing numbers of people dying in the Mediterranean Sea (IOM, 2015). When someone dies during their asylum migration attempt, governments may imply that it was the individual's fault, often stressing the 'illegal' nature of their behaviour to migrate in this manner, rather than acknowledge how their necropower created conditions in which such deaths are not only possible but probable. Even if someone manages to migrate in such contexts, the health impact of the journey and/or detention is often un(der)recognised and under-supported, since access to health systems can be restrictive to migrants (Castañeda, 2022). Looking at migration through the lens of necropolitics allows an appreciation of how policies can have intended and unintended consequences that put certain people in situations that are more likely to impact their health and may result in their death.

Researchers have also used necropolitics to explain how queer people, through different policies and political actions, are made vulnerable and increases their mortality risk (Haritaworn, Kuntsman, and Posocco, 2014). On one hand, this can be quite explicit, with some countries having laws that physically punish people, including using the death penalty, for same-sex sexual activity. According to the Human Dignity Trust, '12 countries have jurisdictions in which the death penalty is imposed or at least a possibility for private, consensual same-sex sexual activity. At least 5 of these implement the death penalty – Iran, Northern Nigeria, Saudi Arabia, Somalia and Yemen – and the death penalty is a legal possibility in Afghanistan, Brunei, Mauritania, Pakistan, Qatar and UAE'.[2] This is an example of where governments determine that certain ways of living – and in this example, particular ways of being sexually active – should be directly punishable or have the threat of being punishable through death.

Even in places where queer people do not need to fear the death penalty for expressing their sexuality, they may still experience situations that put their lives at risk due to how policy impacts their lives. For example, several studies show that access to trans-specific healthcare, including gender-affirming treatments, serves as suicide prevention (Alasuutari et al., 2021). Anti-trans legislation, such as that being proposed in many parts of the United States, that limits, prevents, or even punishes those pursuing such treatments risks worsening people's mental health due to gender dysphoria and can be a factor in people's deaths. Similarly, such legislation can fuel anti-trans and anti-queer sentiments within society, placing queer people at greater risk of physical and emotional abuse and/or violence (E.A. Stanley, 2021). The notable deaths of trans people may also inspire social and political action in terms of how their deaths are mobilised in society afterwards, sometimes used to promote racist and xenophobic policies that can further marginalise people (Riley Snorton and Haritaworn, 2022). Therefore, there is a layering of how policies impact lives and death and the layering of risk. Additionally, people who are multiply-marginalised – due to, for example, sexuality, ethnicity, and wealth – are even more likely to be deemed to be relegated to the status of 'living dead' as proposed by necropolitics, as their lives are not protected, and their deaths not prevented.

Lastly, necropolitics and policies can impact funeral practices and how afterlives are honoured – policies can have power over what and how deaths are grievable. The processes of 'Othering', which is often exacerbated in war, may mean that the people are treated as socially dead during life and that, once physically dead, are not given the same care and rituals as others or what would typically be expected in their culture. For example, sociologist Daher-Nashif (2020) has illustrated that during times of conflict in the 1960s, Israel had a policy that would not release the bodies of Palestinians, instead burying them in numbered but unnamed graves or the 'secret cemeteries of numbers' or in 2015, in refrigerators.[3] These policies prevent the family and friends of the dead Palestinians from being able to hold funerary rituals or visit the deceased. Other studies have shown that being able to conduct funerary rituals can be important for one's own bereavement and processing of grief (Burrell and Selman, 2022). Because of that, Daher-Nashif (2020, 945) argues that 'necropolitics includes the coloniser's management of the colonised grief and bereavement, and the decisions about how, when, where and with whom the colonised should die'. Others point to the use of mass graves in conflict (Hope, 2018) or during pandemics (Iliadou, 2023) as another way to marginalise people even after their deaths in similar ways as described earlier. The power in such practices is that it removes the ability to recognise both the life and the death of the person or groups affected, removing political agency as well as dehumanising their existence and those who mourn them.

Using the term necropolitics is helpful for understanding more concretely how policies and the technologies of states can influence death and dying, especially those who are more at risk of death due to political choices and (in)action. By looking at three different examples here – migration, policies around queerness, and war – it is evident that necropolitics operates both in contexts where death is directly evident (e.g. war) to ones in which death may be positioned as an unintended (although known) consequence of the policies. Critically exploring these areas then challenges one to understand who has power and how power is exercised over people's existences, deaths, and even afterlives.

Conclusion

Policy – whether formal law or stated guidelines aimed to impact action – has the potential to influence how death and dying occur and are experienced. This chapter used several examples to show how states exert power over issues of death through governmentality, biopolitics, and necropolitics. By looking at EOLC policy, it is possible to see how particular forms of dying and death are deemed to be within the remit of the state's interest. By looking at migration, policies controlling queer lives, and actions around war dead, it is also possible to see how policies that are not directly about dying or EOLC also shape who dies, when, and how, or how their dead bodies are controlled. Therefore, critical approaches to death studies can encompass examining policy and the consequences of policies, including challenging the power within them through academia and activism.

Notes

1 The Liverpool Care Pathway (LCP) was a set of guidelines developed in the United Kingdom to be used in the last few days of a person's life. The guideline is intended to enable people to adopt 'good' hospice care in other settings.
2 For a map of the countries that criminalise LGBTQ+ people, see www.humandignitytr ust.org/lgbt-the-law/map-of-criminalisation/.
3 This chapter was written before the 7 October 2023 attack in Israel by Hamas and the subsequent bombardment of Gaza by Israel.

4

MASS DEATH EVENTS AND SHIFTING DEATH PRACTICES

Introduction

There are many events across the globe and throughout history where a large number of people have died related to a specific cause, such as disease, natural disaster or violence, including war.[1] In this chapter, these are called 'mass death events', and a key feature in them is that death – as an actual or perceived risk – is brought to the fore. The monitoring and reporting of death rates[2] during and after such events frequently drive the social, political, and cultural response to the event and is also used as a way of making sense of the event in terms of its impact on a population or how it may impact others in the future. A focus on death rates can emphasise many people were directly impacted by what may be considered a 'bad' (or 'untimely') death. Whilst not all cultures have the same view about what a good death is, unexpected deaths and mass deaths can challenge people's views about the acceptability of death. This chapter uses examples of mass death events from disease, natural disasters, and war to consider what such events can reveal about social life and how death is managed. The first section critically examines how pre-death and post-death ritual practices were impacted by social responses to AIDS, Ebola, and COVID-19. The following section uses examples of natural disasters and war to focus on recovery and mourning. The chapter demonstrates that how these events are managed is not apolitical and can be used to reflect on societal values, inequality, and power.

The language used to describe such events varies and can include 'disaster', 'major incidents', and 'mass casualty incident/events', often drawing on the terminology of emergency services responding to the events. According to McEntire (2007, 159), a mass-fatality incident is a disaster 'situation where there are more bodies than can be handled using existing local resources'. On the one hand, calling

DOI: 10.4324/9781003318002-5

these incidents or events implies that they can be clearly defined in time, location, and population as if they could be clearly identified and readily understood in terms of causes, mechanisms, and outcomes. Yet, it is important to remember that these are often declared 'events' retrospectively or after they have 'started', reflecting a human interpretation of the sequences of unfolding experiences that register them as warranting such a label and thereby granting a level of graveness to the 'event'. For some events, this can be linked to the number of people who died in a relatively short period and/or from unexpected causes. For other events, the number of deaths may be lower. Still, the social significance attributed to the deaths is such that it receives considerable media, political, and societal attention, often with the intention of changing minds and/or practices.

Although several examples are discussed in this chapter, this does not imply that they are viewed as 'equal' in terms of their importance – this is because what is deemed necessary depends on the perspective of the person(s) making such a judgement. The selection of examples is deliberate in that they are varied in terms of 'cause' – disease, natural disaster, violence – and, as such, challenge interpretations and proposed solutions that may focus on only medical, societal or political issues. Instead, each example shows the interrelatedness of these elements, and for death studies, focusing on and thinking through this interrelatedness is vital when adopting a critical approach. Moreover, the writing of this chapter has occurred at a time in which several mass death events are coalescing and competing for media headlines: the COVID-19 pandemic, war in Ukraine and Gaza,[3] shootings in schools and universities, climate emergency and multiple natural disasters in many countries including earthquakes, floods and fires. Given this, focusing on only one example or even one type of event is disingenuous when reflecting on how social worlds are confronted by and remade through mass death events.

Contaminated Bodies and Refracted Rituals

This section focuses on social responses to a disease, highlighting impacts on practices around death and dying, especially as these impacts are not equally distributed in society. This includes care of the dying (notion of contaminated bodies), treatment of the dead (change in funeral practices), and funeral practices (putting social restrictions in place). Concern about disease and death goes beyond biomedical approaches, remaking identity and society in the process. Some of the new practices stay/continue woven into social practices and cultural traditions. Three case studies are used to examine these issues: AIDS, Ebola, and COVID-19.

Since epidemics and pandemics are often linked to infectious diseases, there has typically been a concern about the risk of disease spread from either the corpse and/ or those who care for bodies before and after death. This has resulted in the care of the dead person and body being affected during such outbreaks, with care of the dying and traditional funerary and ritual practices being impacted.

During these outbreaks, there can be a concern about who is likely to be susceptible and potentially die. During the COVID-19 pandemic in 2020, in many countries, there were statements about particular sectors of the population being more 'vulnerable' and needing to 'shield' (or be protected from others). On the one hand, this connection between disease and individual was attributed to physical or biological characteristics, such as existing morbidity, stratification of death rates and concentration of deaths in particular areas and populations, indicating that such differences could not be explained by biology alone. Instead, racial and socio-economic differences were also observable (Abedi et al., 2021). As early as the 1830s cholera outbreaks in England, people were beginning to notice that disease outbreaks do not affect all members of a society equally, with areas of deprivation experiencing higher rates of illness and death (Connisbee, 2020). The prominence of death during epidemics and pandemics can, therefore, bring to the fore issues of social and economic inequality.

This inequality can also be expressed in terms of the stigma that people with a particular disease are treated with by others in society. A well-studied example of stigma and death is presented in the context of HIV/AIDS (Herek and Glunt, 1988). In the 1980s and 1990s, when AIDS was first being 'discovered' and treated, those dying from HIV/AIDS were often secluded within hospital wards, with large signs to denote them as a 'danger' and medical professionals wearing layers of personal protective equipment to reduce disease spread.[4] As very little was known about their conditions or how they were becoming ill, as they laid unwell they were stigmatised and considered to be 'unclean' or 'risky'. In places like the United Kingdom, such assumptions were also linked to the stigma many of them had experienced in their daily lives due to their engagement with bisexual and homosexual sexual practices at a time when homosexuality was only recently decriminalised. Over 1,000 people who were treated with blood products for haemophilia were infected with HIV in the 1980s in the United Kingdom; they were referred to as 'innocent victims', a reminder that socially others were considered to be 'guilty' or to have been personally, and morally, responsible for their disease (Weston, 2021). Stigma, both of disease and behaviour prior to being unwell, were therefore impacting those who were dying of HIV/AIDS in the early decades of the disease.

Over time, the stigma around HIV/AIDS has shifted; in part, this is due to understanding how the disease and illness are passed between individuals and noting that dying bodies are not particularly contagious. This is different, however, for other viruses, such as Ebola, where bodies infected by Ebola are known to be most infective for several days before and after death (Osterholm et al., 2015). Ebola was an epidemic in 2014–2016 in parts of West Africa, most notably Guinea, Liberia and Sierra Leone, where over 11,000 people died (Park, 2020). Public health research into the spread of Ebola has linked body handling and funerary practices to the spread of the disease amongst communities, with 60% of infections linked to care and mortuary rites (WHO 2015a in Fairhead, 2016), more than 365 deaths from Ebola were linked to one funeral of a traditional healer in Sierra Leone

(WHO, 2015b). Liberia's minister for gender and development noted that 75% of Ebola deaths were women who were known to have cared for the ill and prepared bodies for funerals (Akanni, 2014). As noted by Fairhead (2016, 8), 'control over the epidemic requires addressing matters of care and mortuary practices'. Due to this risk of disease spread, the human remains were considered to be 'serious public health threats', particularly in the context of 'improper burial practices' (Park, 2020, 76); note how the language is judgemental and dehumanising, prioritising a medical interpretation. Based on other case studies, one could expect that in such a scenario, those dying of Ebola would be stigmatised.

To combat the spread, public health officials argued that burials needed to be made 'safe' (by, e.g., omitting ritualistic washing and reducing the number of mourners) and that those infected with Ebola needed to be housed in specific, isolated treatment centres. Contrary to expectations of stigmatisation resulting in social exclusion and isolation, in several locations, these approaches were met with both 'noncompliance' (e.g. not travelling to such centres) and violent resistance (Fairhead, 2016); people hid illness and bodies and falsified death certificates to avoid direction creation (Manguvo and Mafuvadze, 2015). Park (2020, 73) explains this by emphasising the social and cultural importance of rituals in various groups of people in this area that link the living and ancestral spirits. Instead of being stigmatised locally within cultural groups, stigma was located on a national and global scale with news coverage stressing how particular funeral practices increased the risk of infection (both locally and internationally), intensifying notions of 'otherness' and positioning some peoples as being 'uncivilised' or being 'less intelligent' for not following public health advice. As Park (2020, 83) summarises, reflecting on the work of Manguro and Mafuvadze (2015), 'the Ebola outbreak in West Africa demonstrated that even if scientifically effective and efficient methods are available, they are unlikely to be implemented successfully unless they are culturally and religiously accepted'. This assertion could apply to all examples discussed so far and can relate to pre- and post-death practices.

Impact on Post-Death Practices

Whilst the previous two examples show that there are concerns about the dead body as being contaminated, there are other examples where post-death rituals have been adapted due to concerns about disease spread amongst the living. During 2020, in many countries such as the United Kingdom and Australia, funerary practices were drastically changed to accommodate 'social distancing' to reduce the spread of COVID-19 between attendees. In this example, there is less of a concern about people becoming unwell at the funeral due to contact with the dead body, but rather that they may infect each other due to the proximity of funeral practices, such as sitting close to one another or hugging. Several examples of funerals being a site of disease spread were published over the years, including reports on how funerary practices of singing or sharing food may have contributed to this (Jaja, Anyanwu, and Iwu Jaja, 2020). These limitations included restricting the number of people who could attend a funeral in person, leading to some adapting 'live streaming' to enable online viewing and participation (Riley et al., 2023). In many places, although COVID-19 is still in circulation (i.e. there is still a risk of catching the virus), the funerary guidance has reverted chiefly to pre-pandemic practices in most places from 2022 onwards.

However, how funerary practices were changed was not universal. Not only was there international variation in how different countries made recommendations in line with their other COVID-19 policies but there were also differences in terms of religion and who had died. In one UK study, researchers found the funerary restrictions impacted those from ethnic minorities more than in White populations, linking this to a range of funerary practices that were impacted by social distancing (such as viewing the body; Routen et al., 2021). Moreover, some governments had policies of forced direct cremation rather than allowing burial with a funeral, which contradicts some religious practices, including for Muslims (e.g. Sri Lanka; Human Rights Watch, 2021). This disparity is important as research indicates that 'the benefit of after-death rituals, including funerals, depends on the ability of the bereaved to shape those rituals and say goodbye in a way which is meaningful for them' (Burrell and Selman, 2022). Whilst some people have welcomed the return to a supposed 'normal', it is expected that some changes in funerary practices may persist, especially around live streaming, optional direct cremation, and limiting who attends funerals.

Changes Within the Deathcare System

As demonstrated in the example of Ebola, how people respond to managing a disease can also impact how they manage the dead body. Whilst for Ebola, this at the time resulted in suggested practices – like direct cremation – being rejected, in other examples, there have been significant changes that have lasted even beyond the initial 'mass death event' to change how deathcare and body disposal are practised.

In the United States, handling bodies after a death from AIDS required new ways of treating the dead. Troyer, drawing on Waldby's work, claims that the HIV/AIDS corpse became a 'politically productive body that altered both institutional codes and technological conventions' (Troyer, 2020, 65). This is because funeral directors at the time had to assume that all bodies could be 'contaminated' with HIV or be vectors of the disease, and so had to adapt their practices to mitigate this 'biohazard risk' unless that 'tag' on the body indicated that their cause of death was non-infectious. The embalming tactics developed to handle infected bodies have not changed much since the 1990s (Troyer, 2020). However, it should be noted that embalming is not a technique that is widely used across the globe, and some religious groups prefer that no embalming occurs before burial (see Chapter 10).

There are not only changes to how bodies are handled after the death but also where they are placed. In the context of COVID-19, as well as many other mass death events that 'overwhelm' a deathcare system, some places resort to the use of mass graves to manage the volume of dead bodies. This contrasts with typical practices in these areas of single burial plots and/or cremation. A widely reported example of this is how New York used Hart Island as a large graveyard, burying 1,000s of people within months in 2020 (Kenney, 2024). This has continued its use as a public cemetery for marginalised deaths: it is used for unnamed and/ or unclaimed bodies since the late 1800s as well as being a site for mass graves resulting from other epidemics (1918 influenza and HIV). What is also notable, though, is who had to dig the graves – during the COVID pandemic, it was not uncommon for New York to use prisoners as gravediggers. Mass graves, like Hart Island, therefore, are not only sites of burial for the marginalised dead but also the marginalised living, placed in roles that expose them to the elements, potential illness, and social stigma.

Politics of Memorialisation

The previous section shows how mass death events can shape care practices and rituals – of the dying, dead body, and also funeral rituals. This section will look at how some mass death events are managed in other ways in terms of broader-scale disaster recovery and memorialisation. Doing this reveals that how mass death events are managed is not apolitical and can be used to reflect on societal values, inequality, and power.

Who Can Access the Deceased

Mass death events, by the very nature of their definition, typically have multiple people who have died in a short time. In some events, this may have occurred within the same few hours, and depending on the nature of the event, it may not be readily manageable to determine how many people or even who has died. This can occur at various events caused by natural disasters, violence, traffic accidents or when infrastructure, such as buildings, collapses. This means that access to the dead is not readily straightforward and can occur alongside rescue efforts to find survivors. Responding to and managing such events may involve a wide range of people and organisations, including aid relief, a field known as 'disaster management'.

Over the past 50 decades, principles for disaster management have been evolving, reflecting lessons learned from previous events and changes in technology and infrastructure to support disaster relief (Tidball-Binz, 2007; Hilhorst, 2005; Morgan et al., 2006). One area of this is how to identify and handle the care of dead bodies in a disaster. Reflecting on the Indian Ocean/South Asian Tsunami that occurred on 26 December 2004, Morgan et al. (2006) noted that previous mass fatality management policies were not directly transferrable to this context, designed more for accidents and terrorist attacks, leaving many lessons to learn from how the dead and bereaved were taken care of in Thailand, Indonesia and Sri Lanka. Across these three countries, it is reported that over 200,000 people died as a result of the tsunami. This overwhelmed local deathcare systems. For instance, there was not enough refrigeration space to store bodies prior to identification, resulting in the use of alternative methods of shallow graves to attempt short-term preservation or mass graves without identification. Thailand and Sri Lanka both 'turned over the handling of the dead to multinational emergent organisations involving 34 countries' (Scanlon, 2008, 1). These organisations were deemed to bring in expertise, structure, and technology – and whilst this can be helpful, it can challenge usual lines of power, undermine local expertise and familial connections, and requires collaboration between individuals and organisations during heightened emotional states (Binder and Baker, 2017).

To facilitate identification, many aid organisations travelled to provide assistance. A 'Disaster Victim Identification' (DVI) team from Belgium that aided identification of bodies in Thailand reported on their process (Beauthier et al., 2009) noting that they arrived about a week after the tsunami, which impacted the ability to identify bodies due to various decomposition levels. Some organisations systemically photographed bodies and noted key factors (sex, height, and/or existence of personal items), other places used dental records and fingerprints, and very few used DNA analysis (Petju et al., 2007). Other released bodies were based on visual recognition (i.e. by family) before formal identification processes were established (Petju et al., 2007). Methods for identification have been studied in this disaster in Thailand, where the majority of bodies recovered included heads, enabling the use of dental techniques. Those with dental records were more likely to be identified and returned to family members than those without (Petju et al., 2007). However, this does not mean people were easily identified as less than 10% of dental records in Thailand could be used, and few local people have them; the use of dental records was more 'successful' for foreigners (Petju et al., 2007.). This lack of records and the ability to use them has been suggested as one of the reasons that hundreds of bodies remain unidentified. Due to the usefulness of forensic dental identification, some governments incentivise dental record keeping, and even placing unique identifiers in dentures and dental implants and encouraging the storage of dental records has been one of the recommendations from this mass death event. How these technologies are recommended and implemented can be seen as an extension of biopower, with governments planning for potential mass death.

The stage just described is part of the body processing and identification before enabling the body to be provided to family (where possible) and funerary practices. Over the years, there have also been changes to how the families are informed about these processes and what materials are provided to them. These are often called 'personal effects' within disaster management. However, people may also use other terms, including possession, property, and valuables, all of which indicate a notion of (previous) personal ownership of the item. Lucy Easthope, an experienced disaster responder working over decades specialising in returning items, charts in her book – *When the Dust Settles* – how this has changed after many years and events to work towards a more compassionate approach (Easthope, 2022). For instance, there have been changes in practices around what personal effects are provided to the family and when/how they can have access to them, recognising that they may be important for people as part of their grieving process. She describes how the items, like a watch, can be viewed by emergency responders as very mundane or ordinary objects, whilst also being incredibly meaningful to family and friends. Receiving such items can help people understand and make sense of the death, including in instances where they may not have been able to see the body. There and elsewhere, Easthope has argued that 'without an "ethic of care" from all responders toward personal effects, the items are highly vulnerable and have in the past been removed to landfills or incinerated. I campaign that response plans should therefore aim to prioritise personal effects with a principal aim to identify, locate and restore personal property in a timely and accurate manner that allows survivors and bereaved to make as many of their own choices as possible' (Easthope, 2019, 123). This is important to note because there are potential power imbalances here in terms of who makes decisions about what is done with personal items, how they are provided (or not) to surviving connections, and how the process of providing such items can influence bereavement and ongoing grief. It has taken people like Easthope, who have argued for acknowledging the role of 'care' in this, that has enabled a change in practices.

Politics of Mourning

Whilst personal items can be important for acknowledging a death and for grief work, other rituals and mourning practices can help and hinder grief for both individuals and collectives. Mass death events provide a useful lens through which to consider what deaths are acknowledged (or even whose deaths with mass fatalities are noted) and what social practices are done or (re)made to make mourning visible.

In many countries across Europe and North America, the politics of mourning is noticeable through war memorials, especially commemorating the First and Second World Wars. These may include statues or walls with the names of people who died during the wars, and in the United Kingdom, they are annually adorned with red Flanders poppies (Iles, 2008). These events can be understood as cultural memory messaging (Sheehan and Davison, 2017), informing how people are supposed to make sense of and remember historical events; this messaging can change over time. Notably, these statues and plaques of remembrance often showcase the names of those in the armed forces rather than civilians impacted by violence. Judith Butler has called attention to this by highlighting which lives are deemed grievable (Butler, 2004; see also Chapter 1); this has been taken further by others for analyses of how different military lives are grieved in the context of war in terms of considering who was put in more danger or risk (Zehfuss, 2009). Around such wars and acts of remembering can be messaging that reaffirms that these people have died for the freedom of others or a nation (Sheehan and Davison, 2017).

Commemoration and remembrance of the (war) dead can be a function of national building. In some examples, this can perpetuate particular notions of power, sovereignty, and citizenship. Anzac Day is the national day of remembrance in Australia and New Zealand for those involved in wars and conflict; it is celebrated on April 25th. The day is significant for the enactment of collective belonging that is part of many of the organised events and practices, as well as for maintaining a sense that nations are made through war (McCreanor et al., 2019). Through this, very specific notions of what it means to belong and what the country represents are perpetuated. It has been noted that the media discourse around this day stresses it as a day of 'respectful remembrance', silencing any perceived dissonance that challenges settler identity and colonialism (McConville et al., 2016). Therefore, it is evident that commemoration is socially regulated, with the ability to further marginalise certain groups of people who's identity and beliefs do not align with nationalistic interpretations and current power structures.

Additionally, it is important to note that messaging about mourning can change over time and is not apolitical.[5] Research on war mourning has demonstrated that how politicians talk about the war dead changes depending on the regime and 'how the dead are mobilised'. For example, in Romania, Bucur (2009) notes how various aspects of the Second World War were made sense of differently, especially as the Romanian army at one point fought in aid of the Nazis and at another time during the war were allied with Soviet troops. Framing Soviet involvement as 'liberation' within the late 1940s meant that war memorialisation typically glorified Soviet soldiers and iconography. In the 1960s, when a nationalist Romanian government was in power, the shift to war memorialisation focused on the 'Great War', minimising Soviet-focused celebrations. Whilst the grand stage politics matters, Bucur also notes that it is important to realise the agency of people in this politics of mourning – working within and outside of the system to find ways to commemorate the war dead that are meaningful to them, even if this is counter to the prevailing political ideology and drawing on a wide range of ethnic and religious traditions.

In some places, there are questions about whether there should be large-scale mourning or commemoration of war, or even other mass death events. One example of this is how Japan has had a 'memory war' – disagreements aired socially about how to commemorate the dead – about how to remember socially the Asian-Pacific War that occurred during the Second World War (Lee, 2015). Japan had over 3 million soldiers who died during wars occurring between 1931 and 1945 (Lee, 2015). Research from Japan has indicated that political decisions not to have state-driven mourning or remembrance could leave generations unable to grieve and disenfranchise their grief (Morris-Suzuki, 1998; Lee, 2015). Therefore, two examples of how mourning is managed include the Yasukuni Shrine in Tokyo, used to commemorate those who 'died in service' – such as war dead from the armed forces – since the late 1800s, and the national memorial month of August. During this month, there are several large-scale memorial activities that focus on significant events, including marking the locations where nuclear bombs were detonated and killed many and public discussions about how society should commemorate and mourn the deaths of war victims.

Conclusion

There are some events where many people die, such as due to a pandemic or disaster. Mass death events are often considered to overwhelm a deathcare system, and such events typically attract media and political attention. Dying, death, and mourning may be experienced differently during and after such events. This chapter showcased several examples that critically explored how social and political responses to such events impacted the ways in which death was managed and how the dead could be grieved. Ultimately, social worlds are confronted by and remade through mass death events. Critically attending to how this is done enables an analysis that understands the role of governments in this, how it impacts relationships and grieving, and the ways in which deathcare practices and technologies can change because of mass death events.

Notes

1 There are also considerable extinction events that cause mass death of fauna and flora, and many so-called natural disasters are influenced by human activities (e.g. where and how settlements are built).

2 See Chapter 2 for a discussion of mortality statistics and issues around counting death. In mass death events there can be added complexities with counting depending on circumstances that may hinder body recovery and identification.

3 As well as many other wars and civil unrest in other countries, which have received less or no attention in the UK and Finnish mainstream media.

4 This is discussed in a three-part BBC documentary focusing on England using archive interviews. More information about the programme can be found at: www.bbc.co.uk/pro grammes/m0018t1c.

5 Research has shown that mortality salience influenced by the events on 11 September was linked to be people being more inclined to support George W. Bush (and his policies for war) as a presidential candidate (Landau et al., 2004). During 2023, commentators expressed concern that Jewish grief was being used to legitimise war (see, e.g. Fox, 2023).

5

SOCIAL MOVEMENTS AND DEATH

Introduction

Social movements comprise group(s) of people who share a collective interest in particular political and/or cultural issues, often made up of informal interactions to further their interests (Diani, 1992). They can play a crucial role in generating social change. Whilst most of the research on social movements focuses on those from the 1970s onwards, the term is thought to have been first used in 1850 by German sociologist Lorenz Von Stein (Martí and Biglia, 2014) and some scholars claim that the root of social movements dates to ancient times (Berger and Nehring, n.d.). Researchers have sought to understand social movements in a variety of manners, especially in terms of how they are structured, how they lead to change, the moral visions of social movements, and even down to the micro-interactions and the role of emotion (Jasper, 2010).

Death – either directly or indirectly – is a frequent theme for social movements, from peasant revolts that protested starvation to abolition that highlighted the unfair treatment of enslaved peoples to anti-globalisation and anti-capitalist movements that critique financial systems that perpetuate inequalities (that often are the social determinants of health and death). Others include the anti-death penalty movement (Haines, 1992), advance care planning in Taiwan (Lai et al., 2011), extinction rebellion, which often uses death in its public actions (Walter, 2022), mothers in Argentina marking the disappearance of young men (Hernandez, 2002), AIDS activism and memorialisation through social movements (Jaramillo, 2023), and even animal rights movements that challenge the death of animals for product testing and clothing (Guither, 1998). Death, or the concern about possible death, including social death, can therefore be a core concern to generate social movements around and be the site of potential change.

DOI: 10.4324/9781003318002-6

When writing about the anti-death penalty movement, Haines (1992) stresses how the social movement was integral to 'transforming underpublicised or affect-neutral events into suddenly realised grievances' through the use of media. In other words, an act (the killing of persons convicted of crimes) that was usually socially considered to be unremarkable became something that was written/broadcasted about and articulated in such a way that people (beyond the social movement) could identify injustices. Tapping into the effect of injustice is an element shared by many of the social movements listed previously. Moreover, many of them extend beyond the effect of injustice to mobilise emotions of grief, either in their actions or to influence people's perceptions of what is worthy of grief. Judith Butler (2009) uses the term grievability to point out that whose life is considered mournable – or something that can and should be grieved – is not to be assumed but is culturally and socially contextual. Although they were focusing on war, this concept of grievability is useful in the context of social movements, as such movements may challenge societies about who is or is not being grieved or considered worthy of grief and what that grief can look like.

This chapter focuses on two social movements that have issues of death as part of their core moral issues – Black Lives Matter and Death Positivite Movement. At first glance, these two movements seem like odd companions. The former seeks to centre the value of Black lives and deaths in cultures which enact Black death as dispensable. The latter seeks to shift social perceptions from being 'death-denying' or having taboos around death to being 'death positive' and accepting death as part of life. Neither section provides a complete history of the movements; instead, key aspects are highlighted to demonstrate and reflect on the links to death, dying and grief. The third section of this chapter provides a discussion of both the movements and broader social issues. By juxtaposing these social movements, it illustrates how people are dissatisfied with how death is socially and culturally 'handled' and their calls for shifting social sensibilities.

Black Lives Matter

Black Lives Matter (also known as BLM and various spin-offs linked to specific geographical areas or organisations) started in 2013 in response to the verdict court case *State of Florida v. George Michael Zimmerman* (Chase, 2018). Trayvon was shot to death on 26 February 2012; George Zimmerman was acquitted of murdering the Black teenager. Media coverage leading up to the trial focused on potential racist intent, and post-verdict social discourse focused on issues of race (Chase, 2018).

Taking to social media as part of their reaction to the verdict, many commented on it what this reflected about American society more generally. Including Alicia Garza, who wrote 'A Love Letter to Black People' reflecting on the verdict and noting her surprise at how little Black lives appeared to matter in the United States. Responding and amplifying the message, Patrisse Cullors began to use the hashtag

#BlackLivesMatter. Together with Opal Tometi, the three women are recognised for growing the social movement from dissatisfaction and a hashtag to galvanising people internationally around the issues of police brutality, inequity, and civil and human rights (Vernon E. Jordan Law Library, n.d.). Crucial to the movement's history is recognising the three founding women, even if they are no longer as actively involved.

Garza, Cullors and Tometi established the Black Lives Matter Global Network Foundation. The movement is intended to be decentralised – meaning there is no one single person or group of people running the social movement. There are local branches in different states and countries – and it can be found in over 40 chapters globally (Black Lives Matter, n.d.-b); most of these are in the United States and Europe. Over time, the structure and organisation of the movement have been questioned, and the foundation has sought to address such critiques through added transparency on its website, including about its financials. As Konadu and Gyamfi (2018) note, these critiques are because 'it has followed a pattern similar to other social movements driven by individuals and organizations…[becoming] more of a conventional hierarchical organization, centralizing its operations and leadership'. They also note that founders have won awards, book deals and notoriety. Such accolades can bring criticism against the movement in terms of who it represents and who is represented, and taken even further, could question the value of winning awards in the context of wider Black death and police brutality.

According to the official website of the Black Lives Matter Global Network Foundation, BLM are working for 'a world where Black lives are no longer systematically targeted for demise' (Black Lives Matter, n.d.-a). This links to the discussion of necropolitics (see Chapter 3) that reflects on how political and social forces can disproportionally make some lives riskier. Whilst some have said that BLM is an extension of the abolition movement and civil rights movements (the latter also sparked by the death of a young Black man, Emmitt Till), due to the anti-racist stance that is shared between them, others argue that the stress on human rights in BLM extends beyond the realms of these previous movements (Chase, 2018). Lebron (2023) contends that the phrase 'black lives matters' does not just call on whites to acknowledge the worth of Black lives but is also an inflexion point for Black people to consider what it means to be in the United States and what other possible futures there could be. In this way, it is important also to note that BLM has also been extended to reflect a wide range of positionalities within it, including supporting queer and trans lives, those with disabilities and those who are undocumented (Black Lives Matter, n.d.-a). It, therefore, can be seen to seek to transform the experiences of a wide range of people who are often marginalised in American (and other similar) societies.

Whilst the three words 'black lives matter' emphasise the word 'lives', much of the movement is driven by a concern about death, and as noted earlier, was sparked by death. The names of the dead are often listed as a stark reminder of the need for the movement (see Lebron, 2023), this practice of recording and listing the names of those killed through racial violence is also seen at the National Memorial for Peace and Justice in the United States that has a memorial dedicated to those who have been lynched. The practice of naming people is key to reaffirming their personhood, especially within Africentric perspectives where 'no person is considered a person without a name' (Nkechi and Benjamin, 2023). There is a legacy in the United States where enslaved people were buried without burial markers, so their histories and names are more readily forgotten (Cann, 2020); the BLM movement seeks to keep these histories living. Importantly, even within the BLM, there are moves to ensure that the Black women also killed by police brutality are remembered (Chatelain and Asoka, 2015). As Asoka notes in an interview about gender and BLM, within the United States, people 'tend to see violence and racism against black men as a barometer of racism against the black population at large, whereas violence against black women is often invisible' (Chatelain and Asoka, 2015, 56). Resistance and remembrance, therefore, exist both within and beyond the movement.

Another act of resistance that can be observed in relation to BLM and cultural practices more generally of marginalised Black groups is how the deaths are commemorated. Commenting on George Floyd's golden casket, Black death studies scholar Kami Flechter highlighted that African Americans use death material culture as a form of resistance, 'using last rites as a tool to subvert the racist, stereotypes caricature of thug and brute' (Social Media post cited in Cann, 2020). BLM extends this further by encouraging people to question the official memorials around them in their societies – some within the movement protested (and removed) statues, racist street names, and memorial plaques to highlight the selective history and absence of marginalised lives and deaths (Leyh, 2020). Whilst these two forms of resistance linked to the BLM movement are not the same, they both serve to challenge who is remembered and how within society, especially challenging white supremacy within memorialisation.

One of the recurring questions around social movements is whether they are 'successful' – to fully understand the question and any answers supplied , it is helpful to consider what is understood as success and who determines this. With regards to BLM, success can be seen in terms of raising awareness of continued social inequality and injustices. For example, studies have been conducted to see if BLM activities reduce racial bias in people; Sawyer and Gampa (2018) found that white people were likely to become less implicitly and explicitly pro-White during BLM moments in the early years of the movement. Lebron (2023) notes how the popularity of the movement, mainly amongst white allies, rose around the death of George Floyd in 2020 and has abated again over time. He repeats what some social commentators at the time reflected as potential boredom and availability from COVID pandemic lockdowns (that were in place around the time of Floyd's death) as inspiring and enabling people to partake in marches and social media action who may otherwise consider themselves too busy to do so. Yet, because social injustices continue to exist, it could be argued that the movement has not yet been entirely successful in terms of meeting its intended aims and that the longer-term impact on racial bias is not yet known.

User-generated maps indicate that most of the BLM-related activities were located in the United States and Europe.[1] Several scholars have noted that the movement is not active in all places where Black lives are marginalised, such as in South Africa (Pillay, 2022) and Egypt (Dewedar, 2022). Pillay (2022) observed that African institutions and media ignored the murder of Collins Khosa, until George Floyd's death brought international attention to police brutality (which was also linked to Collins Khosa's death); Pillay notes that the Black Lives Matter movement centres the gaze on Black American lives and reinforces geopolitical power imbalances. Similarly, Dewedar draws parallels between examples of deaths that appear to have racialised motives – George Floyd's death in 2020 in the United States and Gabriel Tut, a South Sudanese man in Egypt who died in 2017. Whilst Floyd's death received extensive national and international media attention and protests around the grounds of social justice, Tut's death received minimal local media coverage. One of the reasons this may be, as Dewedar suggests, is that Egyptian (national) identity tends to be anti-African and, therefore, by extension, anti-Black. Moreover, Dewedar argues that Black people in Egypt, many of whom are asylum seekers and refugees, do not have the power to mobilise in the manner BLM has operated. This is due to forms of censorship, the absence of powerful black voices and the lack of awareness (and potential societal acceptance) of injustices. Burcu and Wang (2023) note that in China, the media coverage of BLM is used to reinforce pro-Chinese propaganda. They said that Chinese reporting of BLM in 2020 was predominately negative when portraying protests (as these can disrupt social stability) and tended to frame racial inequity as an inherent problem that was present in the United States rather than something that many societies, including China, face (Burcu and Wang, 2023). So, whilst BLM is considered a 'global' movement, it is evident that its effect and to achieve social justice globally is not equal.

Death Positive Movement

The Death Positive Movement – sometimes referred to as Death Positivity (Movement) – is generally concerned with normalising death and dying. It does not mean one has to 'be positive' about death or always accept it. Instead, the movement is about one's attitude towards the subject and seeking to educate people on decay, dying and death in a way that does not perceive death as inherently something to be avoided. As with the BLM, the coinage for Death Positive started on social media, with Caitlin Doughty wondering 'why we had movements like body positivity and sex positivity, but we couldn't use that same umbrella to be forward thinking about our own deaths' (The Order of the Good Death, 2018). Doughty, together with others working on death-related topics or in death industries, is one of the founders of The Order of the Good Death.

The Order of the Good Death is one of the public faces – and lays claim to naming the movement – of the Death Positive Movement, especially in the United States. The Order was founded in 2011, with over 30 founding members (most of whom are women), with the goal of making death a part of life, showing how death is natural but that death anxiety is not (The Order of the Good Death, n.d.-b). According to the Order,

> People who are death positive believe that it is not morbid or taboo to speak openly about death. They see honest conversations about death & dying as the cornerstone of a healthy society.
>
> *(The Order of the Good Death, n.d.-a)*

The Order does not accept death systems as they are but seeks to reform how society engages and manages death, especially in the funeral industry.

The Order of the Good Death notes the more extended history of their movement with ties to what was happening in the 1970s and 1980s (The Order of the Good Death, n.d.-a). Especially with the hospice movement (see also Chapter 7), Natural Death Movement (linked to living wills and refusing treatment), civil rights movements that used imagery and rituals of Dia de Muertos (Day of the Dead), the Death Acceptance Movement (linked to palliative care), and AIDS Activism. Some of this is what Lofland (2019) previously coined as the 'Happy Death Movement' of the 1960s and 1970s as societal awareness about the medicalisation of dying grew, however, as noted in the Order's history, some of the movements occurring at this time were not all 'happy' in that they emphasised gross inequities happening in the United States. Later, the Order also note the Green Burial Movement (encouraging natural burials) and home funeral movements (encouraging family-led funeral and deathcare) in the 1990s, and then in the 2000s, the rise of Death Cafes, Death Doulas, and human composting as all are influencing what would then become the Order; others have grouped this range as the 'New Death Movement' (Westendorp and Gould, 2021). A more comprehensive history of the Order also acknowledges the ways in which individuals in the Order were active in death awareness and funeral industry reform activities before 2011; for example, Caitlin Doughty's YouTube video series *Ask a Mortician* seeks to demystify funerals and remove some of the fear around death. Therefore, the Order acknowledges how the Death Positive Movement is informed and influenced by previous social movements and actions, as well as the contributions of individual members.

Scholars writing on the topic note that the Death Positive Movement is linked to death awareness movement(s) more generally (Incorvaia, 2022). Death awareness movements, according to Walter (2020), seek to generate a 'more humane way of dying' (101), often cast against modern, medicalised depictions of death (see Chapter 6). He characterises them as a response 'to the physical, psychological, social and spiritual risks caused by modern' dying (101), which emphasises 'post-material values of personal expression, personal autonomy and personal spirituality' (102). Both the Death Awareness Movement and the Death Positive Movement seek to bring conversations about death into public spheres, with the general premise that this is good for individuals, those around them, and societies more generally.

One of the main ways in which the Death Positive Movement is rendered visible in society is through the use of social media, digital platforms and the content creation of The Order of the Good Death members. For example, Caitlin Doughty has a YouTube video series and is active on several social media platforms. The Order also had an Esty shop selling death positive goods, including clothing stating 'future corpse' (now there are other sellers promoting 'death positive' wares). Zibaite (2020), who has studied such items, notes that they not only centre death as a theme (i.e. to raise awareness) but do so in a playful or jovial manner. She notes that 'the affective aspect of communication... in this movement is inseparable from the message' (Zibaite, 2020, 157), and therefore, the 'fun' aspects of the messaging are part of the death positive message. Zibaite argues that this has encouraged others to engage with the movement, especially younger demographics online, but risks alienating some who do not connect with the dark humour. Gieseler (2022) notes that the use of social media in these ways has helped others see that they can shift rituals, and indeed, in contemporary times, enables them to create rituals that are meaningful to them, even if, at times, these are (perceived as) comical memes. The creation and consumption of death positive content on social media is not just a way to connect with audiences nor change social discourses, but also can generate a death positive identity that is viewed as a lifestyle formed around personal choices and social networks.

Various other activities have also been associated with the Death Positive Movement, from writings by The Order of Good Death to more expansive understandings of how death cafes[2] have evolved (Koksvik and Richards, 2023), video games (Nicolucci, 2019), Death Positive Libraries (Lerum, 2023; Pitsillides et al., 2023), and even considering how teaching is delivered in university courses about death rituals (Lerum, 2023). These activities have gained the attention of the media, millions of social media users, and academics who are studying death positivity as a phenomenon (see, e.g. Wilde, n.d.). Across many of these activities, people are encouraged to encounter, explore and even possibly reshape whatever fears of death they may have.

Despite being active for over a decade, social polls indicate that people living in places where the Death Positive Movement is active still may fear death (e.g. approximately 40% of US adults state they fear death; Statista, 2019). While some may interpret such findings as showing that the movement is ineffective, generally, this points to one of the tricky aspects of understanding the effectiveness of such social movements – how to measure progress and link activities to changes in behaviour. Others have noted a shift in some end-of-life care and body disposal trends, which they link to a broader notion of the death positive movement as changing people's attitudes and choices about death. For example, Hale (2018) notes an increase in home funerals, the use of death doulas,[3] more simple earth burials, and greener cremations and considers such changes as an outcome of the movement.

Central to the Death Positive Movement are narratives about the pervasiveness of death denial and the societal taboo about death. As Koksvik (2020) notes, 'set against a maintained narrative of societal denial and death taboo, death positivity's mission to increase talk about and engagement with death positions them in opposition to stated oppressive societal norms'. In her research on the movement, she notes how death-positive approaches are presumed to be 'right' or 'better' and that those who adopt such a stance are to expect resistance from those around them. She flags this as concerning because it shows a 'disregard for alternative cultural interpretations offered by researchers and academics over the last thirty years as well as ... [demonstrating] sweeping assumptions of Western cultural homogeneity' (Koksvik, 2020). This is a critique that is not unique to the Death Positive Movement and has been levelled at other revivalist movements that seek to change how death and dying are viewed in society.

Talking about death awareness movements more generally, but also noted by others in relation to those who identify as death positive at Death Cafes (Koksvik and Richards, 2023), Walter (2020) observes that such movements are often comprised of individuals with privileged backgrounds. His concern is that the views of these individuals – often from similar demographics including age, class, gender, race and education – do not necessarily represent the views of a diverse society. In particular, the drive towards self-actualisation in death may ignore or even downplay how others in societies, both within countries like the United States and the United Kingdom and beyond, are striving for survival to avoid premature deaths.

Discussion

The intent of this chapter is not to equate these two social movements but to use them to highlight several aspects of how death features in social movements and how one may think critically about social movements and societal change. As demonstrated by these examples, social movements are an example of social critique that seeks to shift societal views and practices; they both present a view on how people should or could behave. Each example is multi-layered in terms of what they seek to shift. Still, Black Lives Matter (on one level) is about the treatment of Black people in (American) society, especially by police forces. For the Death Positive Movement, it is about encouraging people to be more open to death and accept it as natural. Examining social movements, it is helpful to consider what messages are promoted and by whom, who can connect with the movement and how, and what constructs (e.g. denial of death for the Death Positive Movement) are needed for the messages to be mobilised. By their very nature, social movements are bound to be partial, representing the perspectives of some rather than all, and are often resisted as they seek to speak against norms and established power.

Gender is something to consider when thinking about these social movements – both in terms of who has founded or seen to be the main actors in the movement and who the key audiences are for the movement. In both examples discussed before, women have played crucial roles in establishing, naming, and organising the movements. This resonates also with other death-related movements. For example, the modern hospice movement is often linked to Dame Cicely Saunders, who is seen as key in establishing the hospice model and gaining support for it (see Chapter 7). Another example is the Argentinian mothers known as the Mothers of the Plaza de Mayo, who are known for their often silent performative mourning for those who have disappeared (and possibly died) under military dictatorship (Bosco, 2006). In many societies, women are associated with primary roles in caring and grieving and these social movements can be interpreted as an extension of these gender roles.

In both examples in this chapter, social justice is used as a motivator for some. This is more readily apparent in Black Lives Matter, with clear messaging and use of protesting (online and in-person). For the Death Positive Movement, social justice issues are highlighted in the Order of the Good Death's telling of history in terms of what has informed it as well as how some have claimed that by embracing a death-positive stance, society may be able to address mass death in the Anthropocene (Skakum Jorgensen, 2018). However, both of the movements highlighted in this chapter have received criticism in terms of questioning who they benefit and how, both within a country and the global reach of the movements. There are also questions about the extent to which they have been 'successful', although this is difficult to measure, and social change can take a considerable amount of time to realise fully.

One reason for selecting both examples is that they bring specific questions about the 'social' in contemporary social movements. Social media is used extensively to raise awareness and to mobilise others to be part of the movement (either in activities or in adopting the lifestyle it promotes). Social media allows people to craft identities as activists (Liu et al., 2017) and for people to connect across geographical locations. Linked to this is the potential for both social movements to be decentralised (which both claim to be) by enabling others to generate content, organise activities, and use the movement's messaging in new ways. A third aspect of social, therefore, is also about the social discourse – understood on one level to be what and how people talk about things in a society. Therefore, social movements in contemporary societies can use technological tools, such as digital platforms, to shift power structures and social discourses.

Lastly, both examples of social movement in this chapter illustrate how death can be at the core of social movement. Indeed, this is also noted for other historical and contemporary social movements. Devich-Cyril (2021) argues that grief belongs in social movements and is, at their core, a way to connect, since people cannot grieve in isolation. Whilst this is generalising about how people grieve (and could grieve more optimally), it is helpful to reflect on how the two social movements highlighted in this chapter use grief or the potential of grief to mobilise people into action. In Black Lives Matter, grief is at the core; not just grief about specific deaths, but also grief about how Black Americans are treated more generally and the devaluing of their worth. In the Death Positive Movement, grief is treated like death – something that should be considered normal and therefore not to be afraid of – and can be planned for. People have responded to this by posting about their grief and thoughts about death on social media.

Conclusion

Death and grief can be a motivator and core issue of a range of social movements, either to focus on injustices that people face that place them at greater risk of death or to focus on how death, dying and grief could be different. This chapter has focused on two social movements – Black Lives Matter and the Death Positive Movement – to illustrate these issues and consider how death is used as a motivator for social change. This is not to equate the two social movements; instead, each example demonstrates the different ways in which people seek to change how death occurs and the types of grief people experience. Black Lives Matter is about recognising how race influences experiences of life, violence, and death, especially in the context of police actions. For the Death Positive Movement, the focus is less on social injustices and more on shifting social and cultural approaches to death more generally, encouraging a more accepting approach to death and grief. A critical approach to such social movements highlights the structural factors that have motivated those who originate the movements and the critiques levelled against the movements. For both of these movements, this chapter has discussed the role of gender and social media; these both frame and mobilise the movements differently. Social movements can potentially shape individuals' and society's approaches to death and dying, and the two examples discussed in this chapter provide an overview of how people have sought to do this in contemporary times.

Notes

1 For a live overview, see www.arcgis.com/apps/dashboards/6bc361d72b0048068eae2 c3d29ac734c.
2 Death Cafes have 'globally' spread but there are tensions in how they are run in terms of adapting to socio-cultural differences whilst maintaining the format (Richards et al., 2020). Death Cafes registered with on the Death Café website have featured in 89 countries, but many tend to be in Europe and North America (https://deathcafe. com/map/.
3 Some end of life doula or death doula training emphasises similar messaging to the Death Positive Movement, including normalising non-medical death and facing death as an opportunity for personal and societal growth (Incorvaia, 2023).

SECTION II
Dying

6

MEDICALISATION OF DYING

Introduction

If you live in an area where matters to do with the body often involve considerations of health and medicine, you experience 'medicalisation'. Medicalisation can be defined as 'to make medical' (Conrad, 2009). It is the process through which conditions and practices are considered legitimately under medical treatment and care remit. Medicalisation can involve identifying something as a disease or illness and seeking to primarily rectify it through medical means such as pharmacological or surgical interventions. Some readers may be thinking 'of course matters of the body are linked to medical issues' but it is important to remember that the body can also be thought of and engaged within a wide range of ways, including spiritual and social, that are not focused on medical understandings of the body.

Sociologists interested in medicalisation argue that it has become embedded in many societies, particularly in Europe, North America and Australia, due to a combination of factors. Medicalisation has been a process over centuries, with a decrease in religious authority (Kellehear, 2007), an increase in the professionalisation of medical practitioners and an increase in their oversight of a broader range of issues (Conrad, 2009). There has also been an increase in biotechnology and the pharmaceutical industry, expanding the range of potential interventions and types of 'conditions' that can be or become treated (Kaufman, 2015). There has also been a growing demand from 'consumers' to have medical products to address long-standing human issues, including ageing (Everts Mykytyn, Courtney, 2010; Kaufman, 2010; Joyce and Loe, 2010). The notion of medicalisation has often been used to critique medicine's expansion over people's lives and medical professionals' role in social control (Szasz, 1970, 2007; Illich, 1975; Busfield, 2017).

DOI: 10.4324/9781003318002-8

This chapter looks at the medicalisation of dying. The first section provides an overview of what medicalisation is and why medicalisation matters in terms of dying. The chapter critically explores what this may mean for how people experience dying, how the dying process is managed, and the social consequences of medicalisation. Subsequent sections examine different ways in which people have sought to challenge or modulate such medicalisation, as well as how advancing medical technology plays a role in medicalisation. The final section looks at medicalising dying through a lens of inequity, considering unequal access to palliative and end-of-life care.

Viewing Death as a Medical Event: Medicalisation of Death and Dying

Viewing death as a medical event is a highly socio-cultural practice. That means how death is identified as a medical issue depends on social and cultural issues, and how and if this occurs varies over time and across places. There are many definitions of what death is and when it happens (Black, 1977; Sarbey, 2016). Within biomedicine, death is marked by an absence of certain features considered vital for living. Previously, this was a pulse and the ability to breathe (Knudsen, 2009). Technological improvements in clinical interventions can occasionally reverse these conditions, rendering them inadequate for defining the permanence of death (Engelhardt, 1999; Pernick, 1999). Today, brain death – understood as 'the absence of cerebral responsiveness' (Knudsen, 2009, 29) – is the primary definition used within hospitals, particularly as a criterion for organ donation (Bruno, Ledoux, and Laurey, 2009). Defining death in such biological terms can medicalise death, reducing physical presence to materiality (the physical matter) that can be measured technologically. Moreover, the shift to brain death means that the notion of death is increasingly medicalised through the technological and clinical expertise that is required to ascertain the presence or absence of death in these terms.

The medicalisation of death is also identified by some based on where death occurs. Focusing on location, this is often about the shift from dying at home or in the community to dying in hospitals. Since the 1950s and 1960s, social scientists have been writing about how death within certain countries – such as those in Europe and North America – has become an issue that is under the purview of medicine. The interpretations portray how societies have shifted how death has occurred and been handled over time (Ariès, 1975; Illich, 1975). This shift includes a change from dying earlier in life and predominately from accidents and infectious diseases to dying later in life and from non-infectious diseases, like cancer. These theorists suggest that people viewed accidents and infections as issues of fate, whereas over time, health was viewed as something to manage by specialists, emerging as societies became more technological. Whilst this perspective is not inclusive when thinking about societies globally, it points to a connection being made between technological advancements, professionalisation, and the medicalisation of life processes such as death.

One notable theorist about this transition is Ariès. Ariès (1975) noted that in the mid-20th century, new cultural values (often claimed to be from America) created the sequestering of birth, illness and death into clinical spaces, creating new societal taboos and destroying social practices – death had become unknown, 'invisible' and 'wild' (611). Before this, Ariès argued that there was 'Tame Death' – death was something that people expected, talked about, and had rituals for. Over time, as death became linked with disease, as Ariès argued, this led to death itself being viewed as dirty; people did not only suffer from the disease but also the agony of this dirtiness. Consequently, he argues that part of the medicalisation of dying is not just about seeing it as linked to disease processes but the desire to contain the perceived dirtiness and agony, typically in hospital spaces. He adds that hospitalisation of dying people also enabled families to manage the dying processes differently in terms of managing visitors and balancing care with other social responsibilities (571). Rather than presenting the move to medicalising dying to be purely about healthcare professionals seeking to control dying as it is linked to non-curable diseases, Ariès' account illustrates a nuanced shift in how dying is perceived and managed within society and social networks.

Similarly, building on Ariès' work, Kellehear has argued that as societies have become more industrialised and modern, there has been a corresponding shift in how death is managed and by whom, becoming less community-based and overseen less by religious leaders. He has argued, however, that dying remains a social process, and whilst it may be medicalised, it is important to remember that the vast amount of 'dying' (i.e. living towards the moment of death) occurs outside of clinical spaces (Kellehear, 2008; Sallnow et al., 2022).

Illich (1975) critiques the deaths happening in US healthcare in the 1970s, mainly as many of these occurred in hospitals. He viewed this as people dying anonymously in large bureaucratic and consumer-driven settings (29), values he did not believe should be associated with death, especially not what he viewed as a natural death. Clark (2002) has summarised Illich's critique of the medicalisation of dying as focusing on four main points. First, Illich viewed this shift to deaths occurring in hospital as indicating a societal and individual loss of the ability to accept death and suffering as meaningful and part of life. Second, he viewed the sequestering of death as part of a 'total war' against death across the life course. Third, whereas Ariès points out that people may benefit from dying people being hospitalised, Illich viewed it as damaging personal and family care as well as devaluing traditional rituals. Lastly, he noted that when dying or bereaved people resisted 'patienthood' (i.e. taking the role of a patient), they were perceived to be deviant and that this was a form of social control. Similar to Ariès and Kellehear, who note the social change over time, Illich is more vocal about how this shift can impact social values and be a form of (unwanted) control.

Natural Death, Ordinary Dying, and Doulas

Medicalised dying has been challenged on several fronts, from the location of death to how the process of dying is managed to who is involved. This section explores some of these critiques and the attempts there have been to challenge a norm of medicalised dying. Notably, some of these do not seek to de-medicalise dying completely but remake what aspects of dying are under the medical gaze and how people respond to dying as part of a life and social process.

One of Illich's (1975) critiques is that death in a hospital was not a 'natural' death because of the interventions and setting. In some contexts, the phrase 'allow natural death' is linked to the withdrawing or even with-holding of medical interventions that may be deemed to be life-extending (see, e.g. Knox and Vereb, 2005). Some countries that do not legalise medical assistance in dying may even have laws around this provision, such as the United Arab Emirates; in other countries, such practices of withdrawing treatment are understood within medical ethics and seek to reduce overall harm, even if death is an unintended consequence.[1] Palliative medicine (discussed more in Chapter 7) has also been associated with supporting natural dying processes (Ashby, 2009). This section concerns itself with how the dying process – rather than the moment of death – is seen to be something that is under the threat of medicalisation.

Yet what is perceived to be 'natural' is not a given. Seymour (1999, 2000) poignantly illustrates this point in her work in intensive care units. Through her sociological study, she saw how clinical professionals will manage technology so that symptoms and stages of dying are managed in a way to be perceived by the family as 'natural'; it may even manage to achieve an 'ideal death'. And yet, this very technological intervention means that the dying processes are not unfolding 'naturally' (i.e. on their own). For example, through the descriptions of cases, Seymour shows how the use of technology and medication ensures that death is neither prolonged nor too sudden after treatment options have been explored. Therefore, it is collectively understood that bodily death is the likely outcome (Seymour, 1999). This kind of dying could even include 'orchestrating dying so that the family experience a gradual, quiet and dignified event' (1999, 698). Seymour's work is critical of how other authors have polarised deaths as either technological or natural. In doing so, Seymour illustrates that what matters is how people attribute meaning to the technology rather than merely its presence or absence when determining what is perceived as 'natural' death. Acknowledging the importance of meaning-making is important to note because it allows for a nuanced understanding of how deaths can be both considered 'medicalised' and 'natural'. The critique of medicalisation, therefore, is not just about the place of death, the role of professionals, and the use of technology – it is about how it shapes understandings of death.

A more recent attempt to combat medicalising drives around dying is Kathryn Mannix's concept of 'ordinary dying'.[2] Her work focuses on demystifying for the general public the typical phases a person goes through as they die based on her decades of experience as a palliative care doctor. For example, she explains how a person may lose their appetite days before death, how their breathing may change, and that they are likely to become sleepier. Although not explicitly articulated as such, Mannix's approach to awareness raising aims to indicate where (medical) interventions are not needed towards the end of life – artificial hydration and nutrition are implicitly indicated as unnecessary for the dying person experiencing a loss of appetite. As her work has developed, she also focused on the non-bodily changes that may occur, such as the sharing of 'last messages' (Downe and Mannix, 2023). This aligns with her palliative medicine background, which seeks to provide a holistic approach to dying. Palliative medicine – and palliative care more broadly – asserts that dying is something that can occur under medical supervision but in a way that celebrates the individual and their life and may be supported with symptom management to minimise distress and pain (MacDonald, Herx, and Boyle, 2021). As such, hospice and palliative care seek to humanise the experience of death rather than view it as a medical condition (Fontana, 2009, 39).

Doula-supported dying is another example of an attempt to destabilise the assumption that death and dying must be medicalised or under the domain of clinicians by providing community-based death support (Krawczyk et al., 2022). The essence of a doula is someone who can provide non-medical support as they accompany someone on their dying journey. Doulas provide support to those with terminal or life-limiting illnesses and those around them, as well as providing support and education to communities around issues of death, dying, and bereavement (Rawlings et al., 2019). The focus of doula provision can include but is not limited to presence with the dying person, advocacy and administrative support (e.g. for completing wills and linking with professional services), and emotional and spiritual support. Some argue that doulas can support people to have good-quality deaths by advocating for the dying person in clinical contexts, helping them to avoid 'inappropriate' [medical] treatment as well as receive timely care (Flaherty and Meurer, 2021). However, there is considerable variation nationally and internationally regarding what doula support looks like and the training (if any) they undertake (Rawlings et al., 2021; Krawczyk et al., 2022). Moreover, since the role of doulas is still relatively new, and it is not a professionalised role (Rawlings et al., 2019), the terminology used and definitions of what they are based on what they do are in flux; terms include end-of-life doula, soul midwife, death coach, dying guide, death midwife, and palliative care doula. There is therefore both variation in what the doulas do and what the role is referred to as, but what unites across this is an aim to practice a different approach to the end of life than orienting only around biomedicine.

In all these examples, there remains a paradox within them – namely, whilst dying can be considered a process human bodies go through at the end of life that needs not to be medicalised, it can still be 'supported' with medical treatment and/ or by medical professionals. None of these examples presumes that 'end-of-life care' involving some form of professional and/or symptom management should not exist. In different ways, these approaches to challenging medicalisation are about reframing how death and dying are understood rather than removing medicine's role entirely – from curating a 'natural' appearing death in hospital to raising awareness of bodily and personal changes towards the end of life. Given that some level of medical intervention is presumed in these contexts, the following section examines the role of medical advancements and technology.

Dying and Technology: Illusions of Choice

As noted in the previous section, medicalised dying is not without treatment but rather concerns itself with if, how, and when treatment is provided. On the one hand, palliative medicine has specialised symptom management towards the end of life, including, but not limited to, pain relief, breathlessness, and agitation (Lipman, Jackson, and Tyler, 2000). On the other hand, concern about medicalising dying also questions the potential overtreatment of a person towards the end of their life, especially when the aim of intervention is no longer curative or perceived as 'futile' (Cardona and Greenaway, 2019). Attempts to resolve this tension have led to two main approaches – patient-centred choice about treatment and structural influence over what treatment is on offer.

When critiques of the medicalisation of death were very socially prominent in the United States, the concept of living wills (also known as advance directives) was introduced in legal circles (Kutner, 1969). This would allow individuals to state, prior to occurrence, what treatments they would not like to receive, such as resuscitation. It would be an expression of choice that could have some legal bearing, formal documentation that is the patient's property. This approach to planning ahead has been adopted in a broader range of practices, from advance care planning to funeral planning (Lyons and Winter, 2021; Borgstrom, 2015a). Encouraging people to make decisions about treatments is often a part of palliative care and doula support, promoting a particular template for dying, which includes preparing for death (Walters, 2004). There is a considerable amount of research on how to support such planning, if and how people want to do it, and cultural variation in approaches to planning (McDermott and Selman, 2018; Jimenez et al., 2018; Thomas, Lobo, and Detering, 2018). Others critique the use of advance directives as providing a sense of 'false control' over dying (Perkins, 2007), as such ways of thinking do not always appreciate the underlying biological processes and may encourage people to think they can control the timing of death.

Another sense of controlling the dying process that is considered medicalised in some contexts is through the use of medical assistance in dying. Whilst there is a wide range of what can be regarded as assisted dying, medical aid in dying is specifically about the role of healthcare professionals in providing and administering the means to die after a person has requested it and had an assessment. Whilst not legal in most countries globally, data from Canada, for example, illustrates that people opt for medical assistance in dying due to symptoms from their disease, a sense of lost autonomy, and a fear of suffering (Wiebe et al., 2018). Whether these forms of assisted dying are available in any specific country is linked to local morals and laws (see also Chapter 8). In other contexts, what treatments are even offered is highly influenced by the cost of the treatment, healthcare funding structures, and the use of medical insurance. Kaufman (2015) has illustrated how technological advances can shift what is considered 'standard' treatment in healthcare as procedures become adopted by insurers and expected by the public. She notes that these are often envisioned to extend life, seeking to postpone when dying occurs, even if the intervention impacts the quality of life. On the other hand, in the United Kingdom, treatment may be rationed based on calculations about the impact of quality of life and cost (Edwards, Crump, and Dayan, 2015). The notion of rationing is not limited to the United Kingdom, with research demonstrating that doctors consider resource limitations as a factor that influences if they feel a treatment 'futile' or possible to offer in other countries, including Australia (Close et al., 2019) and sub-Sahara Africa (Ashuntantang, Miljeteig, and Luyckx, 2022; Rao et al., 2022). Therefore, the availability of medical interventions at the end of life is not only limited by patient choice but also what resources are present and societal norms around appropriate treatment towards the end of life.

How dying is medicalised raises questions about what aspects are socially and culturally considered under the scope of medical treatment and care and for whom, when and how that is decided. The examples provided here indicate that this is neither stable nor universally applicable. They are often linked with other structural issues, such as the financing of healthcare, values around personal agency and decision-making, and societal expectations of levels of medical intervention. Critically appreciating these issues recognises that claiming dying is medicalised so not mean the same thing for everyone everywhere.

End-of-Life Care and Access to Treatment: An Unequal Picture

End-of-life care can be defined as the support for people who are in the last months or years of their life (NHS, 2022), whilst this definition may not be explicitly referencing medical care, this type of definition is typically used in healthcare contexts and implicitly assumes the care includes professional healthcare. Medicalising dying through end-of-life care has implications for who receives this type of care, as well as when, where, and how; embedding end-of-life care within healthcare systems means that access to end-of-life care can be inequitable and variable. So, whilst there are some critics about the medicalisation of dying – claiming that there should be less medicalisation – in other contexts, there are people who are not receiving medical interventions that could benefit them, such as pain relief, even near the end of life.

For example, the United Kingdom is currently ranked as a world leader in end-of-life care provision due to the history of the modern hospice movement in the United Kingdom and recent policy developments promoting end-of-life care (Economist Intelligence Unit, 2010). Nevertheless, various reports indicate that within the United Kingdom, as in other countries, access to good multi-professional end-of-life care is not guaranteed for every person dying (Burles, Peternelj-Taylor, and Holtslander, 2016; Walshe et al., 2009). Research indicates that many people throughout the United Kingdom who would benefit from palliative-focused end-of-life care are still not receiving it (Richards, 2022). On a global scale, inequalities in receiving end-of-life care are also noted (Sallnow et al., 2022). This can be caused by policy differences (e.g. restricted access to certain medications in some countries), differences in healthcare financing and infrastructure, and cultural differences in discussing and planning for death (Economist Intelligence Unit, 2015).

In a wide range of countries, certain groups of people tend to be disproportionally disadvantaged in receiving end-of-life care, particularly in receiving specialist end-of-life care. These include older people (particularly those living in nursing and residential homes), people from ethnic minority groups, homeless people or those living in prisons, and people from socio-economically deprived geographical areas (e.g. Haines et al., 2018; Rosenwax and McNamara, 2006; Stajduhar et al., 2019). People may experience a double disadvantage in accessing end-of-life care if they belong to more than one of these groups, such as having dementia and being from an ethnic minority background (Connolly, Sampson, and Purandare, 2012). People from different religious backgrounds, the LGBT+ community, and people who have mental health issues may also anticipate discrimination, which can affect if and how they access end-of-life care services. Overall, people who may be generally marginalised in healthcare systems are also disadvantaged in accessing and receiving end-of-life care; Koffman (2023) has noted that receiving palliative care is a privilege. If a medicalised form of dying is held up as an ideal, even with minimal medical intervention, it is important to question who has access to this form of dying, as well as if they want it.

There is also the assumption that dying is culturally less medicalised in some settings than in others, particularly in lower-income countries (e.g. Economist Intelligence Unit, 2010; Sallnow et al., 2022), the presumption is that community care is the default and preference. This approach is quite generalising and does not recognise the interplay between health, medicine, and culture in many places. For example, a review focusing on research from and about Africa shows that there needs to be 'a reconsideration of the assumption that in Africa the extended family care for the sick, and that people prefer home-based care' (Gysels et al., 2011). Even if home care is viewed as an ideal in palliative care, other research has shown that it can be unrealistic. Olenja's (1999) study of community attitudes towards home care for patients with AIDS in Kenya illustrated how home care was seen as unrealistic in the context of poverty, stigma and lack of knowledge of how to care for a person with AIDS. Another example is Risat's (2024) work in Bangladesh, which demonstrated that when families no longer had the means to care, they would bring relatives to healthcare settings to improve the end-of-life care they received. Therefore, rather than demonise medical intervention during dying, it was presumed to be more appropriate than potentially receiving 'poor' care at home. Moreover, in other countries, people may purposely seek out technology-intense end-of-life care settings, such as intensive care units, viewing this as preferable and in alignment with their beliefs about life and death. Nevertheless, it can be helpful to remember who can access such interventions, as Mpho Tutu van Furth notes that 'most people in the world do not have to wrestle with an over-medicalised death, they have minimal access to quality health care' (Sallnow et al., 2022).

On the one hand, there may be an idealistic vision of de-medicalised dying and a presumption that this occurs in some countries more than others due to differences in cultural structures and healthcare systems. Yet, there should also be caution in assuming that this form of dying is desired and feasible in these settings. Instead, exploring such assumptions can expose inequalities to access to care, structural factors impacting life and care more generally, as well as opening up space to explore cultural, religious, and social perceptions of death alongside medical approaches.

Conclusion

In 2022, the *Lancet* – a leading medical journal – published a commission entitled *The Value of Death* (Sallnow et al., 2022). Within it, it raises many of the concerns addressed in this chapter: changes to where death has occurred, concerns about medicalisation, inequitable access to treatment and concerns about overtreatment. It notes that:

> A striking inconsistency with the progressive medicalisation of death and dying is that it has not led to a parallel increase in relief of symptoms such as pain with low-cost, evidence-based methods, nor has it led to universal access to palliative care services at the end of life.
>
> *(Sallnow et al., 2022, 845)*

As demonstrated in this chapter, whilst concerns for the medicalisation of death and dying are rooted in particular social histories, it has become an everlasting concern within medicine and end-of-life care itself, leading to tensions around to what extent, what kinds of, and for whom medicalisation – in terms of intervention, medical professional involvement, and location – is deemed appropriate and legitimate. This chapter has considered critiques of medicalisation, attempts to remake dying under the medical gaze, and issues of unequal access to medicalised dying. As demonstrated here, whilst medicalised dying may seem the norm for many, this is a situated practice and discussions of medicalisation should acknowledge this.

Notes

1 See Chapter 8 for a more detailed discussion of assisted dying and the different terms used to describe a range of practices linked to it.
2 Borgstrom and McArtney wrote a blog post reflecting on Mannix's use of the term 'ordinary dying' on social media in relation to Queen Elizabeth's death. www.mariecu rie.org.uk/blog/ordinary-dying-queen-elizabeth/357885.

7

PALLIATIVE CARE AND THE MODERN HOSPICE MOVEMENT

Introduction

The word hospice is based on the Latin term *hospitium*, linked to hospitality and means guest house. Historically, religious organisations, like a monastery, would have run hospices to provide lodging for travellers (Vocabulary.com, n.d.). But in the 20th century, the word became more frequently linked to a place and/or type of care, rooted in specific values, for those who are terminally ill. Now, depending on the country and context, people may use the word 'hospice' to mean a place where people are cared for – such as they are 'in the hospice' – or to refer to the type of care that they are receiving, such as being 'on hospice'. These ways of thinking and talking about hospice are due to the Modern Hospice Movement, often attributed to Dame Cicely Saunders and the opening of St Christopher's Hospice in London in 1967. This chapter describes the Modern Hospice Movement, how it is linked to concepts of good death, and issues of inequality when it comes to idealised deaths linked to hospice care.

Since hospice is linked to the care of people with terminal illnesses, there is overlap with other related types of care, such as palliative care, palliative medicine, and end-of-life care. How these terms are used varies in each country and has varied over time and caused conceptual confusion (Billings, 1998; Radbruch et al., 2020a); there have been multiple attempts to find consensus on the terms (e.g. Radbruch et al., 2020b; Ryan et al., 2020; Schüttengruber et al., 2022; Xiao et al., 2021). For clarity, here is an overview of how the terms will be used in this chapter. Hospice refers to the buildings, the philosophy, and the kind of care that hospices and hospice workers provide. In some countries, the term hospice is used to refer to palliative care, and, for example, many of the clinical staff working in UK hospices are specialists in palliative care. Palliative care is the holistic,

DOI: 10.4324/9781003318002-9

individualised care of someone who has been diagnosed with an incurable or life-limiting condition (Department of Health, 2000); palliative care is not limited to those who are imminently dying. It also provides support for the dying person's family and friends during illness and bereavement (WHO, 2015b). It often includes providing care that addresses physical, psychological, social and spiritual needs. Palliative medicine is a recognised medical speciality in some countries, such as the United Kingdom in 1987 (Murie, 2006), but not in others, such as Denmark (Graven, Petersen, and Timm, 2021), specialising in palliative care; the rise of this as a distinct speciality is linked to the rise of hospice care (Higginson, 1993). End-of-life care is care that helps people with advanced, progressive, incurable illnesses to live as well as possible until they die. It enables both patients' and families' supportive and palliative care needs to be identified and met throughout the last phases of life and into bereavement (Department of Health, 2008). So, whilst hospice is linked to palliative and end-of-life care and often involves delivering this type of care, all palliative care, palliative medicine, and end-of-life care is not provided by hospices or hospice workers. Consequently, when talking about international contexts, researchers tend to focus on palliative or end-of-life care rather than 'hospice' as the key term in order to ensure greater clarity about what is being discussed.

The Modern Hospice Movement has played a crucial role in the development, growth and professionalisation of caring for dying people. It was founded partly to respond to the medicalisation of death (see Chapter 6), yet, during the latter part of the 20th century, hospices became incorporated into the healthcare system (Bradshaw, 1996). The very idea that care at the end of life is supported by and within a medical system has been fundamental to the expansion of hospice and palliative care nationally and internationally (Economist Intelligence Unit, 2010). This chapter shows how the Modern Hospice Movement was created and how it envisioned a change in how dying is experienced. This is important to attend to since it has impacted not just the United Kingdom, where the first hospice was opened, but has spread globally and informed international standards of palliative and end-of-life care. Attending to the Modern Hospice Movement with a critical lens enables an appreciation of how it has shaped death and dying in many societies and how it may continue to shape these issues over the following decades.

Modern Hospice Movement

The Modern Hospice Movement is considered to be rooted in the opening of St Christopher's Hospice in London in 1967. St Christopher's Hospice is a building in London which currently describes itself as 'a friendly, vibrant place, and as unlike a traditional hospital as we can make it' (St Christopher's Hospice, 2024). When it opened, the hospice focused on people with terminal illnesses and a team of staff dedicated to their care and committed to discovering the best ways to care for people in such situations (Baines, 2011). The choice of the word hospice was deliberate, linking to a tradition of welcoming those who needed care with honour and respect (Saunders, 1996). What distinguished St Christopher's from previous hospices or care homes was the combination of medical input alongside nursing and spiritual support, as well as the publicity that came with it (Goldin, 1981). Since its opening, St Christopher's has been recognised as a site of innovation and education about palliative care.

Medical historian and sociologist David Clark has written extensively about its history and its founder, Dame Cicely Saunders (e.g. Clark, 1998, 2004, 2022). Some call Dame Saunders the 'hospice mother' (Graven, Petersen, and Timm, 2021) due to her role in envisioning and creating hospice care; others recognise her as the founder of palliative care due to her role in developing symptom control practices (Baines, 2011). Clark notes that Saunders wrote her first paper on the care of the dying in 1957, an entire decade before St Christopher's was opened, and has documented the social, political, and strategic work she undertook to establish the hospice, noting the complex interplay between her charismatic influence and the context in which she operated (Clark, 1998).

Dame Cicely Saunders was trained originally as a nurse and social worker. In her own writing, she cites a meeting in 1947 with David Tasma, a young patient from Warsaw, as inspiring her later work both in his words and in providing her £500[1] via his will (Saunders, 1996). Clark also notes that she had a strong sense of 'personal calling, underpinned by a powerful religious commitment' (Clark, 1998, 46); the combination of her training, experiences and personal values influenced the hospice philosophy. Quotes attributed to her still frequently adorn policy papers and hospice walls, reminding people of some of her core values, such as

> You matter because you are you, and you matter to the end of your life. We will do all we can not only to help you die peacefully but also to live until you die.
> How people die remains in the memory of those who live on.

These point to a fundamental belief that their dying, death or grief does not diminish a person's worth. Significantly, she also believed that how a society treated the dying reflected its fundamental values, saying, 'A society which shuns the dying must have an incomplete philosophy' (Saunders, 1961, 50). As demonstrated by the continual use of her quotes and thinking, Dame Saunders has a continual and ancestral-like legacy in the hospice and palliative care field.

When St Christopher's was founded, there were concerns about the deaths from wars and increasing medicalisation, with people dying in hospitals and being ignored once it was apparent they were no longer curable. Hospice was therefore designed to create a space for the dying person where they could be cared for in a way that would 'help dying people to a good and peaceful death characterised by values such as open awareness, acceptance and reconciliation with dying' (Graven, Petersen, and Timm, 2021). One way of ensuring this was through the treatment of what Saunders called 'total pain' – addressing suffering from physical symptoms, social problems, mental distress and emotional problems (Saunders in Clark, 2014). Rather than focusing on the disease, hospice care was to be focused on the 'syndromes of pain' (Saunders, 1967), and this focus on total pain has been a core value of hospice and holistic palliative care since. Through the development of hospice, underpinned by Cicely Saunders' values and actions, an idealised version of how people could die and be supported to live their lives towards death was created.

Over the years, this notion of hospice has spread beyond London and the United Kingdom, and similar hospices have been opened up in over 136 countries (Lynch et al., 2013). Over the years, St Christopher's has been a site for pioneering innovations around patient care, including symptom management, as well as educating people about palliative care.[2] Not only does it care for dying people, but it provides a range of educational resources (online and in-person), is a site of in-person training for professionals, and has a network of shops to raise charitable funds to support its mission. Whilst hospices were initially designated as places that could support dying people outside of critiques medical institutions – namely hospitals – this rise in focusing on symptom control, education, and functions beyond care has led some social scientists to comment on how hospices have become over time reordered around organisational logistics that are not too dissimilar from medical institutions. Hospice care has itself over time become professionalised, medicalised, and routinised. In particular, the development of palliative medicine as a speciality evolving from hospice care has meant that there has been a shift in foregrounding more secular humanistic values instead of the original religious ones (Clark, 2002). Graven et al. (2021) have used empirical research in Danish hospices to illustrate how hospice managers have felt the need to pragmatically accept some medicalisation to accommodate specialist palliative care and symptom control whilst also still holding onto language rooted in existential values and virtues. The international growth of this movement, on one hand, then provides an opportunity for changing how dying people are cared for on a large scale, whilst at the same time, may not provide as great of the shift from medical models as originally conceived.

McKnight (1995) has argued that the commodification and professionalisation of hospice actually betray the original values of the hospice movement. Furthermore, it is argued that creating a new institution that specialises in the care of the dying may actually undermine people's confidence and capacities to care for dying family and friends. Baugher (2008) has noted that within the hospice field, there is sometimes the tendency to view them as absolute specialists in palliative care and, therefore, end-of-life care (see also Connor, 1998). However, it should be noted that in the United Kingdom since at least 2008, there has been a policy rhetoric that end-of-life care is 'everyone's business' and implication that most forms of non-pharmacological palliation can be provided by a wider range of professionals and the public (Department of Health, 2008).

Good Death

Hospice care is often associated with notions of 'good death', and the term is frequently discussed within academic and practice journals focusing on hospice and palliative care. Whilst it is acknowledged that there is no consensus about how to define a 'good death' (Meier et al., 2016), many of the features used to define it can be linked to hospice values and palliative care practices. Since hospices and the hospice movement champion a particular way of caring for the dying, this has implications for how the dying experience is expected to ideally occur. This section will examine the topic of 'good death' in more detail as a way of critically understanding how the hospice movement both promotes a notion of 'good death' as well as the practical issues that arise.

The notion of 'good death' existed long before the Modern Hospice Movement, and this history is thought to have influenced the values and practices in hospices (Walters, 2004). In the 15th century, the *Ars Moriendi* were two Latin Christina texts, translated as *The Art of Dying*. These texts are viewed as presenting a protocol on how to die well or achieve a 'good death'. The primary audience was thought to be friars, enabling them in their work of supporting those who were dying, specifically in overcoming earthly problems as they transition to eternal glory (Ariès, 1987). Since then, people have provided many interpretations about why the texts existed, how they grew in popularity, and in what ways they resonate with contemporary notions of a good death or, indeed, need to be revived (Feror Ruyes, 2014; Thornton and Phillips, 2009). Whilst the *Ars Moriendi* are rooted in European Christianity, several have also sought to identify if such 'art of dying well' and spiritual care guides exist in other religions, for example including outlining what exists in Islam (Coppens, 2023) and Tibetan Buddhism (Bayer, 2013). The interest in *the Ars Moriendi* continues to circulate in ethics, palliative care and spiritual discussions, with some advocating that societies develop modern or contemporary versions that reflect the issues faced by dying people today, including how to promote agency, issues about treatment decisions, and reconciling relationships and spirituality (Leget, 2007; Ughetti, 2019).

Yet, what is a 'good death' in contemporary society supposed to look like? As noted earlier, there is no consensus on the concept. When reviewing discussions about 'good death' in the academic literature, they vary in terms of what aspects of 'death' are focused on: they describe the proprieties of the dying process, the event of death or the status of being dead (Kastenbaum, 2013). Consequently, good deaths can be viewed as a complex set of preparations and relations (McNamara, Waddell, and Colvin, 1994), including a series of events which may be highly ritualised and individually evaluated as 'good'. This evaluative part is important to note, especially if, on the one hand, there is an expectation that societies could have something like an *Ars Moriendi* or an established set of practices or principles. If there is scope for individual evaluation, then people may value elements of the dying process differently and describe the same death in dissimilar terms (McNamara,

2004). Moreover, cross-cultural studies of good death (Flaskerud, 2017) highlight the importance of context, which can also cause death to be evaluated differently and foreground diverse expectations about the dying process.

Despite this known variation and causes for variation, several studies have attempted to define a 'good death'. For example, one study found that people want these top three things for it to be a good death: to be able to make decisions about themselves, be pain-free, and have emotional well-being (which can be related to holistic care in hospice; Meier et al., 2016). Here, there are links to how good death is being conceptualised and the values and practices of hospice care. Being able to make decisions about one's care is linked to a hospice focus on the person, honouring their self-identify and self-worth. Within hospice care, people are often encouraged to be part of decision-making and even to make advance statements of preferences for care and the setting of their death (Borgstrom, 2015a). The aspect of being pain-free is common in many definitions of good death, sometimes noted as 'symptom free'. This links to Dame Saunders's notion of 'total pain' and is one of the reasons that people advocate for hospice and palliative care towards the end of life as a way of enabling this aspect to be met (Krawczyk, Wood, and Clark, 2018). Lastly, attending to emotional well-being as part of a good death also resonates with hospice values, both in terms of attending to total pain, which may have emotional aspects and holistic care that also considers psychological, social and spiritual elements. Cultural concepts of a good death and hospice practices have considerable overlap, and there is likely an interplay between hospice being influenced by cultural norms while at the same time hospice practices influencing cultural scripts about what a good death could and should look like (Seale, 1998).

The setting of a 'good death' also features in several definitions, including in end-of-life policy definitions in England (Borgstrom, 2020). Here, there is a reference to the dying person being in 'familiar surroundings', often implying that a good death occurs at home (Visser, 2018). Research on people's preferences about the place of death has shown that considerable proportions of the population would like to die in a hospice. However, most people may state they prefer to die at home when asked if they are not currently being cared for in the hospital (Hoare et al., 2015). Culturally, hospices also have to do performative work to display themselves as good places for dying and death, including hosting open days and managing the images they share (e.g. Borgstrom, 2016b). However, in the United Kingdom, approximately only 4% of deaths can occur in hospices, so focusing on hospice as an 'ideal place' may be a misnomer when it comes to the notion of good death.

The term 'euthanasia' is based on the Greek for 'good death' (Norwood, 2007), and this way of dying – the intentional ending of someone's life to end suffering – is sometimes included in peoples' notions of good death (Richards and Krawczyk, 2021; Meier et al., 2016). However, it is often purposefully excluded from definitions in medical settings, including in hospices, depending on the legal context (Borgstrom, 2020). The key element here that causes controversy is the intentionality of the act. In contexts where euthanasia or assisted dying is illegal, hospice and palliative care may still provide pain relief and, as noted earlier, has specialised in symptom management. Although some people may be concerned that the use of such medication may shorten someone's life, since the intention is for symptom management rather than to prematurely end someone's life, this practice is considered ethical within medicine (Arolker, 2017). This is because it is an example of the doctrine of double effect, where the intention is symptom management, but the consequence of death is an extra, even if foreseen, effect of the action taken but is not the intended outcome. This focus on symptom management is also used by anti-euthanasia campaigners who support palliative care and argue that if people had access to adequate symptom care, they would not necessarily want to opt to end their lives earlier. In this way, in some countries, hospice and palliative care may not be able to fully fulfil all notions of 'good death' but still act in a way that seeks to reduce suffering.

The concept of 'good death' has been extensively researched within the context of hospices – from driving philosophy to how different people – such as nurses, patients, and family – perceive what a 'good' death under hospice care is. Within hospice and palliative care, 'good death' encapsulates an idealised concept of dying and that modern hospice philosophy revolves around this concept (Palgi and Abramovitch, 1984). McNamara and colleagues in the 1990s studied good death in Australian hospices, noting that in the United Kingdom and United States at the time, the institutionalisation of hospice care could threaten this ideal (McNamara, Waddell, and Colvin, 1994). They found that nurses expected good deaths to occur in hospices, seeing them as routine, and would often romanticise the re-telling of them by noting aspects like family presence and sunsets. The nurses also wanted to be part of the good deaths, supporting patients and encouraging openness and acceptance of death (McNamara, Waddell, and Colvin, 1995). Interrogating this further, they observed that since hospice nurses are continuously confronted by mortality, working towards the process of 'good death' can affirm the notion of living. This led the researchers to conclude that 'good death' becomes routinised and objectified in hospices, benefiting not only the individuals but also the organisation by 'acting as a symbolic vehicle and guide to future action' (McNamara, Waddell, and Colvin, 1994).

Yet, what a 'good death' is in hospice varies depending on who one speaks to. Nurses may perceive it to be about openness, acceptance, and preparedness (McNamara, Waddell, and Colvin, 1994, 1995), with sudden deaths or where patients are viewed as 'reluctant' deemed problematic (McNamara, Waddell, and Colvin, 1994). Factors like symptom control, family involvement, and when death occurs within the life course are also factored into the evaluation, with perceived distress or uncontrolled symptoms troubling nurses (Payne, Langley-Evans, and Hillier, 1996). Therefore, the process of dying is important and not just the moment of death, with deaths more likely to be identified as 'good' if it goes well overall (see also Taylor, 1993).

However, what patients view as a good death differs and is more diverse according to the research literature. Interviewing patients in the United Kingdom, researchers have found that they consider the following to be part of a good death: dying in one's sleep, dying quietly, with dignity, being pain-free and dying suddenly. These may contradict what staff expect (Payne, Langley-Evans, and Hillier, 1996). When exploring the possible intersection between hospice philosophy and major religions, Coward and Stajduhar (2012, 307) note that responses to pain control and symptom management differ within religions, especially around the experiences and expectations of death. Others have noted that what may be deemed 'good' to the deceased may not be evaluated as 'good' by the relatives or staff at the time (Masson, 2002). Reviewing the research evidence for how bereaved relatives evaluate if a death was good or not, Tenzek and Depner (2017) demonstrated that what is important to family is having opportunities for family to be present during the end-of-life process and a sense of continuity of care, including into bereavement. Looking across perspectives, a review of 'dying well' studies found that common themes include 'dying at the preferred place, relief from pain and psychological distress, emotional support from loved ones, autonomous treatment decision making, avoidance of futile life-prolonging interventions and of being a burden to others, right to assisted suicide or euthanasia, effective communication with professionals, and performance of rituals' (Zaman et al., 2021, 1). Many of these align with palliative care values although are not reliant on them. Therefore, a more nuanced understanding of 'good death' should to be adopted, which considers different perspectives, needs and provision types whilst still considering the socio-cultural context in which the death is occurring.

McNamara (2004) first suggested thinking about 'good enough' deaths in hospices as a way to appreciate how hospice staff strive to achieve 'good deaths' for their patients but that this may not always be possible. Masson (2002) extends this to patients and families who are often aware of the tensions and paradoxes in divergent perspectives when it comes to dying – 'good' is perceived as too absolute to accommodate complex emotions as well as the changes that occur during the process of dying. Masson (2002) further argues that if hospice and palliative care focused more on 'good enough' death rather than 'good death', it would allow for more engagement with the complexity of the experience and not detract from striving for professional standards.

While these suggestions to move from 'good death' to 'good enough' death were made in the late 1990s and early 2000s, policy and palliative care discourse from the 2000s onwards continue to discuss 'good death'. A discourse analysis of policy in the United Kingdom illustrated that policy explicitly defines a good death as having the following attributes: being treated as an individual, with dignity and respect; being without pain and other symptoms; being in familiar surroundings; and being in the company of close family and/or friends (Borgstrom, 2020). Implicitly, a more elaborate understanding was identified: the person receives holistic end-of-life care; the dying person is treated with dignity and respect; the death is not sudden and unexpected; people are prepared and have ideally done some advance care planning; people are aware that someone is dying and openly discuss this; upon knowing the dying person's preferences, all involved are to work towards achieving these; the place of death is important; the person's family is involved; and the needs of the bereaved are considered. Most of this resonates with descriptions of what hospice staff viewed as part of good death, illustrating how this philosophy and idealised driver of care has continued. However, this analysis points to the importance of care, rather than the event of death per se, as a focal point. Consequently, it is recommended that due to the discursive power of policy – and, by extension, how the term is used in the Modern Hospice Movement – there should be a shift away from using the term good death and related ways of evaluating deaths to outlining what quality dying and care should look like. This shift would enable a more explicit emphasis on the processes that could change outcomes whilst not prescribing that all deaths are similarly good and would be in line with appreciating the tensions in dying in hospice and the diversity in perspectives that previous research has discovered.

Inequality in Accessing an Idealised Death

As noted in the previous section, the Modern Hospice Movement and the focus on good death have at their core, idealised notions of how death occurs. Whilst the ideal can be a motivating factor for work and help sustain the organisational processes, ideals can also be exclusionary. This section explores some of the ways in which hospice care – both as an ideal and how it is practised – can be a site of inequality and inequity.

First, it is known that more people could benefit from hospice and palliative care than currently do (Tobin et al., 2022). Part of this is down to access to hospice and palliative care in geographical terms – hospices are not equally or equitably distributed within countries or even globally (Clark et al., 2020; van Steijn et al., 2021). Even within the United Kingdom, with a longer history of hospice provision, one's distance to a hospice depends on where one lives, with some areas having more hospices than others. One of the reasons for this is that hospices are heavily funded through charities, and so their location is not purely based on population health assessments. In several countries, it has been well documented that people in rural areas are less likely to have access to hospice (van Steijn et al., 2021), this mirrors a general trend of less access to healthcare in these areas, especially to specialist services. If hospice care is deemed to be a 'gold standard' for the care of the dying, it is essential to question who can access this 'gold standard' and what structural barriers there may be to access.

Another factor that impacts access to hospice care is linked to what disease or condition a person is dying from. Although the modern hospice was not envisioned to be exclusive to people with cancer, there is a major critique within the field that this has been their predominant focus (Sallnow et al., 2022). This is partly due to cancer being understood to have a more clearly defined and identifiable dying trajectory (Murray and Sheikh, 2008), as well as being an area in which pain relief and symptom management – key specialist traits of palliative care – have been more extensively researched and developed. Being able to identify that someone is dying and/or would benefit from hospice care is a crucial step to accessing hospice because it often relies on a referral process. In many countries, access to hospice for people with non-malignant diseases (i.e. something other than cancer) has been variable (Lau et al., 2021; Sallnow et al., 2022). Specific interventions to increase access have been designed, including hospices that have explicitly adopted or developed a speciality in treating other diseases, such as HIV/AIDs or neurological conditions.

Besides location and disease, other factors act as barriers to hospice care. These vary depending on context, but systematic reviews highlight that they include age, ethnicity, and possibly gender, sexuality, and marital status (see Tobin et al., 2022). The palliative care community are aware of inequalities in access, especially as there is growing research literature demonstrating the scope and impact of these (see Koffman et al., 2023). In turn, as a sector, there are attempts to address a range of inequalities and re-envision hospice care for the future. It is beyond the scope of this chapter to outline them all, but here are a few examples: providing technology to enable access to hospice-level expertise in a person's home, virtual reality, and using more community-based peer support to provide care where a person lives (Moutogiannis et al., 2023; Webb et al., 2021). Both are about trying to change the perimeters and parameters of hospice care, relocating it from focusing on specific places and people to widen access.

Nevertheless, even if one manages to access a hospice, not all hospices can provide the same level of service. This is particularly poignant in relation to access to morphine globally, with data in many low- and middle-income countries showing that access and consumption of morphine are below estimated levels of need (Clark et al., 2022). Variation in access depends on several factors, including legislation that impacts availably of the drug, cultural perceptions about the drug and its effects, and the cost of the medication. Access to morphine is considered such a problem internationally that it has been the focus of several high-profile reports (Sallnow et al., 2022) and WHO activities (WHO, 2023a). This relates to issues discussed in Chapter 6 about inequalities and the medicalisation of dying.

Conclusion

Current palliative and end-of-life care is linked to the Modern Hospice Movement. The start of this movement is often attributed to Dame Cicely Saunders who set up St Christopher's Hospice in London in the 1960s. Since the 1960s, hospice care has spread across the world, although there is variation in terms of how it is practised, who has access, and questions about if and how it adapts to local contexts.

The hospice model of care seeks to be holistic, covering symptom management, as well as psychological, social and spiritual aspects of well-being in order to address 'total pain'. This approach to care has influenced palliative and end-of-life care with palliative medicine emerging as a distinct medical speciality in some countries. Part of this approach is a focus on 'good death', an idealised version of how death and dying can occur often placing emphasis on symptom management, a person's preferences, and place of death. Whilst the notion of a 'good death' can be a motivating factor for professional work and help sustain the organisational processes, it is important to remember that ideals can also be exclusionary and to think critically about how they shape the way care is provided and experienced.

Notes

1   Worth approximately £24,000 in 2023. For perspective, hospices in the United Kingdom report that it often costs several million to run the hospice per year in 2023 with the sector facing a £186 million funding deficit (Hospice UK, n.d.).
2   The hospice provides a range of educational programmes and has links with several academic institutions. It is also the base for several research studies on a wide range of topics from symptom management to community engagement. More details about the hospice can be found at their website: www.stchristophers.org.uk/.

8

ASSISTED DYING

Introduction

Assisted dying is a controversial topic. While assisted dying is often portrayed as a polarising topic, with people either firmly in favour or opposed, the reality is more nuanced and complex. People might approve or reject assisted dying, depending on the scenario. Furthermore, lived experience might again alter these perceptions. Yet many people strongly oppose it for moral and religious reasons. Only a few countries across the globe have a legal framework that allows for this form of dying, but several countries are debating whether they should adopt this practice and, if so, in what way. Ideas around assisted dying are constantly in flux; countries which have legalised this practice continue to have debates about the ethical, moral and social implications of this form of dying.

Technological developments in medicine have caused a shift in understandings of dying and death and have, for example, introduced the notion of 'brain death', which has drastically altered understandings of who is alive and who is dead. Developments in medicine have made it possible for life to be extended and prolonged, and consequently, dying has become a prolonged process as well. It is sometimes argued that these technological developments, and the prolongation of life that can be achieved with them, have introduced the debate around the ending of life by means of assisted dying. Yet evidence shows that even before the introduction of these technologies, discourse existed around autonomy and choice in death (Buchbinder, 2021).

Anthropologists Richards and Krawczyk (2021) suggest that life-extending treatments and treatments that hasten death are 'two sides of the same coin' that point to a 'Western' denial of dying. They ponder to what extent assisted dying affects the cultural value of dying and note that it is another way in which dying

DOI: 10.4324/9781003318002-10

can be erased, and that it is not a cause but a symptom of societies uncomfortable with acknowledging that dying indeed occurs.

In contrast, it has been suggested that the legal availability of assisted dying opens a space for people to discuss dying. Anthropologist Frances Norwood (2009) suggests that the availability of euthanasia has created an environment in the Netherlands in which talking about death and potential endings is more socially acceptable. She termed these discussions 'euthanasia talk', as the assumed availability makes it possible for people to reflect on their mortality. It is important to keep in mind that access to euthanasia is still highly restricted, and it is very much *assumed* availability that drives these discussions. In the Netherlands, euthanasia is something that people can request, yet it is not a right. Still, these types of conversations are much more difficult to have if they are purely an academic and abstract exercise. This type of legislation thus creates a discourse, or a way of talking about death and dying, that would not be possible if euthanasia was not an 'option'. Studies in Oregon and Vermont have similarly demonstrated that assisted dying is far more discussed than it is actually performed (Buchbinder, 2021). This shows the impact of legislation for people then consciously reflecting on and discussing death and dying.

Assisted dying is inherently social. There are various 'stakeholders' involved in assisted dying including the dying, their relationships, medical professionals, policymakers and law-enforcers. These groups will all have different understandings and views regarding this topic. As this chapter will show, despite ideas of autonomy and choice underpinning ideas around assisted dying, assisted dying always takes place in a social realm. Whilst debates around assisted dying often revolve around its legality, the law is not an abstract thing but is interpreted and carried out by people. When discussing assisted dying, it is easy to slip into legal language, yet it is pertinent to keep in mind that all of this is inherently social, and about the interactions between people.

This chapter offers insight into different definitions used to describe assisted dying, and what these terms reveal about socio-cultural and moral attitudes towards this form of dying. The chapter outlines the countries that currently have a legal framework and how assisted dying is conducted in their particular context. As assisted dying is not available in every country, access to this form of dying is not evenly distributed across the globe. Importantly, as will be shown in this chapter, even within the countries that have legalised or decriminalised assisted dying it is evident that some people are more likely to receive an assisted death than others. The final section considers various arguments for and against assisted dying demonstrating the ongoing debates on the matter.

Terminology

There is a myriad of terms that describe assistance in dying. The 'assistance' refers to the fact that death is acted upon and is often defined in opposition of so-called natural deaths in which no interventions to hasten death have occurred. The increased medicalisation of death and dying means that the boundary between 'natural' and 'assisted' dying is blur and not straightforward. The sheer number of terms to describe assisted dying both reflect the different societal contexts this practice has developed in, and that terminology does not simple travel or translate. Concepts and terms are not neutral and often reveal much about the cultural or legal context in which they are developed. Buchbinder notes that in Vermont a politics of language underpins the use of, for example, medical aid in dying, physician-assisted suicide and death in dignity.

> Proponents find the language of suicide offensive and inaccurate (because terminally ill people very much want to live), while opponents view 'aid in dying' as euphemistic and misleading and assert that there are many other ways to 'die with dignity'.
>
> *(Buchbinder, 2021, 4)*

While we predominantly use the term 'assisted dying' throughout this chapter, it is important to specify which definition you use when writing about this topic; when citing others' work, we use the terms they employ. For those interested in legal definitions, Downie et al. (2022) have written a comprehensive paper outlining the legal definitions that are used in countries that allow assisted dying. It is important to note that in addition to *legal* definitions of assisted dying, there are also *clinical* definitions, definitions used by policymakers and definitions that are used by the general public. Many of these terms overlap, and certain terms might be used interchangeably in public discourse.

Assisted dying is an umbrella term for a range of practices and 'could be considered to fall on a spectrum of additional practices including withholding or withdrawing potentially life-sustaining treatment, assisted voluntary stopping eating and drinking, and palliative/terminal sedation' (Downie et al., 2022, 1547). It often focuses on physician-assisted dying. Depending on local rules around eligibility, it allows patients to request a prescription for oral medication that will end their life upon self-administration (Singer et al., 2022). In all these cases, it is a medical professional that offers the assistance in supplying the medication that will end the person's life. Family members or friends aiding in a person's death can risk prosecution for attempting murder. This makes assisted dying a death that is strongly embedded in the medical realm. Assisted dying is also known as physician-assisted death or 'aid in dying'. In some places assisted dying is referred to as 'dying with dignity', which mimics the language used in the Oregon legislation. A form of assisted dying practised in some states of the United States and Canada is Medical Assistance in Dying (MAiD).

Euthanasia from the Greek 'εὐθανασία' literally means 'a good death' (eu = good, thanatos = death). In relation to assisted dying, euthanasia refers to the termination of a life by a doctor on request of a patient. A further distinction can be made between 'passive' and 'active' euthanasia. Active euthanasia refers to the *administering* of a life-ending substance or procedure. Passive euthanasia is the deliberate *withholding* of a life-preserving substance of procedure (Brassington, 2020). Both in active and passive euthanasia, it is doctors who are in charge of either administering or withholding medication or treatment.

Physician-assisted suicide or assisted suicide is a death, or suicide, effected with the assistance of another person, especially the taking of lethal drugs provided by a doctor for the purpose by a patient with a terminal illness or incurable condition. This term most explicitly reveals moral connotations involved in assisted dying. Anthropologist Anita Hannig (2022) observed that during the development of assisted dying laws in Oregon, administrators and health officials were divided on which terminology to use but a term popular at the time was physician-assisted suicide. Hannig notes that

> By equating medical aid-in-dying with suicide, opponents of the former can tap into the persistent social taboos and moral outrage that surround the latter— even if no longer primarily seen as a sin, the act of taking one's life remains strongly suspect.

As can be read in Chapter 12 on suicide, for a long time, this was considered a crime, and in some countries, it still is. To this day, deaths by suicide can be met with stigma and cause disenfranchised grief. Terminology can thus reflect moral frameworks and local legislations and understandings.

Countries With Legislation Around Assisted Dying

There are only a limited number of countries in the world that have legal frameworks around assisted dying. In most of the world, it remains illegal or ill-defined within existing legislation. Whilst in some countries, ongoing discussions are occurring around whether assisted dying should be legalised, in other parts of the world, these discussions are absent or limited. Assisted dying might be a low priority in countries that struggle with the provision of basic healthcare, and certain religions strongly oppose assisted dying.

There can either be country-wide legislation, which is found in Belgium, Colombia, Luxembourg, Switzerland, Spain, the Netherlands and New Zealand, or state-wide legislation, which is the case in Australia, Canada and the United States. Most of these areas are considered 'Western' in terms of their legal systems and cultural values. In Table 8.1 you can see all the jurisdictions that at the time of writing have developed a legal framework around assisted dying. Even in countries that have legalised a form of assisted dying it can be difficult to know how many people access and/or die through these means as there are different mechanisms for recording deaths in the various jurisdictions (see also Chapter 2 about mortality statistics).

TABLE 8.1 Characteristics of Jurisdictions With Legalised Assisted Dying[1]

Jurisdiction	Term used	Year authorised	Diagnosis/prognosis required	Method	Waiting period	Age
Switzerland	Assisted suicide	1937	None specified	Patient administered only	None specified	None specified
Netherlands	Euthanasia Physician-assisted suicide	1994 First legal review 2002 Procedure	None specified	Both physician and patient administered	None specified	12
Colombia	Euthanasia and physician-assisted death	1997 Decriminalising active euthanasia 2015 2022 Medical-assisted suicide added to legislation	Terminal	Both physician and patient administered	Within 15 days after committee approval	18
Oregon, USA	Physician-assisted suicide	1997	Terminal, <6 months	Patient administered only	15 days oral request	18
Belgium	Euthanasia and physician-assisted suicide	2002	Adults: incurable condition Minors: terminal	Both physician and patient administered	None specified	None (terminal) 1 month (non-terminal)
Luxembourg	Euthanasia and physician-assisted suicide	2009	Incurable condition	Both physician and patient administered	None specified	18
Washington, USA	Physician-assisted suicide	2009	Terminal, <6 months	Patient administered only	15 days oral request, 48 hours written request	18

Montana, USA	Physician aid in dying	2009	None specified	Patient administered only	None specified	None specified
Vermont, USA	No specific term used	2013	Terminal, <6 months	Patient administered only	15 days oral request, 48 hours written request	18
California, USA	Aid in dying	2015	Terminal, <6 months	Patient administered only	15 days oral request	18
Canada	Medical assistance in dying	2016	Grievous and irremediable medical condition	Both physician and patient administered	10 days written request	18
Colorado, USA	Medical aid in dying	2016	Terminal, <6 months	Patient administered only	15 days oral request	18
Washington, DC, USA	No specific term used	2017	Terminal, <6 months	Patient administered only	15 days oral request, 48 hours written request	18
Victoria, Australia	Voluntary assisted dying	2017	Terminal, <6 months (or 12 months for neurodegenerative conditions)	Patient administered only	9 days written request	18
Hawaii, USA	Aid in dying	2018	Terminal, <6 months	Patient administered only	20 days oral request, 48 hours written request	18
Maine, USA	No specific term used	2019	Terminal, <6 months	Patient administered only	17 days oral request, 48 hours written request	18

(Continued)

TABLE 8.1 (Continued)

Jurisdiction	Term used	Year authorised	Diagnosis/prognosis required	Method	Waiting period	Age
New Jersey, USA	No specific term used	2019	Terminal, <6 months	Patient administered only	18 days oral request, 48 hours written request	18
Germany	Assisted dying	2020	Information not available	Patient administered only	Information not available	Information not available
New Mexico, USA	No specific term used	2021	Terminal, <6 months (or 12 months for neurodegenerative conditions)	Patient administered only	Information not available	18
Western Australia, Australia	Voluntary assisted dying	2021	Terminal, <6 months (or 12 months for neurodegenerative conditions)	Patient administered only	9 days written request	18
Tasmania, Australia	Voluntary assisted dying	2021	Terminal, <6 months (or 12 months for neurodegenerative conditions)	Patient administered only	9 days written request	18
New Zealand	Assisted dying	2021	Terminal, like <6 months to live	Patient administered only	None specified	18
Spain	Euthanasia	2021	A serious and incurable illness	Both physician and patient administered	15 days after initial approval, 10 days after second approval	18

[1] This table is adapted from Buchbinder and Cain (2023), these authors prefer the term MAID and we have changed this to assisted dying. Other terms used come from Mroz et al. (2021). Additional information for New Zealand was taken from the End of Life Choice Act (Ministry of Health, 2019) and Spain (Velasco et al., 2021).

The Netherlands has had a euthanasia law since 2002. It is also referred to as 'hulp by zelfdoding' – literally assistance during self-killing, but more commonly translated as assisted suicide. In the Netherlands there are ongoing discussions whether the law should broaden to allow, for example, poor mental health to be a reason to qualify for euthanasia. It has been debated that those who feel their life is 'complete' should similarly be allowed to choose to die (van Wijngaarden, Leget, and Goossensen, 2015, 2016).

As can be seen in the table, there are differences in terms of whether the medication is self-administered or given by a medical practitioner. This will have an impact on who is able to receive assisted dying in certain locations. Colombia is the first Latin American country to decriminalise euthanasia. In 2022, legislation changed to include assisted suicide (Erazo-Munoz, Borda-Restrepo, and Benavides-Cruz, 2023). Whilst euthanasia, where a doctor administers a legal injection, had been legalised, it was still illegal to assist a person who would like to take lethal medication themselves. Currently, Colombians thus have the option to either self-administer or let a medical professional administer the medication.

Eligibility is also dependent on residency and/or citizenship. Switzerland is exceptional in that it allows foreign nationals to travel there to complete an assisted suicide. This allowance has meant that, for example, people from the United Kingdom, where no form of assisted dying is currently legal, travel to this country to complete an assisted death. The phrase 'going to Switzerland' has become a euphemism in the United Kingdom to refer to assisted dying (Richards, 2017). In New Zealand, citizens and people with permanent residence are eligible to request assistance in dying (Ministry of Health, 2019). In Spain any person of legal age and of Spanish nationality, legal residence or with a registration certificate that certifies at least 12 months of stay in Spain has potentially access to assisted dying (Velasco et al., 2021). Other countries only allow their own nationals to make use of assisted dying legislations. How assisted dying is perceived legally also differs per country. For example, Medical Assistance in Dying (MAID), the term used for assisted dying in Canada, is considered a constitutional right. This means Canadians have a right to end their life; whereas, for example, in the Netherlands it is a request that can be accepted or rejected.

Assisted Dying and Inequality

Who receives assisted dying and, importantly, who does not, reveals some important insights in terms of how access is linked to class, gender, and/or ethnicity. There are practical and structural barriers that determine who has access to assisted dying. This section critically highlights examples of structural aspects that influence access to assisted dying.

Geography is one major factor as the number of countries that have legalised assisted dying is limited. For example, there is no country in Africa that allows for assisted dying or euthanasia (Amzat et al., 2023), and research around the topic in this continent is limited. Studies available show a strong opposition to the practice; a high majority of participants in a Ugandan study considered assisted dying to be murder (Kalanzi, 2013). A study with medical students in Sudan indicates that most of these students opposed euthanasia for ethical and religious reasons (Ahmed and Kheir, 2006); Islam is the dominant religion in Sudan. Assisted dying is forbidden in Islamic doctrines (Madadin et al., 2020) which explains why people in Islamic countries might strongly oppose the practice. Nuance is warranted with statements like these as it has been noted that the withdrawal or withholding of treatment for an imminently fatal illness is permissible (Madadin et al., 2020). However, research with South African medical students (2018) showed a growing consensus that some form of assisted dying should be legalised in the country. Access to assisted dying is thus non-existent in Africa, and little is known about public attitudes on the topic.

Even in countries that do have legislations access is not distributed equally. Legalised assisted dying does not equate immediate access. It is known that there is implicit bias and structural barriers to access any form in healthcare for specific groups. Research has shown that there are 'implicit assumptions by health-care providers based on race, gender, class, sexuality, size, and dis/ability' (Sikka, 2021). These assumptions are also prevalent in access to assisted dying, and are compounded by medical distrust that is experienced by certain groups who are therefore less likely to request an assisted death (Sikka, 2021). In the United States, race and religion are significant predictors of access to assisted dying and, for example, the states of Oregon, Montana, Washington and Vermont are all considered majority white, rural and secular (Buchbinder, 2021). Marginalised communities, for example people in prison, have more limited access to assisted dying compared with those in the general community (Driftmier and Shaw, 2021). The majority of assisted dying deaths are cancer deaths, as this illness has a more predictable illness trajectory compared with other illnesses, sufferers from other illnesses are often less likely to receive an assisted death (Norwood, 2009).

Key Arguments Around Assisted Dying

Assisted dying does not have a simple binary of people being in favour or against the phenomenon. Recent research on citizen's values in New Zealand showed that 'the same moral, ethical and ideological discourses can be used to support arguments for and against assisted dying' (Jaye et al., 2021, 77). This is not unique to New Zealand. There is a myriad of legal, ethical or personal arguments that can influence micro- and macro-level understandings of the topic. Whilst New Zealand recently adopted an assisted dying law, it remains illegal in the United Kingdom. In 2021, the British Medical Association (BMA) adopted a 'neutral' position towards assisted dying which 'means [they] will neither support nor oppose attempts to change the law' (BMA, 2021). This neutral stance is highlighted here as an example that there is more to the assisted dying debate than a simple yes/no binary. Importantly, being 'neutral' is still taking a stance. The following sections will introduce arguments that are often part of assisted dying debates. This is not a comprehensive list, but instead an introduction to some ideas that highlight the multi-layeredness of this issue.

Autonomy, Control and Choice

A common reason for people to desire assisted dying is that they want *some* level of control over their own ending. Autonomy is the ability to decide for oneself and is often linked to agency, the ability to pursue an action in relation to that decision. Empirical evidence of countries where assisted dying is available shows that notions of control, choice and autonomy are not straightforward.

Buchbinder (2021) notes that in Vermont assisted dying has resulted in a new script around dying and death. Assisted dying offers a scripted death in which certain steps can be followed. Yet, Buchbinder highlights that ideas around an assisted death are often aspirational as there are many barriers in receiving an assisted death. Whilst people feel they have agency and choice, evidence from both Vermont (Buchbinder, 2021) and the Netherlands (Norwood, 2009; van der Geest and Satalkar, 2021) show that agency is relational and that decisions around the end of life are never solely made by an individual.

> With medical aid in dying, both agency and control over death are distributed among a range of actors and institutions. It is not simply the case that the medical system exerts control, while patients exercise agency. Instead, agency and control are necessarily shared between patients, families, health care providers, medical institutions and the state.
>
> *(Buchbinder, 2021, 11)*

Van der Geest and Satalkar (2021) suggest three elements that complicate the notion of autonomy for people in the Netherlands who desire an assisted death. First, doctors have the final say in measuring the amount of pain of the patient experiences. Second, these types of decisions are not solely made by the individual dying, but involve a complex web of relationships that will impact this decision. Lastly, increased frailty and ageing of people can result in others taking over the decision-making for the dying person. These three obstacles noted by Van der Geest and Satalkar show the complexity of decision-making and notions of choice related to assisted dying.

Preventing Suffering and Unwanted Futures

A reason why people might want to opt for assisted dying is to end current suffering or to pre-empt future suffering. Whilst pain and suffering for a long time were deemed to be a way to atone for sins on the deathbed, any form of suffering (both physically and mentally) is increasingly considered to be part of a bad dying experience (Richards and Krawczyk, 2021). As noted by Richards and Krawczyk (2021, 3), 'the increase in lawful assisted dying is already a *result* of the growing cultural belief that pain and suffering at the end of life are meaningless, biographically disruptive, and therefore need to be eradicated'. In the Netherlands, suffering is a prerequisite, as 'unbearable suffering' is a requirement to qualify for euthanasia. In such contexts, it is expected that the person can demonstrate how the suffering is unbearable for them and is unlikely to be resolvable via other means. Such suffering can be perceived as challenging a person's sense of dignity (Quah et al., 2023). Some people argue that if there was enough palliative care (see chapters 6 and 7) assisted dying would not be required as suffering would be alleviated through symptom and spiritual support and dignity could be provided through person-centred care (The Economist, 2018).

Another aspect of suffering is perceived future suffering, in the notion of unwanted futures. Researching people with dementia and their families in the Netherlands, Lemos Dekker (2021) notes that the potential of an unwanted future was a strong reason to request euthanasia. There are ongoing debates whether people with dementia should be entitled to euthanasia deaths as they are often not able to consent to the procedure at the time of their death. This unwanted future can, on the one hand, be seen as a way for people to have agency and control over their own deaths. On the other hand, 'not wanting to be a burden' is often part of the reason these people with dementia opted for euthanasia, which challenges if this is an autonomous decision. Lemos Dekker (2017) highlights the tensions in assisted dementia deaths as, for example, family members welcomed these deaths as they considered their loved one's life 'not worth living'. Here is the blurring of individual and social understandings of unwanted futures and potential suffering.

Vulnerability and a Slippery Slope

In societies, certain groups are considered more vulnerable to illness and/ or structural inequalities than others. People with disabilities and people with dementia are often thought to be at risk if assisted dying laws are implemented, potentially because of a perceived notion of burden and care as well as potential inabilities to consent and voice their preferences. This worry can be linked to the notion of a slippery slope. As Benatar notes

> Slippery slope arguments, which are regularly invoked in a variety of practical ethics contexts, make the claim that if some specific kind of action (such as euthanasia) is permitted, then society will be inexorably led ('down the slippery slope') to permitting other actions that are morally wrong.
>
> *(Benatar, 2011, 206–207)*

The argument thus posits what the future of societies would be if assisted dying were allowed. What types of death would be deemed acceptable. The notion of 'lives worth living', as noted by Lemos Dekker (2017), is one of the reasons why people can be wary of the availability of assisted dying. In countries that have legalised assisted dying, ongoing discussions occur on who should be deemed eligible and who not. It is suggested that safeguarding is needed for vulnerable populations as it could be argued that allowing assisted dying changes attitudes, or enforces attitudes towards older people, people with disabilities and people with severe mental health problems and changes the way people think about lives worth living and lives that are expendable.

The Involvement of Doctors

The role of medical professionals in assisted dying is used as an argument both in favour and against assisted dying. On the one hand, it is argued that the role doctors play in assisted dying gives them too much power and that they should not be involved in the practice at all. On the other hand, it is argued that doctors should not be involved at all. The Hippocratic Oath, a set of rules on how medical doctors are supposed to conduct themselves, which includes a note on not doing harm used as proof that medical professionals should have no part in this (see, e.g. Rosen, 2012).

Time

Time plays a role both in arguments in favour and against assisted dying. Time comes up in terms of legislation, frequently in terms of terminal prognosis and/ or time between approval of assisted dying and when it is done. There are also concerns by some that assisted dying causes an untimely death in that death is hastened. Assisted dying has the opportunity to change the timing of death. Some people will know precisely when they are going to die and this offers opportunities for new ways of saying goodbye or to potentially have a 'funeral' with the dying person present. New grief and dying rituals can emerge as a consequence of this practice.

In terms of legislation, time can be a factor in determining who is eligible or not for an assisted death. For example, in MAID in Vermont the person dying has to receive a prognosis that they will die within 6 months (Buchbinder, 2021) but timeframes might differ depending on local legislations. Some legislation also provides a 'cooling off period': an intentional gap between being approved for receiving assistance and the use of such assistance to enable the person to change their mind.

In theory, people who opt and are approved to receive an assisted death will know exactly when they are going to die. But as can be shown by examples mentioned later, this 'knowing' is not that simple as there is often a time gap between opting for assisted dying and the assistance (or self-administration) occurring. In contexts where a person must ingest the lethal medication themselves, there is a fear, particularly for people with muscle diseases to lose the ability to swallow and therefore be 'too late' (Hannig, 2022; Buchbinder, 2021). The timing of death was an important consideration in the euthanasia requests of people living with dementia in the Netherlands. 'The prospect of decline motivates the request for euthanasia, but it is also precisely what threatens the possibility to receive it, as the request must be made before one loses the ability to understand and confirm the request' (Lemos Dekker, 2021, 815). Like people with muscle degenerative diseases, people with dementia found themselves in a bind between fearing a euthanasia death would come either 'too soon' or 'too late'.

The notion of death coming 'too soon' or, in other words, hastened is an argument often used by those rejecting assisted dying as it is felt that people's lives should end 'naturally' without medical intervention at the end.

Ongoing Debate

The legalisation of assisted dying does not end the debate. Assisted dying allows for the ending of lives under very specific circumstances and there are various discussions on whether rules and regulations should either be widened or narrowed. The actual implementation of assisted dying laws continuously raise more questions. As Buchbinder points out, laws are inherently social, as people interpret and act upon them, like the terminology around assisted dying, the laws that make them possible are indeed also value-laden and never neutral. Countries that have a legal framework around assisted dying by no means have a consensus throughout the entire population that assisted dying should be legal. Furthermore, in places where assisted dying is legal, there are continuous debates about who should be included, and excluded. Or in other words, who should be able to receive assisted dying, and who should not.

To take the Netherlands as an example, there have been various debates considering whether people with severe mental health problems should be allowed assisted dying. Recently, discussion focused on whether or not feeling that your life is 'completed' should be reason for people to end their life via euthanasia (van Wijngaarden, Leget, and Goossensen, 2015). In 2023, the decision was made to widen the law to include terminally ill children (Reuters, 2023). There has been discussion whether children should be allowed assisted dying and what this means in terms of capacity and consent.

Conclusion

This chapter has examined assisted dying, engaging critically with the social nature of it. There is a wide range of terminology to describe assisted dying, and several of the key concepts and their distinctions have been discussed. Various forms of assisted dying are found across the world, mainly in 'Western' societies; some examples of variations in different judicial contexts have been provided previously.

Even where assisted dying is legal, who can access it and how they are able to access assistance is influenced by structural inequalities.

There is a wide range of beliefs about the topic, and these are often in flux. Assisted dying is often presented as a binary; people are either strongly in favour or strongly opposed. The chapter has highlighted how both proponents and opponents of assisted dying can use similar arguments to argue their case, which highlights and can amplify ambivalence around the topic.

9

DISENFRANCHISED DYING

Introduction

Dying well with access to care is considered a human right by some, especially in relation to diagnosing dying and through the provision of palliative and/or end of life care (Ellershaw, 2024) When someone is dying, there are universal human rights that particularly come to the fore. This can include dignity, physical integrity, health, and freedom from torture (Negri, 2013). Whilst there are debates as to the extent to which human rights are indeed universal (Freeman, 2022), the connection between human rights and someone's experience of dying and how their care is managed is useful for thinking about how privilege and social norms impact one's understanding and experiences of death and dying.

Disenfranchisement is the state of being deprived of a privilege or right. In death studies, the concept of disenfranchisement is typically used in relation to grief. Doka defines disenfranchised grief 'as grief that results when a person experiences a significant loss and the resultant grief is not openly acknowledged, socially validated, or publicly mourned' (Doka, 2014). This means that even if they are feeling grief (or emotions in the aftermath of a death or loss), this is not recognised by others around them, and people do not have access to social right to mourn and having their mourning recognised. Therefore, they may receive no sympathy, social support, and/or care from professionals linked to their grief. Various authors have considered how there can be 'rankings of grief' – social hierarchies about who can be mourned and who can mourn (Robson and Walter, 2013; Peskin, 2019; Rosbrow, 2019) – especially in relation to deaths or relationships that are stigmatised (Robson and Walter, 2013).

Social norms and stigma can, therefore, influence how grief is experienced, resulting in a sense of disenfranchisement. Whilst not yet articulated as such

DOI: 10.4324/9781003318002-11

in the literature,[1] something similar can be said of dying – that dying can be disenfranchised, with people being deprived of rights linked to their dying is identified, with a deprivation of care (or different standards of care being provided to them linked to lower perceived social worth of their lives or a focus on curative rather than palliative care), and with their deaths being less likely to be grieved or spoken about (or deemed grievable, see Chapter 1). Ultimately, disenfranchised dying is an example of deaths that challenge the 'good death' ideal because of the circumstances of the dying experience and how they are socially managed.

To think through the concept of disenfranchised dying, this chapter focuses on two examples: maternal mortality and deaths in prison. Both deaths in prison as well as maternal mortality raise questions on what types of death and dying are 'grievable' (Butler, 2004). They highlight how both individual as well as social responses to death and dying are strongly affected by not only the type of death but also the person who is dying. There are also social determinants that influence who is likely to die in both contexts, including links to race, age, geographical location, and socioeconomic status. This chapter explores to what extent the social phenomena of maternal dying and dying in prison are acknowledged on an individual and social level, considering how they may occur out of sight, often with a lack of care and a lack of attending to the dying.

The first part of this chapter focuses on maternal mortality, discussing why it is an issue and how dying during and shortly after pregnancy can be a form of disenfranchised dying. It also explores how the grief linked to these deaths can also be disenfranchised. The next section of the chapter focuses on dying in prison. As outlined above, deaths in prison can be 'out of sight', and institutionalisation may impact a person's ability to access healthcare, including palliative care. For both sections, the concepts of necropolitics and grievability (see Chapter 1) are important to consider as they help to reveal how social inequalities impact dying in these contexts. The third section briefly covers examples of where these scenarios overlap – when migrant pregnant women are detained as part of immigration procedures.

Maternal Mortality

According to the World Health Organization (WHO), maternal mortality is 'unacceptably high' with a reported 28,700 women dying during or following pregnancy in 2020. In other words, a maternal death occurred almost every two minutes in that year. The WHO defines maternal mortality as:

the death of a woman while pregnant or within 42 days of termination of pregnancy, irrespective of the duration and site of the pregnancy, from any cause related to or aggravated by the pregnancy or its management but not from unintentional or incidental causes.[2]

Most cases of maternal mortality are considered to be preventable. While the number of women who die during childbirth or pregnancy is decreasing overall, this decrease is unequally divided across the globe. In 2020, almost 95% of all maternal deaths occurred in low and lower-middle-income countries.

But even in higher-income countries, such as the United Kingdom and the United States, there are discrepancies in maternal mortality. Petersen et al. (2019) note a discrepancy in maternal mortality between 2007 and 2016 as Black and American Indian/Alaskan Native women had significantly more pregnancy-related deaths compared to other groups. In the United Kingdom, the risk of maternal death in 2019–2021 was almost four times higher among women from Black ethnic minority backgrounds compared to White women (MBRRACE-UK, 2023). Reasons for these differences include a lack of individualised care and not being listened to when presenting symptoms, which can impact the timeliness of receiving life-saving care or timely recognition that palliative care is needed, lack of continuity of care meaning healthcare providers may be unaware of complex medical histories, and microaggressions (M. Knight et al., 2021).

Notably, very little research has focused on the care that can be provided to mothers in the context of potential maternal mortality. Research on the potential triggers to refer mothers to palliative care is relatively new (Davis et al., 2020). This means that dying in these contexts can be disenfranchised in that the mothers are not necessarily able to access levels of care that are aimed at easing suffering at the end of life (see Chapter 6 and Chapter 7). It also raises questions as to what extent the mothers and those around them are aware that they are dying. This is an example of disenfranchised dying because many of these deaths are preventable and, moreover, because the dying phase goes under or unrecognised. This means that the women are unlikely to receive palliative and/or end-of-life care in order to experience a 'good death'.

Hooker (2023) considers maternal deaths of Black women in the United States as political deaths, viewing these deaths as a result of state action or inaction. She notes that 'whilst there are still generalised risks to the mother's health associated with childbirth, an individual Black woman's death from complications as a result of maternal mortality is not "natural" but political in light of current racial disparities in health care' (Hooker, 2023, 10–11). Furthermore, she suggests whilst some of these deaths can be due to economic reasons and lack of access to healthcare, there is evidence that minority patients tend to receive lower quality care even when they have the same types of health insurance as non-minorities (Hooker, 2023). Physiologically, there is no reason why Black women in various geographies are more likely to die in childbirth, so other social determinants and necropolitics (see Chapter 1 and Chapter 3) are at play.

The most common approach to reducing maternal mortality numbers has been to address biomedical reasons for these deaths. Still, less effort has been made to understand and reduce the social determinants that underpin these deaths (Souza et al., 2023). It has been argued that increased awareness not only of social determinants but also structural determinants such as racism, classism, and the political structure of environments is crucial to take into account for understanding and preventing future maternal mortality (Crear-Perry et al., 2021). This is linked to what Leith Mullings (2021) has termed the necropolitics of reproduction, which she considered 'not only policies that value some lives more than others, but the use of political power to determine who will live and who will die' (Mullings, 2021). In the necropolitics of reproduction, both policies and power determine which mothers survive pregnancy and which do not, and which mothers are more deserving to be mothers and achieve motherhood.

Political implications and policies can also be found in how maternal mortality is spoken about. This mainly refers to the socioeconomic costs as, for example, there can be financial implications if the mother was one of the breadwinners. Still, these deaths have various social implications as well. A qualitative interview study in KwaZulu-Natal, South Africa, showed that maternal mortality has potentially complex and multi-layered impacts on both the surviving children throughout the life course and for the families and individuals tasked with their care (L. Knight and Yamin, 2015). The death of a mother brings risks to children, as there is a higher chance of infant mortality due to the absence of breastfeeding and less access to healthcare (Yamin et al., 2013). A study in rural Tanzania showed that maternal death has broad-ranging effects. This includes delays in access to healthcare, limited access to breastfeeding or other nutrition, and limited access to education. There are exacerbated effects, specifically on orphaned girls. Care dynamics also change as it is common for children to be separated from their biological fathers and other siblings to be placed in the care of a female relative (Yamin et al., 2013)[3]. Maternal mortality thus has wide-ranging implications, not just for the person who had died but the rest of the family network, especially children. Maternal mortality can be viewed as depriving the mother of an active role in her motherhood, and the absence of these mothers is also evident in the absence of their role (or potential role) in such accounts. This is a further example of how maternal mortality can be considered a case of disenfranchisement in the context of death.

Dying in Prison

Prison as a space is probably not the first place one considers an appropriate place for dying. But wherever people live, there is always the possibility of death. This section considers how dying in prison can be an example of disenfranchised dying. This is important to consider as prison populations in several countries are 'ageing', with people given long sentences that mean they are likely to spend their last years of life in prison. But first, it is useful to understand the potential scale of prison deaths.

It is unclear how many people are currently in prison across the globe, but in 2020, it was estimated that between 10.77 and 11.5 million people were in prison worldwide (Fair and Walmsley, 2021). Mortality rates are 50% higher for people in prison compared to those in the general community (Penal Reform International, 2022), but the number of deaths in prison worldwide is unknown. There is no global definition of what constitutes a 'death in custody'. Some countries only count deaths that occur within a detention facility. In contrast, other countries also include deaths in pre-trial detention, deaths on temporary leave, and deaths occurring shortly after prison release (Penal Reform International, 2022). Ireland classifies a death as a 'death in custody' up until a month post-release; in Turkey, only up to ten days, whereas other countries do not include these deaths at all (Penal Reform International, 2022). Whilst international standards require all deaths in prison to be investigated, this by no means is done everywhere (Penal Reform International, 2022). It is also known that the first 14 days after someone is released from prison prove to be a high risk as people take their own lives during this time (PPO, 2023). These deaths, though statistically perhaps not 'prison deaths', show another complex layer of the relationship between life, death, prison, and punishment.

Tomczak and Mulgrew (2023) note that the current means of collecting data about prisoner deaths makes various groups invisible. Prisoner death is a gendered phenomenon, predominantly involving males, and little is known about women dying in prison. Importantly, transgender deaths are entirely absent from official data (Tomczak and Mulgrew, 2023). Additionally, Tomczak and Mulgrew (2023) indicate that race and ethnicity are not visible in international data sets on prisoner deaths, obfuscating the disproportionate number of deaths amongst marginalised groups. Tomczak and Mulgrew propose three tenets to capture the number of people who die in prison adequately; firstly, they advocate for *counting prisoners who die* as opposed to *prisoner deaths*.[4] Secondly, they advocate for the examination of characteristics of prisoners who die so that age, disability, race, ethnicity, sexuality, and gender are all included and available for analysis. Lastly, they argue in favour of adopting explicitly defined, mutually exclusive categorisations instead of current definitions that conflate different types of death.

Every death in custody in the United Kingdom is investigated by the Prisons and Probation Ombudsman, and the UK government keeps up-to-date statistics on the amount of people who die in prison. In the 12 months to June 2023, there were 313 deaths in prison custody, an increase of 9% from 288 deaths in the previous 12 months.[5] Eighty-eight of these deaths were self-inflicted, 185 deaths were due to natural causes (i.e. illness or 'old age') and 37 deaths were registered as 'other' as causes of death can be very complex. These numbers tell little about the dying experience, whether family and friends were involved in the dying experience and what the broader repercussions of these deaths are. Since being disenfranchised is linked to a deprivation of privileges, these deaths in prison – even if they have different causes – are linked through the fact that the people who died whilst in prison were not able to live fully social lives, even at the end of life.

Whilst there is increased attention to ageing in prison, dying in prison, particularly from the experience of people in prison themselves, has received less scholarly attention (Visser, 2021). This could be due to several reasons: it is harder to get funding for projects on death and dying, access to people in prison is difficult and will be linked to the type of death a researcher might be interested in (i.e. suicide, violent, sudden, or expected death). Prison research, in general, can be quite challenging as prisons can be reluctant to let researchers enter their premises.

There is not one type of dying that occurs in prison: people can die of older age, people can die by suicide, and they can die from both infectious as well as non-infectious diseases such as cancer. People can be killed in prison and some people receive the death penalty as punishment. Scholars also talk about the 'slow death' of being in prison, through stripping away civil rights (Andreescu, 2023) as a form of social death, as well as the use of life sentences (Girling and Seal, 2016).

Liebling (2017, 20) argues that 'the ending of life in custody should be controversial'. Liebling notes that deaths in prison challenge the legitimacy of prisons and that

> we should be disturbed by the punitiveness of a judicial system that keeps people in custody for longer than they have been alive, or that aims to keep them until they die, and the culture and practices of a prison system that can make life unendurable.
>
> *(Liebling, 2017, 28)*

Focusing on three types of dying in prison, which Liebling argues are quite common: suicide, murder, and the 'whole life sentence', which she argues is a form of 'dying without death', Liebling suggests that 'end of life in prison should be avoided wherever possible, but where unavoidable, it should be approached with dignity, choice and relationships in mind' (Liebling, 2017, 21). As officially 'loss of liberty' is considered as a punishment in the United Kingdom (Turner, Payne, and Barbarachild, 2011), dying in prison is an additional punishment. Arguably, prison will not be people's first choice when thinking about a place to die, yet for some people, prison is their 'home', and particularly long-term prisoners can 'choose' to die in prison. This is an example of disenfranchised dying as it disables the people from making decisions about their care in line with good death ideals (see Chapter 7) and, specifically perhaps, intentionally seeks to ensure their dying experience is one akin to punishment.

It is interesting to look at dying in prison, especially in relation to current policies that emphasise 'choice' around the end of life. Particularly the choice of place of death. People in prison have limited choices available regarding any aspect of their everyday lives. Similarly, they have limited agency regarding the types of deaths they would like and that actually occur. With the rise of the older population in prison, the likelihood of people dying in prison increases. At the same time, due to poor mental health, self-harm is often rife in prisons and some people die prematurely in prison because of this.

People in prison are presumably there because they have committed a crime. It might therefore be easier to consider the deaths of those in custody as 'deserved' and less worthy of grief, yet people in prison often come from marginalised communities and have led difficult lives which have caused them to go to prison. Various social determinants lead to prison; and there are policies and social practices, influenced by necropolitics, which mean some groups of people are more likely to be targeted by police forces, more likely to be found guilty, and more likely to receive more punitive sentences (Broadfield, 2021). Some studies have shown that bereavement might be a reason why people end up in prison in the first place. For example, Vaswani (2018) notes that many of the young men in custody in Scotland have experienced an extraordinary amount of bereavement very young in life. The aggression or events that led to their imprisonment can be partly explained by their not coping with their grief. These young men often come from marginalised communities, and therefore, there are social determinants for them to be in prison that are rarely unpacked and show that the relationship between death, loss, and prison is very complex.

The available research on dying in prison from the experience of people in prison highlights that the experience of dying in prison is not singular. A 2006 study with ageing prisoners concluded that some people in prison see death as an escape from life; others saw dying in prison as the 'ultimate defeat' which would cause stigma and humiliation to their family (Aday, 2006). This study, and a later study with older women in a US prison, found that thinking about death and death anxiety were common occurrences (Aday, 2006; Aday and Wahidin, 2016). As Aday and Wahidin (2016, 314) suggest:

> Behind bars one finds the possibility of dying all alone, no family present to support you, no last goodbyes, and no opportunity for reconciliations. For most people, dying in prison would be the least optimal environment on earth from which to choose. Perhaps it is the thought of dying in such stark institutions that often escalates fear and uncertainty about the dying process.

Stanley conducted ethnographic research on the experience of dying in prison in the United States (2021). Her research offers rare first-hand accounts of the dynamics of dying in prison, including of a man called Daniel. In a maximum- to medium-security prison in Maine, Stanley observed the peer-based end-of-life care that was offered in this prison. Fellow prisoners were trained to help with the provision of care and held vigil shifts with the dying. In particular, Stanley describes the sensory experience of being part of the dying experience of Daniel; she was present when he died.

> I sat in silence at the foot of the bed beside C.R [peer caregiver], who was also experiencing a hospice death for the first time. I listened intently to Daniel's breathing, each breath fewer and further between. (…) I sense a natural intimacy

as Agelu [peer caregiver] tenderly stroked Daniel's head with large hands that experienced nearly a decade of death as a peer caregiver. An electric calm, an impenetrable tranquillity, came over the cell. With ears that I had learned to open in new ways, I caught Agelu's whispered words: 'Enjoy the journey'. As the moon glistened through the small window, Daniel's chest rose in a large breath. Froze. And then fell for the last time.

(D. Stanley, 2021, 62)

Whilst Liebling (2017) highlights the violent deaths that occur in prison, Stanley shows gentle and peaceful dying can equally occur inside prison walls. Stanley notes how Daniel's dying experience highlights how his dying affected everyone working in the prison, the peer hospice workers, and his brother, who was allowed to be inside the prison for his death. Whilst this shows one example, there is a range of dying experiences that can occur in custody and the ageing of the prison population has meant a larger proportion of older people are dying behind locked doors.

Palliative Care in Prison

The increase of an older prison population has meant that, increasingly, prisons need to provide some form of end-of-life care or palliative care to people in prison. It has been suggested that older people in prison face a double burden as they are deprived of their liberty and often do not have their needs met (Turner et al., 2018). Some older people de facto receive a life sentence due to their age and will thus die in prison (Turner et al., 2018). Turner and Peacock (2017) note that the rise of older people in the prison population provides several challenges for healthcare and custodial staff trying to meet the needs of this group. Most prison officers do not anticipate that they will be working in such close proximity to death when they start working in prisons. Research with Irish prison officers has similarly shown that due to the complex power dynamics and relationships in prisons, prison officers feel they cannot tell people how they really feel about the deaths of prisoners (Barry, 2019). The emotional labour of being involved in end-of-life care in prison is complex. This might be made even more complicated depending on the nature of the offence of the person in prison. Turner and Peacock note:

> Prisoners, particularly sex offenders, are frequently vilified in the British media, and many people do not believe that they should be allowed a dignified and pain-free death. This adds a layer of challenges for those trying to improve end-of-life care for older prisoners, many of whom are sex offenders.
>
> *(2017, 63)*

Others have noted that dying well is potentially achievable in a prison environment, yet there are various barriers towards achieving a so-called 'good death' in prison (Burles, Peternelj-Taylor, and Holtslander, 2016). There are various practical barriers to accessing palliative care in prisons, including access to medical equipment and medicine like morphine (Burles, Peternelj-Taylor, and Holtslander, 2016). In some circumstances, as highlighted in Turkey, the paperwork required to access palliative or end-of-life care can require a lengthy process, which means prisoners can die before the paperwork is processed (Can, 2022). Lastly, Lillie (2018) notes that a failure to identify individuals that are dying in prison, or to anticipate those who are dying is equally hindering the dying and support processes for those who are dying in prison.

The principles of palliative care and the purpose of prison do not always match. Palliative care focuses, amongst other things, on comfort and making sure people die without pain. It has been suggested that the availability of palliative care in prisons is challenging what the purpose of prisons is and what types of care should be available to those residing in them (Turner, Payne, and Barbarachild, 2011). Controversially, some view the addition of hospice or palliative care in prison settings, including places like Guantánamo Bay, as an attempt by political authorities to disavow themselves from the inflicted torture of imprisonment whilst still maintaining control over the person (Velasquez-Potts, 2023).

Given the changing demographics of prison populations with many older prisoners who may need end-of-life care, there is an increasing interest in this area. Yet, it is interesting that certain types of death and dying, like the deaths of older prisoners, are receiving increased scholarly attention, whilst other types, for example, the deaths of young men in prison, receive little attention. Consequently, only certain types of disenfranchised dying in prisons are being explored and debated, which can further the disenfranchisement of other forms of dying.

Considering Maternal Mortality in Detention Centres

It might seem odd that these two experiences – maternal mortality and dying in prison – are juxtaposed, but there are examples in which these two phenomena overlap. The border between the United States of America and Mexico is a space where pregnant migrant women who have crossed the border to seek asylum in the United States can find themselves detained and giving birth in a US Immigration and Customs Enforcement facility (Heffernan, 2023). Due to poor access to healthcare, food, water, and basic necessities, as well as exposure to violence in these facilities, these pregnant immigrant women and their unborn babies are at a higher risk of death. The experience of detainment and birthing in these facilities can be dehumanising:

In February 2020, a Guatemalan migrant woman was forced to give birth standing up, leaning over a trash can, in full view of several immigration enforcement officers and other migrants whom she did not know, in the waiting area of a United States (US) Customs and Border Protection (CBP) holding facility in southern California.

(Heffernan, 2023, 31)

Hefferman (2023, 32) argues this is 'part of a continuum of gendered necropolitical violence enacted on the bodies of poor, racialised migrant women throughout their migration experiences'. In this example, pregnant women who have crossed a national border find themselves being labelled as a criminal. This, in turn, affects their birthing experiences and the extent to which their lives are considered important or disposable.[6] Data about outcomes for incarcerated women is inconsistent or sparse (Paynter et al., 2019). More generally, reviews have demonstrated that migration can increase the likelihood that a woman dies during or shortly after pregnancy/birth (Pedersen et al., 2014; Herrera et al., 2019).

Conclusion

This chapter has examined the experiences of maternal mortality and dying in prison to highlight how these can be examples of disenfranchised dying. Disenfranchised dying is a new term, borrowing from the concept of disenfranchised grief. Disenfranchised dying focuses on how the dying person and their experience may be denied, hidden, and how the ways in which their dying and death is managed can have (negative) implications for timely identification and provision of care needs. They may also be subject to a lack of dignity, violence, and silencing about the cause of their deaths. Understanding the scale of these kinds of deaths is difficult. Mortality statistics for maternal mortality are incomplete as are statistics for those who die in prison. Additionally, since there is no universal definition of a 'death in custody' it is difficult to compare these numbers internationally. Lastly, even where statistics do exist, they do not reveal much about the experiences of these deaths. Importantly, there are social and cultural determinants that influence whether someone dies in childbirth and whether someone dies in prison. In both cases, it is helpful to understand how necropolitics can be involved, and how gender, race, and socioeconomic status impact which lives are at risk in these contexts and whose deaths are considered grievable.

Notes

1   Very few have used the term 'disenfranchised dying' in published academic literature. One example is Howarth (2009) who briefly uses the term to talk about dying that is not socially recognised, either because someone is dying in an institution (like a care home) or from a socially stigmatised condition (like AIDS).

2   Trends in maternal mortality 2000 to 2020 https://iris.who.int/bitstream/handle/10665/366225/9789240068759-eng.pdf?sequence=1

3 Yamin et al. (2013) note that in their study, only the stories of children whose maternal death was known by community healthcare workers were included, implying that not every maternal death is acknowledged or recorded.

4 They do this to highlight the human life that is lost. In the phrase 'prisoner death' this can be forgotten or overlooked and people can be reduced to a statistic.

5 www.gov.uk/government/statistics/safety-in-custody-quarterly-update-to-march-2023/ safety-in-custody-statistics-england-and-wales-deaths-in-prison-custody-to-june-2023-assaults-and-self-harm-to-march-2023#:~:text=In%20the%2012%20months%20 to,in%20the%20previous%2012%20months.

6 Access to healthcare in the United States is unequally divided among members of society. As jails and prisons are required to give 'those in their care' access to healthcare, there are examples in the United States of poor pregnant women deliberately committing crimes to get access to prenatal healthcare (Sufrin, 2017). Ironically, for these women, the prison provides a safety net that is unavailable outside of prison walls (Sufrin, 2017).

SECTION III
The Aftermath of Death

10

THE DEAD BODY AND DISPOSAL PRACTICES

Introduction

When someone dies, in human societies, there is an assumption that something must happen with the body. Various biological processes begin when a body dies. Corpses produce various gasses and decompose slowly or more quickly, depending on the location. But typically, dead human bodies are not left lying around decomposing; bodies are washed and dressed, and there is some form of ritual to say goodbye to the deceased. There are socio-cultural responses to a dead body. As social-historian Thomas Laqueur (2015, 4) notes:

> to treat a dead body as if it were ordinary organic matter – to leave it lie as if it were the body of a beast – or wilfully to desecrate and mutilate it is to erase it from culture and from the human community; to deny existence of the community from which it came, to deny its humanity.

Dead bodies evoke an almost universal response that 'something needs to be done' with the body; this response is grounded in the community that that person belonged to. The dead body is often met with discomfort, and this is reflected in the way it has been theorised. Scholars have described the dead body as, for example, a disruptor of the social order, an unwelcome reminder of decay, a symbol of pollution and a symbol of disorder (See: Harper, 2010). Harper (2010, 311) notes 'the dead body is not a uniform entity but one that can hold a multiplicity of meanings and therefore *be* different things'. Harper suggests that the dead body is not merely an object but an entity that has social agency that can affect the actions of the living. Davies (2017, 31) notes: 'the corpse is the prime symbol of death. Its initial silence and subsequent decay enshrine the radical changes of mortality

DOI: 10.4324/9781003318002-13

that challenge the living to respond'. Across the globe, disposal practices differ based on socio-cultural, religious, political and economic practices, and beliefs. A phrase often uttered is that 'we are all equal in death', something that is idealistic in principle but something to be critical of. All means of disposal, be it burial, cremation or something else, have costs involved, which not everyone can afford, and have different ritual, social, religious, and personal meanings attached to them.

Dead bodies not only pose a challenge to the living, who have to make decisions on how to dispose of them,[1] but also prove challenging to define in legal terms. Legislation makes visible the debate of whether a dead body is indeed a person or perhaps a thing (Stroud, 2018). This shows the differences between socio-cultural and legal understandings of dead bodies as those disposing of a loved one will likely not refer to the dead body as a 'thing'. Each country has specific legislation with regard to body disposal. The development of new ways of disposal not only prompts societal debates about whether practices should be allowed, but they also trigger the development of new legislations as, despite the dead bodies' status between a thing and a person, people have to follow current laws when disposing of a body.

This in-betweenness of dead bodies has also been reflected in anthropological research. Anthropologists have long been interested in the significance of the corpse, mortuary practices, and the rituals that are performed by different communities. Arnold van Gennep (van Gennep, 2019) suggests dead bodies are in a liminal state; they are in a world between the living and the dead. Mortuary and funeral rituals can be seen as a rite of passage for the dead to be fully integrated into the world of the deceased and for the living to make sense of the death.

This chapter will introduce some 'traditional' ways of disposal, for example, burial and cremation. It will also introduce newer ways of disposal. Many words linked to disposal practices are often taken for granted and ill-defined in the literature. Some terms, like the word 'disposal', might sound insensitive, yet this is a concept commonly used within death studies (Rumble et al., 2014). Various forces play a role in the changing landscape of bodily disposal practices. This chapter will show how socio-cultural changes, consumer cultures, and a growing critical concern for the environment all play a part in the development of practices around the globe.

Preparing the Body for Disposal

In some places, the body is ritually washed and prepared for the disposal practice that will follow. These practices often reveal cultural norms and ideas around gender and race. For example, in Sunni Muslim funerals in Turkey, touch in the form of kissing, washing, and caressing the dead body of the deceased is considered extremely important (Zengin, 2022). The ritual washing of the corpse is organised amongst gender and familial lines. This strict gendered division has proven problematic for deceased who are trans people as corpse washers and family members might refuse to touch the dead body (Zengin, 2022). In the United Kingdom, the washing of the bodies was traditionally done by women, but the introduction of funeral directors, who were predominantly men, took away this role (Bradbury, 1999). During slavery in the United States, Black women played a key role in the washing and dressing of corpses, and whilst this is not always acknowledged in history, because of these roles, Black women played a key role in the development of Black undertaking (Fletcher, 2023b).

The after-death handling of a body can extend beyond washing and dressing. A practice widespread in North America is the process of embalming, which is a way of treating the body to keep it 'fresh' for longer by inserting chemicals into the body. While embalming has a long history, the practice became common in the United States because of The American Civil War (1861–1865) (Troyer, 2020). Dead soldiers needed to be preserved for their transport back home, and embalming provided the perfect solution.[2] Troyer (2020) notes that embalmment introduced *corpse time* as bodies no longer followed the normal timeframe with regard to organic decomposition.

> The process of embalming was hidden from view, as were the chemicals used by embalmers. What emerged from nineteenth-century mechanical labor on the human corpse was a modern dead body that required embalmed vision to be seen in the proper context and state of vitality.
>
> *(Troyer, 2020, 28–29)*

Embalming preserves bodies and shields mourners from the perhaps more unpleasant realities of decomposing.

Cann (2018) notes that the continued popularity of embalming in the United States is mainly due to the funeral industry and its marketing. The corpse is presented as potentially unhygienic and a danger to society. Whilst the dead body is presented as a potential hazard, it is the process of embalming that requires highly toxic chemicals that require the wearing of complete body protection and a respirator. Embalming makes the viewing of the body more flexible, as the body will be better preserved, and there will be fewer changes of unwanted noises and movements compared to un-embalmed corpses (Cann, 2018). Cann notes that while many people believe embalming is an essential part of funeral services, many consumers do not know the real reason they are being offered this service, which is its significant profit margin (Cann, 2018).

Despite being popular, embalming is not universally practised in the United States. Cann (2018) notes that Jewish people do not embalm the body, nor do they view it, as they find it disrespectful to the deceased. Similarly, Islam also rejects embalmment, and as in Buddhism and Hinduism, most people prefer to be cremated, and embalmment is not part of these rites. Buddhists believe that the soul lingers near the body for days following the death and therefore absolute respect must be given to the body, and the body should be treated as if it is still alive (Cann,

2018). Consequently, embalmment does not happen. As Jews, Muslims, Hindus, and Buddhists residing in the United States tend to reject embalming practices, this practice cannot be solely understood as part of the United States' cultural geography or its socio-cultural influence (Cann, 2018). Similarly, it cannot be understood to be directly linked to Christian belief systems, as many Catholics and Protestants living in Europe and Latin America do not use embalmment (Cann, 2018).

This section has shown that there are various ways in which the body can be prepared before disposal. This is not done universally but, in most places, some form of ritual or the dressing of the dead body is considered necessary. After these practices, the dead body is ready for burial, cremation, or other form of disposal.

Burial

Burial is a form of bodily disposal where a body is placed into the ground, sometimes with objects. It can also be referred to as interment or inhumation. The places where corpses are buried are often referred to as 'burial grounds', which is a generic term that refers to any place where burial takes place (Rugg, 2000). There is a lot of terminology that is used to describe burial spaces, including churchyards, cemeteries, and graveyards. These terms all have different meanings but are often taken for granted and not explained in the literature (Rugg, 2000). Human bodies are typically buried horizontally, yet there are also examples of corpses buried vertically (Gould et al., 2023).

Archaeological evidence shows that some form of burial practices have existed for as long as there have been humans around (Roberts, 2022). It is sometimes difficult to deduce what types of rituals, if any, were used around burials. Archaeologists disagree about the meaning of specific ancient sites where human remains have been found, whether remains were placed there initially or ended up there accidentally (Roberts, 2022). Roberts (2022, 93) notes that 'even if we don't know what past people were thinking when they performed funerary rites, the practices themselves speak of some sort of symbolic thinking – some sort of appreciation of the difference between being alive and being dead, the meaning of loss, the importance of ritual'. Burial practices depend on people's beliefs, not least their beliefs about the afterlife (Davies, 2017). Burial is considered 'a final resting place', in some locations, whereas in other places, the plot will be exhumed after a certain amount of time.

Cremation

Another form of bodily disposal is cremation. This is a means of body disposal through burning. While the presence of burial sites, graves, and human remains reveal that burial practices have occurred for thousands of years, it is more difficult to find archaeological evidence of other means of disposal, such as cremation, as these practices leave fewer traces.[3]

While cremation has been an integral way of bodily disposal in some parts of the world, it has been fiercely rejected in others. In the religious traditions of Buddhism, Hinduism, and Sikhism, cremation is favoured over burial (Cann, 2018). Christianity, for a very long time, has condemned the use of cremation as a means of bodily disposal. In many places in the world, where burial used to be the typical way of disposal, cremation has slowly made way. These changes to cremation have been adopted for a range of reasons, including the scarcity of land and the costs of burial, and changing beliefs around memorials and remembering as some people feel they do not need the physical site of the grave to remember their dead.

In Europe, Britain was the first country to popularise cremation (Jupp, 2005). This was due to several reasons, including concerns about hygiene around cemeteries and other burial spaces (Davies, 2017). Whilst cremation has gained popularity around Europe, not least because it is often cheaper than burial, this development has not occurred evenly across the continent. For example, due to the influence of the Orthodox Church, the number of cremations in Romania has remained low (Rotar, 2018). Rotar notes that whilst the debate over cremation for religious reasons has primarily disappeared in Europe, religious influence in Romania has remained strong. While cremation is becoming more popular in many places, a growing concern is the ecological impact of this disposal practice, and the discussion on whether this practice should be allowed has thus moved from religious grounds to environmental grounds. In other places, the uptake of cremation is driven by financial reasons, with cremations, especially direct cremations with no memorial service, being cheaper (Sunlife Direct, 2024).

Disposal and Land

In some parts of the world, burial is considered 'a final resting place', whereas in other places, graves are temporary. This is often linked to the scarcity of space in specific geographic locations. For example, on the island of Singapore, burial plots are only available for 15 years (Hui and Yeoh, 2002). After this time, the plot will be exhumed to free up space for a new user. This change was implemented after the Second World War and reflects a tension between the state's view of Chinese burial grounds as a 'waste of space' whereas they can be considered sacred by Chinese communities (Hui and Yeoh, 2002). While less extreme, in the Netherlands, burial is often temporary too. People can rent a plot for a number of years. After this time, the lease can be renewed, or the grave will be exhumed to make place for someone else (Venhorst and Mathijssen, 2017). Local contexts, therefore, shape where, how, and for how long people are buried.

Furthermore, certain practices might only be reserved for certain groups and unattainable to achieve for those outside the group. Historically, various groups of people have been excluded from certain burial practices; for example, people who killed themselves by suicide were often not allowed to be buried in church graveyards. In the United States, racial segregation is still visible in death as African Americans and White Americans historically are buried in different cemeteries (Fletcher, 2023a). Cemeteries and graveyards continue to reveal ethnical or racial divisions in society; some cemeteries are only used for members of a specific religion; some cemeteries are divided into blocks of people who belong to the same group.

Societal and technological changes all have an impact on disposal practices and what people do in times of death. Allison (2023, IX) notes how in Japan, people used to be buried 'in a family or ancestral plot in the ground, attached to a Buddhist temple passed down for generations, and tended fastidiously by patrilineal kin'. Allison states that after the Second World War, Japan adopted post-war reforms in 1947, which meant that the status of the grave changed. No longer was it a place to memorialise ancestors, but instead, it became a place for an individual's eternal rest (Allison, 2023). Meaning of graves has changed due to these reforms but also due to urbanisation, which came with different lifestyles, an ageing population combined with low birth rates, and a decrease in marriage and cohabitation (Allison, 2023). Increasingly, people in Japan are living and dying alone. A response to these changing attitudes towards grave tending and memorialisation combined with technological developments has led to the development of automated graves.

> The basic model is a building-style columbarium where remains are stored in boxes or lockers in a storage area but delivered by automation to a handful of beautiful graves when required by a visitor. Once the visit is complete, the boxes are returned to their shelves in an Amazon-like warehouse.
>
> *(Allison, 2023, 176)*

Lack of space is a huge issue in cities like Tokyo, and these automated columbaria are one way to solve this problem. The issue of tending to the grave or not having relatives around to tend to your grave is also fixed by this automated system. Allison points out that these types of graves might sound horrific and futuristic. Still, she argues that

> whereas once urban dwellers returned to rural homes to honour and perpetuate the sacredness of ancestral graves, now remains from those graves are being sent to automated columbaria in the cities in an attempt to rescue them from becoming abandoned materiality and souls.
>
> *(Allison, 2023, 190)*

These automated graves lead to new ways of continuing old traditions as well as make space for new ways of commemorating and memorialising. They can also be viewed as a more sustainable way to keep the dead, as many are warehoused in the exact location. This example shows how burial practices are changing in response to changing cultural norms and technological developments. What might be considered 'normal' now, can be considered outdated or irrelevant or, as we shall see, un-environmentally friendly in the future.

Disposal and Sustainability

A growing concern around disposal practices is their sustainability. McManus (2023) argues that death is currently unsustainable; the interconnected aspects of economic, social, and environmental ways of managing the dead all contribute to its unsustainability. In other words, there are various reasons why disposal practices are not eco-friendly and current practices can have a negative impact on future generations.

McManus notes that cemeteries have often been the focus of writing on death and sustainability. Importantly, cemeteries are not considered green urban spaces by city planners, and therefore they do not have to be as 'green' as other urban spaces (McManus, 2023).

> The perceived gulf between cemeteries and other open spaces is based on a specialness given to the primary users of cemeteries: the grieving. At heart, the specialness accrued to the grieving is the presumption that the social needs of the grieving are incompatible with and have to trump other users and environmental sustainability goals that may be seen to infringe their use of these spaces.
>
> *(McManus, 2023, 5)*

The emotional connotation that cemeteries hold thus affects the way they are thought about. Consequently, these spaces are considered not to be accountable for their environmental impact.

In various places in the world, the importance of the environment and sustainable burial practices have been introduced. Rumble et al (2014) note that since the 1990s the importance of the environment has made its way into the British burial and cremation industry. Various new ways of disposal entered the scene in response to this. For example, so-called 'natural burial' has become increasingly popular in the United Kingdom. Davies and Rumble (2012) note that people sometimes chose natural burial to 'return to nature' or 'to give something back', and over 200 natural burial sites were created between the 1990s and 2011. In Zimbabwe, green burial is also emerging as a practice. Research shows that religion is a successful way to promote this practice as people are moved by spiritual principles and ecological faith (Muposhi, Chokera, and Mudzimba, 2023).

Where Rugg (2000) notes a wild linguistic landscape of terms to refer to cemeteries, Davies and Rumble (2012) similarly observe the wide range of words used to denote more sustainable burial grounds, including ecological, green, natural, or woodland burial. They suggest that 'ecological' carries a science-like validation and 'green' suggests an element of political activism. 'Natural' is deemed to be linked to desires for independence from the 'unnatural' interference of commercial ventures, opting for an alliance with the organic world. Lastly, 'woodland' carries its more specific cultural affinity with British landscape tradition' (Davies and Rumble, 2012, 1). There are various reasons why people choose to be buried this way, but the impact on the environment is often an important one.

While there is an implication that these types of burial are more sustainable, questions remain about how 'green' or 'natural' these spaces are. As the majority of dead bodies in Zimbabwe, for example, are currently undergoing embalmment, the chemicals used in this process often leach into the soil and offer a significant risk of contaminating groundwater (Muposhi, Chokera, and Mudzimba, 2023) and many 'natural' burial grounds have different rules and regulations on what is allowed to be entered into the ground or placed on the burial site.

Cremation can be quite a polluting way to dispose of a body. The release of nitrogen dioxide is the main cause of the environmental problems resulting from cremation. Globally the cremation industry is responsible for 1% of the annual nitrogen dioxide emission (Robinson, 2021). There are also considerations about materials that are not burned during the process of cremation. Both in the United Kingdom and elsewhere the cremation industry has started to 'to recycle implants, scrub emissions and recycle heat in response to financial inducements and legal requirements to protect the environment' (Rumble et al., 2014). Consequently, there are ongoing technological developments around cremation to reduce the environmental impact of the practice.

Alkaline hydrolysis is a new way of bodily disposal that is considered more environmentally friendly, resource-effective, and economically sound (Arnold et al., 2023; Robinson, 2021). It goes by various names and is also referred to as 'resomation', 'water cremation', 'bio-cremation', 'aquamation', 'green cremation', and 'flameless cremation' (Robinson, 2021). It is a chemical process that mimics natural decomposition; it was initially developed in the 1990s to dispose of animal carcasses (Rumble et al., 2014). Through this process, the body would be reduced to bones which can be ground to white 'ash' and a DNA-free residual that can be treated and returned to the water system (Robinson, 2021). It has been suggested that alkaline hydrolysis could be a real contender with burial and cremation, but the lack of public awareness of this method hampers its growth (Arnold et al., 2023). There is public concern about what the fluid that remains after this process could potentially do to wastewater. Plans to install a Resomator in the United Kingdom in 2017 were rejected because of the perception that human remains would enter the water system and due to the lack of regulations and guidelines regarding water standards and disposal practices (Robinson, 2021).

Each new technological development has to contest cultural and religious norms but also local legislation. Currently, in the Netherlands, according to Dutch Law, the body of a deceased person can be buried, cremated, or donated to science (Health Council of the Netherlands, 2020). A Health Council committee has been considering new ways of bodily disposal and whether these should be included in the Corpse Disposal Act. The Committee measured new techniques against three values: safety, dignity, and sustainability and argued that alkaline hydrolysis meets all three criteria. They note that the technical specifications of this technique should be assessed and developed further before this new way of disposal can be authorised and added to the law (Health Council of the Netherlands, 2020). A second new way of disposal, namely human composting, was rejected as, to date, insufficient information was available to make a reasonable assessment (Health Council of the Netherlands, 2020).

The example of alkaline hydrolysis highlights two critical elements that influence the success of new disposal technologies. First, public awareness and perceptions play a role in whether a practice is deemed acceptable. Secondly, legal frameworks need to be adapted to allow for certain practices to occur. Every new way of disposal thus has to be measured against local practices and local law. This means that a particular practice can be legal in one place but illegal in another, or considered acceptable in one area and abnormal in another.

Conclusion

This chapter has examined different disposal practices used around the world. It has shown that critical usage of concepts, such as 'dead bodies' and 'corpses' and the range of terms to describe burial grounds, is warranted. It has examined the traditional disposal practices of burial and cremation and highlighted how socio-cultural and technological changes impact these practices. There is an increased awareness of the environmental impact of these disposal practices. There are developments around more sustainable and environmentally friendly practices, which can be seen in the growing interest in natural burials and the development of new disposal technologies such as alkaline hydrolysis.

As demonstrated in this chapter, a wide range of values and social practices influence how a body is treated after death. This can include religion, social norms, changing technology, financial resources, and environmental concerns. Legal understandings of dead bodies and what is permissible also vary across countries and over time, reshaping how the dead are disposed of. Rather than assume such practices are universal or unchanging, it is important to critically reflect on how the practices are created, done, and challenged, as this reveals much about the different values behind them, potential inequities, and what power structures, such as the law, shape them.

Notes

1   For a visual overview of various disposal practices see these educational videos from the Open University: https://connect.open.ac.uk/society-psychology-and-criminology/inside-the-undertakers

2 The development of embalmment coincided with the development of the rail network in the United States and many corpses were transported via rail, with a first-class ticket (Troyer 2020).
3 This also applies to other disposal practices like sky burials which rely on scavenger birds consuming the body.

11

GRIEF THEORIES AND THERAPIES

Introduction

Grief is an individual response to a loss. This loss can, in many cases, be the death of a person – this is a form of grief. Ideas and understandings of how people are supposed to respond to a loss or bereavement are influenced by the historical and socio-cultural context. Loss is a universal experience, but whether grief is a universal experience is questionable as some places do, for example, not even have a word for grief. Furthermore, how grief is understood and interpreted varies depending on where you live. Breen and O'Connor (2007) note a paradox in the literature on grief and bereavement as, on the one hand, there is an emphasis that grief is unique, depending on a myriad of variables, yet on the other hand there are discourses around 'normal' and 'complicated' grief. They note that 'grief is a unique experience that occurs within a historical, social, cultural, and political context, and our research endeavours need to recognise it as such' (Breen and O'Connor, 2007). In 'Western' societies, there are specific and dominant ideas on what grief is and is not, and these are reflected in the theories that have been developed around grief and bereavement. How one responds to this loss is subject to people's socio-cultural context. It is often suggested that every grief experience is unique, depending on the context.

Understanding the theories underpinning grief and bereavement is essential as they highlight the thinking in various academic disciplines (i.e. medicine, psychology, sociology) and reflect cultural understandings of loss and grief. Theories and ideas are not static but change over time. Yet some notions, despite empirical evidence pointing to other conclusions, remain persistent and influence understandings of grief both in academic circles as well as is in popular culture and media. The theories discussed in this chapter are predominantly rooted in

DOI: 10.4324/9781003318002-14

psychology and therefore centre individual responses to grief. Many grief theories take the individual as a starting point and do not look at collective reactions to grief. Instead, grief is often understood as an individual's 'problem' that they need to work through. But how grief is experienced and framed is shaped by people's social and cultural context and therefore there is no a singular way to grief. Psychology and psychiatry have had a significant impact in our understanding of grief, particularly in viewing it as a psychiatric syndrome (see Klass, 2023). This chapter will look at these theories and give an overview of other theories that view grief more as a social phenomenon. This chapter does not cover a comprehensive review but instead offers some insight in the different ways that grief can be theorised and understood. Whenever you are encountered with a theory or model, it is essential to critically assess what is being talked about and what is not being discussed.

Several definitions of grief are presented in this chapter. There are various ways of approaching grief, and we will teach some ways of understanding the topic. This chapter highlights the assumptions present in psychological and psychoanalytical understandings of grief and introduces social understandings of grief that focus more on relationships instead of the individual griever.

Defining Grief

There is no singular definition of grief – some view grief as an emotion and 'a response to the involuntary loss through the death of a human being who is viewed as significant by the actor of reference' (Lofland, 1985). Ratcliffe (2022) talks about the 'two-sidedness' of grief which on the one hand can be linked to something very particular such as a certain loss, but on the other hand encompass 'everything'. 'Grief is neither an episodic emotion nor an assortment of disparate episodes spreads over time. It is a process, the unity of which derives from the unity of the life disturbance that it navigates' (Ratcliffe, 2022, 17). Klass and Steffen (2018, 9) note grief is now best understood as:

> An interaction between interior, interpersonal, communal, and cultural narratives by which individuals and communities construct the meaning of the deceased's life and death, as well as the post-death status of the bereaved within the broader community.

Grief can thus be viewed as emotions, a process, actions, and a state of being responding to a loss. Depending on the discipline, there can be vastly different ideas about grief.

This variance is further complicated by language. The word 'grief', as currently understood in English, does not exist in every language. Chinese, for example, did not have a word for grief 'until recently when Western ideas about death and dying were introduced through the hospice (Klass, 2014). While researching grief and bereavement in Senegal, Evans et al. (2017) similarly note the challenge of translating specific phrases from Wolong and French to English and the risk of losing meaning.

> Discussing and reflecting on the nuances of how key signifying words and phrases were used in Wolof and French by participants, translators, and researchers has shed light on the cultural specificities of language and wider socio-cultural expectations and taken-for-granted assumptions which construct 'grief' and experiences/meanings of death and bereavement in particular ways.
>
> *(Evans et al., 2017, 131)*

Furthermore, English distinguishes between grief and mourning, which is absent in every language. The work of psychoanalyst Sigmund Freud *Trauer und Melancholie* (1917), has been highly influential in shaping understandings of grief and bereavement. However, where in English a distinction is made between grief (the individual response to loss) and mourning (the public manifestation of grief), this distinction is not present in German and *trauer* can refer to both grief and mourning, yet the work has been translated as *Mourning and Melancholia*. As English is a dominant language in academic research it is crucial to keep in mind that this language offers a particular framework and understanding of grief, that is not universally accepted.

Psychological and Psychoanalytical Assumptions of Grief

There is an abundance of literature available concerned with 'normal' grief. It is argued that grief is often hidden in 'Western' societies. Harris (2010) suggests that in capitalistic 'Western' societies neoliberal values underpin societal and cultural expectations of grief experiences and behaviours; bereaved people are temporarily allowed to grieve a loved one, but this cannot last too long as they should return to be productive members of society. Furthermore, Harris notes specific rules around who has permission to grief, how long grief can last and how it can and should be manifested. Deviation from these norms can result in the pathologising of grief. The *Diagnostic and Statistical Manuel*, Volume 5 (DSM-5) includes diagnoses of 'complicated grief' and 'traumatic grief disorder', which implies that some forms of grief and bereavement are 'abnormal'. Yet, they can contribute to the internalising of beliefs that specific ways of grieving are 'wrong' and, in fact, a mental disorder. Harris (2010) strives for the normalising of death as a natural part of life and for greater acceptance of the different grief responses and their longevity. When researching and thinking about grief and bereavement, it is important to unpack what behaviours and feelings are considered 'normal' and which are not and why certain societies might have more or less space for grief and grieving. This isn't easy, as many of these assumptions can be hidden or taken for granted.

Breen and O'Connor (2007, 200–201) suggest that many of the dominant classic grief theories follow a number of assumptions:

> These are: a) grief follows a relatively distinct pattern; b) grief is short-term and finite; c) grief is a quasi-linear process characterized by stages/phases/tasks/processes of shock, yearning, and recovery; d) the grief process needs to be 'worked through'; e) for people bereaved through illness, the work of grief begins in anticipation of the death; f) meaning in and/or positives gained from the death must be found; g) grief culminates in the detachment from the deceased loved one; and h) the continuation of grief is abnormal, even pathological.

Despite abundant empirical evidence that grief responses often do not adhere to these assumptions, their influence shapes ideas, theories, and beliefs around grief. Many of these assumptions are present in the model developed by Elisabeth Kübler-Ross. Kübler-Ross proposed in the 1960s that dying patients experience a predictable set of stages that they go through before they die. This model was based on research with people who were diagnosed with a terminal illness. The five stages are denial, anger, bargaining, depression and, finally, acceptance of death. In later work, she linked these stages to the experience of grief (Tyrrell et al., 2023). Importantly, there is very little empirical evidence that suggest that people in fact go through these stages, and the model has been critiqued heavily as experiences of grief and loss are not linear (Breen and O'Connor, 2007).

William Worden (1996) created another model of grief. Worden developed a task-based approach to grief called the Four Tasks of Mourning. The four tasks are as follows: (1) To accept the reality of the loss, (2) To process the pain of the grief, (3) To adjust to a world without the deceased, and (4) To find a way to remember the dead while embarking on the rest of one's journey through life. Here again, we see many of the assumptions of grief outlined by Breen and O'Connor (2007); according to Worden, grief needs to be 'resolved', is temporal, and there are precise tasks to successfully move through one's grief. Pearce (2019) notes that the task model of grief does not have to be completed in a set order, but it does put the responsibility of grief work onto an individual and understands it as a set of actions to be completed by the bereaved. Grief here is not a set of stages one has to go through, but instead a set of tasks one can meet to resolve the 'problem' of grief.

Stage models of grief where never developed to become prescriptive models for grief (Lloyd, 2018) but have often started to live their own lives. There are numerous popular culture examples to be found in film, television, and books that all reinforce the message that grief is a set of stages that can be worked through. The lived experience of many suffering people shows that it is more complex and that people can have numerous and varied responses to grief and loss.

Social Models of Grief

At the end of the 20th century, there was a shift in ideas around grief that focused on psychological and psychoanalytic theories towards social models of grief (Pearce and Komaromy, 2022). In these social models the focus is less on the individual griever and more on the relationships between people and the broader social impact of loss. Many theories around grief and bereavement have been developed in the 1990s in response to earlier grief models. A significant transformation has been the focus on continuing bonds with the deceased instead of *breaking* the bonds with the deceased. For example, Walter thus considered the act of talking as essential in creating a durable biography of the dead (Walter, 1996). In this section, we introduce other models developed during this time. These models highlight the broader impact of grief and bereavement beyond the individual. They often challenge the assumption that grief has an endpoint or follows set stages or phases. It is important to note that many of these theories have originated in Western societies and that some of the elements spoken about have been present in bereavement practices in other parts of the globe.

Continuing Bonds Theory

Arguably, continuing bonds theory is one of the most influential theories in death studies. In this theory, Klass et al. (1996) wanted to counter the dominant idea that people 'sever' their bonds with their deceased loved ones. In contrast, they argue that people *continue* their bond. They note 'that it is normative for mourners to maintain a presence and connection with the deceased, and that this presence is not static' (Klass, Silverman, and Nickman 1996, 17). Klass (2006, 244) notes that with continuing bonds theory the authors 'wanted to show that interacting with the dead could be normal rather than pathological'. This theory thus foregrounds the idea that people do not sever bonds post-death. While not using the term 'continuing bonds', sociologist Tony Walter (1996) proposes a similar model that challenges clinical understandings of grief in the same year as Klass et al. (1996). Walter (1996, 7) notes that the purpose of grief is 'the construction of a durable biography that enables the living to integrate the memory of the dead into their ongoing lives'. According to Walter, 'the process by which this is achieved is mainly conversation with others who knew the deceased'. Walter notes that this process is increasingly complex when people no longer know the deceased or are not readily available for these discussions. While he does not use continuing bonds, this *durable biography* highlights the continued relationship between the living and the dead. In a recent paper, Klass (2023) comments that there can be the assumption that continuing bonds lead to 'positive grieving'. He argues that this is not necessarily true and that 'it is not unusual to find conflicted or dysfunctional patterns in the relationship that continue after death' (Klass, 2023, 8). The ties people continue to have with people post-death can thus be harmful. Similarly, Mathijssen (2017) has drawn attention to the fact that posthumous relationships can change over time. As a consequence, Mathijssen points to the notion of *transforming bonds* (Mathijssen, 2017).

The bond between the living and the dead, whilst continuing, can additionally take a different shape. While continuing bonds are considered a significant development in scholarly work on grief, longstanding traditions in various parts of the world indicate that this notion of continuation is not new. While traditions are changing in Japan (see Chapter 10), this country has longstanding rituals and traditions around the memorialisation of ancestors, which show the continued importance of deceased loved ones in everyday life. Another example is the way the Toraja, a people living in Indonesia, integrate their deceased loved ones in their everyday lives.

> For Torajans, the death of the body isn't the abrupt, final, severing event of the West. Instead, death is just one step in a long, gradually unfolding process. Late loved ones are tended at home for weeks, months, or even years after death.
>
> *(Bennett, 2016)*

Dual Model of Grief

In 1999, Margaret Stroebe and Henk Schut introduced the *dual process model* of coping with grief (Stroebe and Schut, 1999). This model was initially developed to understand dealing with the death of a partner but has been applied to other types of losses as well. Stroebe and Schut (1999) note that various stressors are involved during a bereavement. Stroebe and Schut (1999) note that there are various stressors involved during a bereavement. They outline two types of 'stressors' – loss-oriented and restoration-oriented. '*Loss-orientation* refers to the concentration on, and dealing with, processing of some aspect of the loss experience itself, most particularly, with respect to the deceased person' (Stroebe and Schut, 1999, 212). Loss-oriented stressors include grief work, the intrusion of grief, and the breaking of bonds. There is a range of emotions involved, including a potential yearning for the deceased, and this process focuses predominantly on coping with the grief and the loss itself.

The second type of stressor, the *restoration-orientation*, deals with the change that has come about because of the death. This can involve attending to the life changes that have occurred because of the death, doing new things, trying to distract oneself from the loss, denying or avoiding the grief, and taking on or coming to terms with the new identities that have emerged because of the death. Stroebe and Schut consider the broader impact of grief.

> In many bereavements these additional sources of stress add considerably to the burden of loss and cause extreme additional anxiety and upset. They include mastering the tasks that the deceased had undertaken (e.g., the finances or cooking); dealing with arrangements for the reorganization of life without the

loved one (e.g., it may be necessary to sell one's house); the development of a new identity from 'spouse' to 'widow(er)' or from 'parent' to 'parent of a deceased child'.

(Stroebe and Schut, 1999, 214)

Stroebe and Schut (1999) argue that people oscillate or move between loss-oriented and restoration-oriented stressors. They suggest that coming to terms with a loss is a back-and-forth between these two types of stressors. This oscillation between phases makes the model stand out from other models that have predominantly focused on loss-oriented *or* restoration-oriented coping strategies.

Growing Around Grief

Another model of grief, proposed by grief councillor Louis Tonkin, is the notion that people *grow around* their grief (Tonkin, 1996). According to Tonkin, grief does not grow smaller over time; what happens is that people's lives grow around it. As people move forwards with their lives, they continue to have experiences, and while the death and loss might still be significant, other life experiences grow around this sense of grief. This is important, particularly for those bereaved, as it acknowledges that the loss does not go away, which can explain why people still have 'dark' days years later when the grief feels 'smaller' or perhaps even 'gone'. Again, this model has no 'resolution' to the grief or a forgetting or breaking of the bond. Instead, it is another manifestation of how the dead are integrated into the everyday lives of the bereaved and continue to have importance and meaning.

Posthuman Grief

Most of the theories around grief centre the experience of humans. They are based on the experience of individual people making sense of the deaths of other people. Whilst continuing bonds theory, for example, was developed to highlight human interdependence, it is still emphasising individual human agency and the inner relationship between one individual and a deceased other (Pearce, 2019). There are increased calls to decentre the experience of humans and to adopt a more-than-human perspective. This could be considered posthuman grief; grief that does not necessarily start with humans or grief, or which does not focus on the loss of other humans. This includes foregrounding, for example, the relationship between humans and non-human animals more at the heart of research on grief and mourning (Lykke, 2022. Parallel to this are calls to recognise types of grief and mourning that go beyond the loss of humans. It is suggested that the deaths of humans are treated as exceptional and that other types of losses, such as biodiversity loss or even the loss of a pet, are deemed less relevant (Kemp, Jacobs, and Stewart, 2016; Barnett, 2022). For example, Barnett (2022) draws attention to ecological grief, or the grief that can be felt in response to ecological losses, both experienced and anticipated, that are a consequence of climate change. These theories thus draw our attention to a different way of viewing the world, in which the grief of deaths of humans is not considered exceptional, but a small part of a bigger whole. Yet, to date, it is predominantly the grief in response to human loss that is socially accepted.

Grief Therapy

Many of the theories around grief, particularly psychological ones, set up grief as something that one has to 'work through'. One of the ways to do this work is through therapy. People can seek help in treatment for any loss, but it has been suggested that people who have experienced a violent or sudden death can significantly benefit from therapy (Neimeyer, Klass, and Dennis 2014; Neimeyer and Currier, 2009). Which losses people seek therapeutic help for can to some extent reveal a hierarchy of losses and which deaths are deemed socially acceptable to grieve and find support for. Much of the support that people get is available through people close to them. Only a few are considered to need professional support for their grief, yet Harris (2010) notes that increasingly, people are seeking professional help as they are unsure whether their response to a loss is appropriate. Harris (2010)

> realized that much of my work as a counsellor has been spent attempting to normalize grief responses that have been deemed as abnormal by social indices, un-doing the unhealthy suppression of grief, and attempting to re-frame the pathology-based approach to grief that seems prevalent in Western society in order to counteract the paralyzing effects that these influences have upon many of my bereaved clients.

The increase in popularity of grief therapy highlights cultural expectations put on people regarding how they supposedly should feel or behave (Harris, 2010).

Considerable research has been dedicated to understanding how effective different therapeutic interventions are. Meta-analyses indicate that professionally provided grief therapy can be effective when someone is has 'protracted grief'; there is little evidence to support the provision of grief therapy in all contexts irrespective of self-perceived distress(Neimeyer, Breen, and Milman, 2023). Research literature is conflicted as to whether there are sex or gender differences about grief and success of therapy for different groups, as well as the role of age, race, culture, and socioeconomic status. Rather than focusing on sociodemographic differences as a cause of potential differences in how grief is expressed or displayed, Doka and Martin suggest looking at grieving styles as a continuum and understanding how these may be influenced by social norms, culture, and experiences (Doka and Martin, 2011). Importantly, when thinking about these issues, especially expectations around therapeutic intervention or different groups, one should consider what power and prejudices may be behind the theories and models of therapy (Allan and Harms, 2010).

An example for this can be found in the focus on restoration or recover. In counselling or therapy, there can be a focus on so-called 'meaning making' (Neimeyer, Klass, and Dennis, 2014) which helps people make sense of their loss and helps them continue with their everyday lives. Caroline Pearce (2019) has noted how many grief theories are developed on the understanding that someone will 'recover' from grief. Grief therapies can underscore this understanding as well. Pearce challenges this notion and wonders what will happen to those who do not recover from a loss. She questions what full recovery looks like and whether this is, in fact, desirable. As noted earlier, many grief theories find their origin in the psy-disciplines. There is a tendency to distinguish between normal and abnormal ways of coping with grief. Pearce argues that 'non-recovery' is a valid position for a bereaved person to inhabit, thus challenging normative and temporal understandings of grief and loss.

Additionally, grief therapy predominately focuses on talking and cognitive engagement with grief. The body appears absent in much of this literature (Pearce and Komaromy, 2022). There is, however, a recognition that people may experience somatic – or bodily – responses to their emotions; as Keller points, how bodies can be holders of grief (E. R. Keller, 2023). One study based on participants in three regions (United States, Turkey/Iran, Cyprus/Greece), for example, found 'high levels of somatic symptom distress' when someone is bereaved (Hennemann et al., 2023). The symptoms included stomach or bowel problems, headaches, and trouble sleeping. Another study focusing on bereaved students in Belgium noted that they may experience pain, but are reluctant to seek support for somatic symptoms (Chirico et al., 2022). Whilst some consider the physical symptoms as an indication of a lack of coping, others have noted the usefulness of considering how grief is embodied. For example, Gudmundsdottir writing about bereaved parents acknowledges the importance of how people experience in their body, especially as bereaved parents are learning to live in a world without the physical presence of their child (Gudmundsdottir, 2009). Thinking about the body and grief challenges 'traditional' talk-focused therapies and opens up other modes of therapeutic work that may be more oriented to movement, physicality, or embodied.

Conclusion

This chapter has examined the notion of grief. There is no singular understanding of this phenomenon, yet grief theories developed in psychology and psychiatry have strongly influenced normative ideas of grief. They typically centre on the individual experiencing a loss and have historically highlighted the need to 'get over' a loss or 'break a bond' with the deceased. More social understandings of grief and loss have been developed, which highlight the relationality of loss and the continuing bond between the living and the dead post-death. The body appears absent in much of this literature but grief can be considered an embodied experience. Many of the models and theories around grief focus on the impact grief has on the mind and talk about emotional and psychological well-being. The focus of grief as an emotional and psychological 'problem' has resulted in the rise and growth of grief therapy.

12

SUICIDE

Introduction

The World Health Organisation (WHO) (2023b) defines suicide as 'the act of deliberately killing oneself'. Scholarship has noted that it is difficult to fully grasp what suicide is and isn't:

> Suicide as a discursively constituted phenomenon, will always resist complete description, if for no other reason than as a cultural product it lacks any unchanging essence that could act as a stabilizing centre by which to secure such a description.
>
> *(Marsh, 2010, 7)*

Suicide is not a singular phenomenon. There is not one way to take one's own life, nor one reason to do so. Societal perceptions and language have a strong influence on the way suicide is perceived and talked about. The phrase *committing or committed* suicide refers to the time (or in places where) when attempting suicide was/is considered a crime. There has been a call to end the use of the phrase 'committed suicide' by clinicians and in academic writing since the term can be considered inaccurate, stigma-laden and outdated (Nielsen, Padmanathan, and Knipe, 2016). A recent anonymous survey conducted among people affected by suicide found that the terms 'took their own life' and 'died by suicide' were favoured (Padmanathan et al., 2019). Phrases like these are increasingly used to step away from the language that overtly connotes blame and judgement.

It is estimated that globally over 700,000 people die by suicide every year (WHO, 2021). Suicide rates are not evenly spread globally; approximately 80% of suicide deaths take place in low- and middle-income countries (Knettel et al.,

DOI: 10.4324/9781003318002-15

2024). In 2019, more than 1 of every 100 deaths was the result of suicide (WHO, 2021). It is important to know that this figure is an estimate and that the real number of suicides is unknown. In addition to suicide deaths, there are numerous suicide attempts, estimated to be 10 to 20 times the amount of suicide deaths. Yet again the real figures of these attempts are very difficult to quantify. It is suggested, though, that a prior suicide attempt is an important risk factor for future suicide (WHO, 2021). The global suicide figure does not include assisted dying deaths, which were discussed in Chapter 8. Whilst in some places this is referred to as assisted suicide, these numbers are mostly kept separate. Instead, suicide figures include the numerous ways in which people across the world take their own lives, without the assistance of medical personnel.

Suicide is a highly complex issue, and in this chapter, we outline some elements that can be taken into account when researching this topic. In suicide research, these elements are often referred to as risk factors; these include gender, sexuality, and age. A multi-factor analysis of suicide is beneficial as often a myriad of perhaps overlapping or even contradicting elements could lead to suicide. Yet whilst people might 'have' risk factors, it is important to keep in mind that these do not *have to* lead to suicidality. The chapter also looks at media portrayals of suicide as this informs how people think about suicide and can influence actions around suicide and suicidal behaviour.

Whilst global suicide numbers are important to provide a sense of the scale of the problem, the context and the people behind those numbers are equally important to understand. This chapter looks at some of the risk factors for suicide but also considers a critical perspective on the complexity of this issue. This is particularly pertinent as suicide attempts and suicide deaths can receive societal and moral judgement. Some types of death are considered more socially acceptable than others. Suicide is one that is often deemed less socially acceptable. Certain kinds of death may mean that those who are bereaved experience stigma, and so-called disenfranchised grief.

Understanding Suicide: Theories and Methods

Suicidology is the study of suicide. Marsh (2015) suggests three assumptions dominate current suicide research and practice. Firstly, the assumption that suicide is pathological and that people who kill themselves are all mentally ill. Marsh suggests that modern suicidology is founded on this claim and this is often considered an 'unassailable truth' which has come 'to dominate thinking on suicide to such an extent that it is now hard to think otherwise about the issue, or to imagine suicide prevention practices not in some way diagrammed in relation to mental illness and its detection and treatment' (Marsh, 2015, 18). This link between suicide and mental illness has not always existed and prior to this medicalisation narrative, suicide was thought to be a sin and a crime (Marsh, 2015). The framing of suicide as a pathology, or a response to mental ill health, has been evident in much psychological, psychiatric, and psychotherapeutic research. This approach to suicide has a strong impact on how suicide is perceived academically, socially, and politically. Importantly, while this thinking is dominant now in many countries, understandings of suicide are always in flux and can again change over time.

The second assumption is that suicidology is a science and that the topic should be studied 'scientifically' (Marsh, 2015). Marsh notes that, in theory, this stance is unproblematic as suicide is a topic that deserves scientific attention; however, what is meant by a 'scientific approach' has been defined in a very narrow way. Consequently, many studies within the field are quantitative studies using very specific research methods and paradigms. This positivist approach that largely relies on numbers is suggested to be removed from 'the subjective reality and meaning of the suicidal crisis of the self – that is, the actual suicidal person' (Webb, 2010, 40 in Marsh, 2015). Marsh argues that other forms of knowledge and knowledge production are needed to better understand the complexity of suicide.

The final assumption is that suicide is individual, and that suicidality arises from and is located within a separate, singular, individual subject (Marsh, 2015). This means that suicide is conceptualised as an individual problem, and deaths by suicide are reduced to singular, stand-alone events and not a response to wider issues. The understanding of suicide as an individual problem is evident in the suicide prevention agenda as it is understood as 'an undesirable individual action that requires no interrogation into how the phenomenon has come to be constructed over time' (White, 2017, 472). Yet, considering suicide as something located within or about an individual divorces suicide from social justice issues such as practices of exclusion and oppression, politics, stigma, and hate. In his book *Le Suicide: Étude de sociologie* (1897), Émile Durkheim made the case that suicides are not merely an individual's act, but that society or a person's social group can play a part in this.[1] He was interested in understanding why some groups had higher levels of suicide than others. Durkheim noted different levels of suicides between Protestants and Catholics and he suggested that this was because in France Protestants had lower levels of integration compared to Catholics, resulting in more suicide. This ongoing understanding of suicide as an individual act is surprising as sociological evidence for a long time has pointed to the socio-cultural factors that are at play in suicide.

Suicide receives much scholarly attention, yet it is argued that there is a lack of adequate theorisation and models that explain the phenomenon (Millner, Robinaugh, and Nock, 2020). Millner et al. suggest that a lot of current ideas are based on 'verbal theories' which use 'words to specify how the theory components are related to one another and how they produce the phenomena of interest... Because natural language is inherently vague, these theories often contain hidden assumptions, unknowns, or shortcomings' (Millner, Robinaugh, and Nock, 2020,

705). They argue in favour of formalising suicide theories and more rigorous descriptive research. White notes that presently:

> Authoritative knowledge about suicide is produced through scientific research; this leads to the construction of suicide as a particular kind of problem that can be acted upon; this knowledge is then 'applied' to practice; and the goal of preventing and controlling suicide in the population is expected to follow.
>
> *(White, 2017, 472)*

White argues in favour of so-called 'critical suicidology':

> Theoretically, it means engaging with language, discourse, power relations, and social histories, to show how knowledge, practice, ways of being 'selves' and ideas about life, death and suicide are not settled but are always being (re-) produced and coconstituted in multiple and fluid ways within specific social, historical, cultural, and political contexts.
>
> *(White, 2017)*

This critical suicidology approach is in keeping with this book.

Suicide Through the Lens of Risk Factors

There is a myriad of so-called risk factors that can contribute to people's likelihood to die by suicide, or even their suicidality (suicidal ideation or intent). One of the reasons to theorise suicide in terms of risk factors is to reduce attempts and prevent suicide deaths. The following sections will focus on some of those risk factors. It is important to keep in mind, however, that these risk factors do not mean someone will die by suicide. In his auto-ethnography, suicide researcher Mike Alvarez (2024) notes that his specific case includes at least 16 risk factors that make him at risk for suicide, including childhood abuse, sexuality, and post-migration stressors. He argues that this focus on risk factors:

> tells readers *nothing* about the alchemic life processes that make these accumulative risks explosive. It also tells us nothing of the existential dilemmas that plaguing suicidal people as they ponder questions of life and death. For these we will need qualitative methodologies.
>
> *(Alvarez, 2024, 155)*

The following sections will briefly touch on how experiences of gender and sexuality can contribute to feeling suicidal. Bereavement by suicide is also considered a risk factor. When reading these sections, it is important to keep a multi-focal lens in mind, as suicide is unlikely to be reduced to a singular social determinant or reason.

Gender and Suicide

In most places in the world, suicide rates are higher for men than for women (WHO, 2021). For example, in the United Kingdom, men account for three-quarters of suicide deaths (Ridge et al., 2021); similar gender disparities are found in India (Singh, 2022). The gender dynamics of suicide have meant that a lot of research has been concerned with why men take their own lives and how this links to notions of masculinity, including employment. In a UK interview study with men aged between 23 and 50 who had suicidal ideations and/or attempted suicide, Ridge et al. (2021) found that feeling left behind by life, feeling the need to hide oneself, being frustrated when trying to seek help, and relationship problems are all factors that can contribute to suicidality.

Less is known about the reasons why women take their own lives. Mallon et al. (2016) posit that, similarly to men, issues associated with feminine identities can be linked to deaths by suicide among women. They suggest that there is a troubling discourse present in suicide research that often posits suicide as a 'male' problem linked to their masculine identities, yet suicides by women are often separated from their gender identity.

> Within this discourse it is implied that male death by suicide is an indication that masculinity is visibly in crisis. By contrast, female death by suicide is largely invisible and can be accounted for by an increased propensity towards mental illness that is unrelated to their gendered identity.
>
> *(Mallon et al., 2016, 673)*

Gender identity can play a role in suicide. On the one hand, it can cause tensions for people who strongly identify as men or women and feel that they do not live up to normative gender identities. On the other hand, people who do not fit the assumed gender binary can equally feel suicidal because of this.

LGBTQ+[2] and Suicide

It has been observed in several countries that people in the LGBTQ+ community have a higher rate of suicidal thoughts and attempts compared to cisgender and heterosexual peers. LGBTQ+ people are often framed as 'other' or 'different' by society and experience various pressures in everyday life. A study in New Zealand showed that discrimination across their lifetime was linked to higher incidences of self-harm and suicide attempts for transgender people compared to cisgendered people (Treharne et al., 2020). Another study by Marzetti et al. (2022) included interviews 24 LGBT+ people aged 16–24 living in Scotland. They suggest that suicide in this group can be understood as a response to stigma, discrimination, and harassment. They suggest that in many cases suicide can thus be seen as an escape both from the internal conflicts and external harassment that participants were faced with. This study revealed that reasons for suicide are not singular but instead suicidal distress needs to be understood as a complex response or relationship between so-called queerphobia, cis-heteronormativity, and individual psychological states. In other words, suicidal ideation amongst this group is complicated and deserves more scholarly attention.

Youth Suicide

Suicide is the fourth leading cause of death amongst young people aged 15–29 globally (Marzetti et al., 2022). White (2012) invites people to think critically about youth suicide and not view it as a singular, stable, or 'tame' problem that has a potentially simple solution. Instead, it is suggested that youth suicide is viewed as a 'wild' problem with no clear boundaries and no clear, single-cut, solutions. She notes that 'it cannot be solved, nor contained, through an exclusive reliance on pre-determined, standardised, de-contextualised interventions' (White, 2012, 42). Why, how, and when young people try to take their own life is complex and multifaceted. White (2012, 2017) notes that youth suicide prevention programs in the United States are often based on medical and psychiatric ways of understanding suicide, and often do not take the views of younger people themselves into account. In, for example, cognitive behaviour therapy, younger people are individually held responsible for managing their distress and structural forms of violence that might contribute to their state of being are not considered or acknowledged (White, 2017). Consequently, White argues that the current way of trying to prevent youth suicide is often anxiety producing, sterile, regulated, and highly predictable. Whilst White criticises approaches taken in the United States, research indicates that across Africa there is relatively no academically published work on counselling interventions to prevent suicide across the continent (Knettel et al., 2024). This has led to calls for more intervention-based research to understand what can work both for youths and in resource-constrained settings.

Suicide Amongst Indigenous Populations

Suicide also has a disproportionate impact on indigenous populations (Pollock et al., 2018). A systematic review found that in some countries, for example, Brazil and Canada, suicide rates amongst indigenous populations were 20 times higher compared to non-indigenous populations (Pollock et al., 2018). Whilst this review notes that the suicide rates amongst indigenous populations are not universally higher across the globe, these differences can be stark. Here, again, we see the importance of adopting a multi-factor analysis as in many of the studies age and gender played a role, with youth between 15 and 25 having the highest suicide rates in the majority of the studies cited, and men accounted for the majority of suicide deaths (Pollock et al., 2018). It has been suggested that the development of models and theories that centre and situate the experience of indigenous populations are essential in the prevention of future suicides among these groups (O'Keefe et al., 2018). This can include strengthening connectedness to one's culture and fostering relationships between youth and Indigenous Elders, integrating indigenous knowledge, promoting indigenous self-determination, and employing decolonial approaches (Sjoblom et al., 2022). Importantly, there is a need to enable indigenous people to be 'knowledge producers' about suicide rather than only 'research subjects' or quantified populations and to consider suicide research and prevention as social justice issues (Ansloos and Peltier, 2021).

Bereaved by Suicide

Deaths by suicide, like other types of death, cause grief and bereavement to those who are left behind. It has been suggested, however, that suicide bereavement can be different compared to other types of losses. It has particular negative emotions attached to it, which are often not caused by other types of death (Bell et al., 2012). Those bereaved by suicide can experience feelings of guilt, responsibility, and can feel suicidal (Bell et al., 2012). 'Suicide disturbs the very core of one's (existential) belief system. Unanswered questions and searching for reasons, combined with feelings of personal responsibility and guilt brings about a mental torment which cannot be communicated' (Bell et al., 2012, 63). Bell et al. argue that some of these feelings are unique to suicide bereavement as the person chose to die. As suicide bereavement often comes with strong feelings of guilt and questions of whether this death could have been prevented by those bereaved by suicide, it can be considered a *disenfranchised* loss.

It has been suggested that those bereaved by suicide benefit from postvention or 'the care and support activities offered to those who have been bereaved by suicide to promote recovery and prevent adverse outcomes regarding their grief and mental health' (Allie, Bantjes, and Andriessen, 2023, 2). Postvention experts (Allie et al. 2023, 627) have suggested that 'navigating the nature and impact of suicide grief, managing the impact of suicide bereavement on interpersonal relationships, and dealing with the practical challenges associated' are the key challenges for those bereaved by suicide and these should be at the core of postvention initiatives.

Media Portrayals of Suicide

Researchers have pondered whether popular culture portrayals in film and television cause people to mimic these types of deaths in the same way. In their work on suicide contagion amongst young adults bereaved by suicide, Bell et al (2012) note that what is transmitted is the *idea* of suicide. People who are bereaved by suicide are shown through their loss that something like suicide is indeed thinkable and doable. To what extent fictional and non-fictional representations of suicide have the same effect as the experience of suicide bereavement on suicidality is something that is not fully understood. Particularly the 2017 Netflix show 'Thirteen Reasons

Why' in which a young woman leaves 13 cassette tapes to explain why she took her own life has been criticised for graphically showing the actual suicide. This scene has been removed from the show, but various scholars have been concerned with the notion of whether this fictional portrayal caused young adult audiences to take their own life (Rosa et al., 2019).

Suicide has been the topic of numerous documentaries. Analysing three British television documentaries about the aftermath of student suicide, Calver and Michael-Fox (2021) note that these documentaries not only highlight the fact that suicide appears to be an increasing issue amongst university students, but that it reflects a wider social problem amongst young adults. Furthermore, these documentaries show that media constructions of 'being a student' have shifted from being 'carefree' to being 'under pressure' (Calver and Michael-Fox, 2021). Suicide can serve as an escape from these pressures. Perhaps one of the most infamous examples of a suicide documentary is Eric Steel's 2006 film *The Bridge* which focuses on deaths by suicide at the Golden Gate Bridge in San Francisco. The documentary film has received much criticism for showing the real deaths of people jumping of the bridge. Given the potential of suicide contagion in this case scholars have wondered whether depicting suicide in this way is ethical (Malkowski, 2017). Thomas (2024), in line with the maker of the documentary, Eric Steel, has argued that the documentary shows the problem of suicide and its prevention 'inside out'. 'The bridge, which has no barrier preventing jumpers from climbing over the guardrail, might seem like the last failure in a long line of support systems that failed to prevent victims' suicide' (Thomas, 2024, 31). Suicide documentaries depict in different ways the challenges of modern life and the challenges of preventing these types of deaths. They can be seen as a warning but potentially can also create awareness of different suicide methods.

What prevents or contributes to suicidal behaviour are important questions to be asked but they do not come with an easy answer. The internet is a place where people potentially can find help when feeling suicidal as forums can serve as a safe space that are pro-recovery (Alvarez, 2022). SuicideForum describes itself as a 'peer to peer community for people in need' and has clear rules and guidelines on how users should interact, a prerequisite being that users should write in a non-triggering manner and members are, for example, prohibited from sharing suicide methods or discussing potential suicide plans (Alvarez, 2022). While this space to potentially prevent suicides is available online, the opposite is also true: 'pro-suicide' websites also exist. Alvaraz (2022) notes that one of these websites 'is a place where users post suicide means and methods, solicit suicide partners, post suicide timelines, and in extreme cases, share links to live broadcasts of 'real live' suicide, also known as 'deathcasting'. Online spaces are thus complex spaces that both aid and prevent suicides, and it is important to consider how 'new' forms of media intersect with the creation and consumption of suicide-related content.

Journalism, documentaries, and popular culture all contribute to our understanding of suicide. Suicide contagion, a 'phenomenon that occurs when people are exposed to an individual suicide – usually through the media – feel compelled to imitate that suicide' (Malkowski, 2017, 122) is a concern when portraying or reporting suicide. Duncan and Luce (2022) argue in favour of responsible reporting when it comes to writing about suicide. They analysed news stories about suicide and suggest that these types of stories often stigmatise and sensationalise suicide, which is unhelpful and, given the amount of suicide deaths each year, highly undesirable. As a consequence, they have developed a Responsible Suicide Reporting Model (Duncan and Luce, 2022, 1142) which consists of the following six questions:

1   Have I minimised harm to those affected by suicide?
2   Have I told the truth yet avoided explicit details of method and location?
3   Have I taken care in producing the story including tone and language?
4   Have I used social media responsibly?
5   Do I avoid stereotypes, harmful content, and stigmatising stories?
6   Have I provided support via helplines?

Duncan and Luce (2022) argue that if journalists adhere to these questions whilst writing their stories, they can minimise critical risks factors such as stigmatisation and copycat effects.

Conclusion

This chapter has introduced some theories around understanding suicide, researching suicide, writing and reporting suicide, and has discussed several risk factors associated with these types of death. Suicide is a particularly complex topic in death studies. There is no scholarly consensus on what causes suicide, how to prevent suicide, or how to deal with the aftermath of suicide loss, or even how to research and study suicide. A myriad of intertwined elements contribute to suicidality and considering multiple factors in analyses can be beneficial in trying to understand suicide. Suicide by no means is a one-size-fits-all and this chapter has highlighted the complexity of the topic and has introduced some ways one can start to critically assess this issue.

Notes

1   Durkheim used suicide as an example to make the case for sociology as a discipline and is considered one of the disciplines' founding fathers.
2   LGBTQ+ is used in this chapter to a wide range of sexualities and gender expression, including: lesbian, gay, bisexual, transgender, intersex, queer/questioning, asexual, and many other terms such as non-binary and pansexual. There is not a singular LGBTQ+ community; research varies in how sexuality and gender are grouped.

13
CONCLUSION

Introduction

Considering death, dying, and bereavement through a critical lens is not a given – some may even question why it is even important to think about power dynamics, who dies and lives when, and the consequences of such nuances for grief and bereavement. For some, death is a 'natural' occurrence; however, as demonstrated in this book, social, cultural, and political factors all influence how death is experienced, managed, and made sense of. We all have gaps in our understanding, but this book offers a starting point to analyse and uncover what we take for granted in terms of death, dying, and the dead.

In this book we have sought to illuminate the importance of thinking about these issues critically. Firstly, because doing so illustrates how death and dying are not universally experienced in the same way by everyone. Secondly, a critical lens enables an analytical level that attends to issues of power, noting how this shapes death, dying, and bereavement. Attending to power can highlight not only where inequalities lie but also provide insight into potential levers for change and ways to account for the role of politics in death.

In doing so, we have drawn on several key concepts throughout the book, including notions of necropolitics, grievability, and disenfranchisement. These are all defined in Chapter 1. In this chapter, we briefly summarise several of the key points made across the book and think about the future directions for research, scholarship, and activism.

DOI: 10.4324/9781003318002-16

Recurring Themes

There are several recurring themes in this book, and these have been quite intentional. They are themes informed by our own research and orientations within the field of death studies, and they have shaped the book proposal and the writing that we have done. Also, we have acknowledged in the earlier sections of the book how the writing of these chapters has been very much informed by the political, medical, and social contexts in which we were living in during the creation of this text, most notably the COVID-19 pandemic, George Floyd's death and surrounding activism linked to Black Lives Matter movements, various wars, and personal bereavements. Importantly, not only do such contexts influence what we write about, but as we've tried to demonstrate throughout several of the chapters, such events and how they're managed also have considerable impact in terms of how death, dying, and bereavement are done and understood. How death is 'responded to' is both socially and culturally informed, as well as being constantly reshaped. By critically questioning how death is managed, for example, the processes and implications of this can be better understood.

One of the recurring themes throughout this book is that the way people die, and their experiences of dying, are not just about 'health' in the human body. There are multiple social economic, political, and cultural factors that shape what death and dying are and how it is for someone to go through those experiences. This even extends to how it is to care for someone who is dying or grieving a loss. Because of this, we have sought to illustrate the range of qualities that there might be in terms of when people die, what they die from, and the types of medical interventions or care that they may have access to. There is a great deal of emphasis within the palliative and end-of-care field about enabling people to experience or have a 'good death'. The emphasis on 'good death' often notes how this is important for the dying person in addition to having impacts on those that care for them both in terms of family and friends as well as healthcare professionals and therefore influence bereavement outcomes. Yet, who decides what a good death is, and the actual realistic nature of being able to achieve that is often not something solely within the power of an individual or those around them. To achieve the 'ideal of a good death', one has to, perhaps ironically, be able to survive a life that, for some people, is constrained by mechanisms that present higher mortality risks. Ultimately, then, the ideal good death is one of privilege.

This leads to another recurring theme throughout the book, and that is around who is allowed to let live but, more importantly, 'let die'. Whilst the sanctity of life is something that politicians may seek to promote, there are many decisions and policies made that have the (un)intended consequence of promoting death, or at least dying or compounding ill-health from otherwise preventable causes. This links to the notion of necropolitics which we outlined in the introduction and is referenced throughout several of the chapters. It draws on the work of Mbembe who was influenced by Foucault's concept of biopolitics (Mbembe, 2019; Foucault,

2003). While one might hope that we live in a utopia that supports the thriving of everyone, as the research we cited in several of the chapters demonstrates, there are many factors at play that actively make such thriving more difficult, whether it is through the marginalisation of certain groups in different societies to the active creation of policy decisions that essentially place them in very precarious situations where survivability is that much more difficult.

We expanded on this to think about not only how certain lives are made less worthy or less grievable but how, in different scenarios, the very experience of dying is further disenfranchised. This disenfranchisement means taking away certain privileges or assumptions about human dignity to the extent that the dying experience is under-recognised and under-supported. This is most articulated in Chapter 9 where we focus on maternal mortality and examples of palliative care or dying in prison. Here we are also mindful that, potentially, the most disenfranchised of dying is dying that does not even make it into academic papers or warrants media or research attention. As death researchers we are aware that we, too, do not always give voice or include marginalised populations in research as much as is needed.

By using the phrase disenfranchised dying, we were inspired by Doka's concept of disenfranchised grief (Doka, 2014). He uses the concept to note how certain people's experience of grief, either because of the nature of the death or social norms around different aspects of grief, goes under-recognised and under-supported. This notion of grief and what is allowed to be grieved or mourned with the social sanctions that might be around links well with Butler's concept of grievability (Butler, 2009, 2004). Butler's use of the term grievability is important for thinking about how grief is ultimately not just personal but also political. This theme reoccurs through many of the chapters: death, dying, and grief, often considered as an individual or a very personal matter, are shaped by political forces.

Political forces impact people differently. This is for a wide range of reasons including the level of resources they might already have, their relative social power and ability to resist, as well as adapt to and shape social norms. Across the chapters, we have sought to illustrate that who is impacted by what is not always consistent. For example, things may not always impact women more than men or certain ages over others. Rather, whenever considering death, dying, and loss, there is a very complex and nuanced set of issues at hand, and it is important to think about the multi-factorial elements that influence how death is experienced, managed, and responded to. However, we also know that it is often groups that are marginalised in other ways that are also often disproportionately impacted around death, dying, and grief, whether it be in terms of inequality and access to care, more likely to be detained in prison, or be negatively impacted by policies. That means those that are impacted often throughout their life and marginalised across the life course may indeed also continue to be experiencing such impacts and marginalisation while dying (including what cause of death they have), at the moment of the death, and possibly also into bereavement.

State of the Field and Future Directions

Death studies as a field has been growing in popularity over the past several decades. As an area of interest for researchers, as well as activists, the concepts of death, dying, and grief have had waves of interest over the last century or so, most notably in the 1960s and 70s and again in the 1990s and early 2000s as well as now. The recent interest in death and scholarship around dying and grief and loss has been heavily influenced by the COVID-19 pandemic. Many researchers came to the field from other disciplines or other areas of interest because of what they witnessed happening. Some were interested in how and why the pandemic increased death rates and impacted mortality statistics. Others have been interested in social and political reactions that varied greatly in terms of how to manage the mortality risk and loss that COVID-19 presented, as well as considering how such management could have potentially negative consequences.

One of the things that has been noticed within death studies, and is also an issue within this book, is an emphasis and over-reliance on Western perspectives on death, dying, grief, loss, and bereavement (McCarthy, Woodthorpe, and Almack, 2023). Sometimes such perspectives are taken to be understood as 'normal' or used as the 'standard' by which to compare other countries or experiences. One of the reasons for this bias, is in part because of how knowledge production in academic senses is divided globally, with an increasing emphasis on English language within research and scholarship. However, there is the capacity for that to change particularly with in-depth studies using a critical lens. One way of doing this is by challenging the essentialism and universalism that death and dying are sometimes spoken about, both within societies but also within research. Another way for this change to happen is for the sharing of knowledge, customs, and research from a wider range of countries and perspectives and for these to be cited and shared. We have sought to do this but welcome even more action in this area. This is part of a move to decolonise death and bereavement studies (Hamilton, Golding, and McCarthy, 2022).

When thinking about the future of death studies, in addition to decolonising the field, there are three areas that we think will become increasingly popular in research, education, and activism. Firstly, there is a growing interest and literature on technological advancements and digital futures, including digital afterlives and cyberthanatology (Recuber, 2023; Beaunoyer and Guitton, 2021). Technological advancements may also challenge the limits of life and death, with an interest in preservation technologies, transhumanism, and anti-ageing (Hurtado, 2023). Secondly, there is an interest in death studies as being a field that can understand death as something that is more-than-human. This means that there is a recognition that the world is entangled, and that human life and death is entangled with, for example, animals, the environment, and other non-human elements (Castree, Kitchin, and Rogers, 2013). Such an approach seeks to decentre humans as the core element of understanding. This is particularly pertinent when thinking about climate change (for example, see Árnason and Hafsteinsson, 2020). Of course, some may seek to combine these topics in new and novel ways.

Lastly, we can foresee that 'death activism' is likely to continue over the next decade or more. This will build on existing social movements (as discussed in Chapter 5) and wider death awareness campaigns. It may also spring up around social justice issues in different countries, although this will be unequally distributed. The Lance Commission on the Value of Death calls for a realistic utopia with shifted death systems (Sallnow et al., 2022); activism can play a role in realising this by highlighting how aspects of death systems are not currently serving people and society in different ways. It may also be that readers of this book will feel inspired to consider their own role in activism around the issues covered in these chapters. Some have found that being involved in activism, whilst testing of their psychological and political positions, can be personally and socially meaningful and provide collective healing in contexts of grief and death (Elnakib and Turner, 2023)

Conclusion

This book has explored the complex ways in which death and dying are managed and experienced in different social, cultural, historical, political, and medical contexts. The critical lens adopted in this book is rooted in questions of power, inequity, and social norms. In our writing, we have sought to show how, much like the social determinants and contexts of health that are important to understand, the social determinants and contexts of death are worthy of consideration, including in the aftermath of death. We hope this text leaves readers inspired to adopt a critical lens, and to use this text as a building block to continue the conversation in death studies. During this time, death studies has grown as a field and is likely to continue to diversify in terms of topics examined, geographical areas covered, and the interlink between research, scholarship, and activism.

REFERENCES

Abedi, Vida, Oluwaseyi Olulana, Venkatesh Avula, Durgesh Chaudhary, Ayesha Khan, Shima Shahjouei, Jiang Li, and Ramin Zand. 2021. "Racial, Economic, and Health Inequality and COVID-19 Infection in the United States." *Journal of Racial and Ethnic Health Disparities* 8 (3): 732–742. https://doi.org/10.1007/S40615-020-00833-4/TABLES/2

AbouZahr, Carla, Don De Savigny, Lene Mikkelsen, Philip W. Setel, Rafael Lozano, and Alan D. Lopez. 2015. "Towards Universal Civil Registration and Vital Statistics Systems: The Time Is Now." *The Lancet* 386 (10001): 1407–1418. https://doi.org/10.1016/S0140-6736(15)60170-2

AbouZahr, Carla, Lene Mikkelsen, Rasika Rampatige, and Alan Lopez. 2010. *Mortality Statistics: A Tool to Improve Understanding and Quality*. Herston: the Health Information Knowledge Hub . www.uq.edu.au/hishub

Adams, William M., Samantha E. Scarneo, and Douglas J. Casa. 2017. "State-Level Implementation of Health and Safety Policies to Prevent Sudden Death and Catastrophic Injuries Within Secondary School Athletics." *Orthopaedic Journal of Sports Medicine* 5 (9). https://doi.org/10.1177/2325967117727262/SUPPL_FILE/OJSM_727262_APPENDIX.PDF

Aday, Ronald. 2006. "Aging Prisoners' Concerns toward Dying in Prison." *OMEGA* 52 (3): 199–216. https://doi.org/10.2190/CHTD-YL7T-R1RR-LHMN

Aday, Ronald, and Azrini Wahidin. 2016. "Older Prisoners' Experiences of Death, Dying and Grief behind Bars." *Howard Journal of Crime and Justice* 55 (3): 312–327. https://doi.org/10.1111/hojo.12172

Adhiyaman, Vedamurthy, and Indrajit Chattopadhyay. 2021. "Is It Appropriate to Link 'Old Age' to Certain Causes of Death on the Medical Certificate of Cause of Death?" *Future Healthcare Journal* 8 (3): e686. https://doi.org/10.7861/FHJ.2021-0050

Afeworki Abay, Robel, and Yvonne Wechuli. 2022. "'We Are Here Because You Were There': Necropolitics as a Critical Framework for Analysing the Complex Relationship between Colonialism, Forced Migration and Disability." *Globale Zusammenhänge, Lokale Deutungen*, 25–36. https://doi.org/10.1007/978-3-658-37356-6_2

Ahmed, A.M., and M.M. Kheir. 2006. "Attitudes towards Euthanasia among Final-Year Khartoum University Medical Students." *Eastern Mediterranean Health Journal* 12 (4): 391–397.

Akanni, Tooni. 2014. "Confronting Ebola in Liberia: The Gendered Realities." www.opende mocracy.net/en/5050/confronting-ebola-in-liberia-gendered-realities-0/

Alasuutari, Varpu., Stephenson Brooks Whitestone, K. Jaworski, and Olga Doletskaya. 2021. "When I Talk about Queer Death, I Talk about Transnecropolitics and Suicide Prevention." *Whatever* 4: 606–614. https://doi.org/10.13131/2611-657X.whatever. v4i1.XXX

Alfsen, G. Cecilie, and Jan Maehlen. 2012. "The Value of autopsies for Determining the Cause of Death." *Tidsskr Nor Legeforen Nr* 2: 147–151.

Allan, June, and Louise Harms. 2010. "'Power and Prejudice': Thinking Differently about Grief." *Grief Matters* 13 (3): 72–75. https://search.informit.org/doi/10.3316/infor mit.587610363212616

Allie, Sophia Lorraine Noxolo, Jason Bantjes, and Karl Andriessen. 2023. "Suicide Postvention for Staff and Students on University Campuses: A Scoping Review." *BMJ Open* 13 (6). https://doi.org/10.1136/bmjopen-2022-068730

Allison, Anne. 2023. *Being Dead Otherwise*. Durham and London: Duke University Press.

Alvarez, Mike. 2022. "'Life Is about Trying to Find a Better Place to Live': Discourses of Dwelling in a pro-Recovery Suicide Forum." *Qualitative Research in Medicine and Healthcare* 6 (1). https://doi.org/10.4081/qrmh.2022.10437

———. 2024. *Unraveling: An Autoethnography If Suicide and Renewal*. New York: Routlegde.

Amnesty International. n.d. "Refugees, Asylum Seekers and Migrants – Amnesty International." Accessed January 27, 2024. www.amnesty.org/en/what-we-do/refugees-asylum-seekers-and-migrants/

Amzat, Jimoh, Kehinde Kazeem Kanmodi, Abbas Ismail, and Eyinade Adeduntan Egbedina. 2023. "Euthanasia in Africa: A Scoping Review of Empirical Evidence." *Health Science Reports* 6 (5): 1–14. https://doi.org/10.1002/hsr2.1239

Andreescu, Raluca. 2023. "A Slow Death before Dying: Contemporary Stories from Solitary Confinement." *European Journal of American Studies* 18 (18–2). https://doi. org/10.4000/EJAS.20131

Ansloos, Jeffrey, and Shanna Peltier. 2021. "A Question of Justice: Critically Researching Suicide with Indigenous Studies of Affect, Biosociality, and Land-Based Relations." *Health: An Interdisciplinary Journal for the Social Study of Health, Illness and Medicine* 26 (1): 100–119. https://doi.org/10.1177/13634593211046845

Ariès, Philippe. 1975. *Western Attitudes toward Death. Western Attitudes toward Death.* Baltimore, MD: Johns Hopkins University Press. https://doi.org/10.1353/BOOK.20658

———. 1987. *Het Uur van Onze Dood: Duizend Jaar Sterven, Begraven, Rouwen En Gedenken*. Amsterdam: Elsevier.

Árnason, Arnar, and Sigurjón Baldur Hafsteinsson. 2020. "A Funeral for a Glacier: Mourning the More-than-Human on the Edges of Modernity." *Thanatos* 9 (2): 2020. https://journal. fi/thanatos/article/view/137230

Arnold, Michael, Tamara Kohn, Bjorn Nansen, and Fraser Allison. 2023. "Representing Alkaline Hydrolysis: A Material-Semiotic Analysis of an Alternative to Burial and Cremation." *Mortality*, February, 1–19. https://doi.org/10.1080/13576275.2023.2174838

Arolker, Milind and Erica Borgstrom. 2017. "Death and Dying Seminar: The Use of Sedation in Dying Patients (March 2017)." The Open University. https://doi.org/10.21954/ ou.rd.5513605.v1

Ashby, M. 2009. "The Dying Human in Palliative Medicine." In *The Study of Dying: From Autonomy to Transformation*, edited by A. Kellehear. Cambridge University Press.

Ashuntantang, Gloria, Ingrid Miljeteig, and Valerie A. Luyckx. 2022. "Bedside Rationing and Moral Distress in Nephrologists in Sub- Saharan Africa." *BMC Nephrology* 23 (1): 1–14. https://doi.org/10.1186/S12882-022-02827-2/FIGURES/6

Baines, Mary. 2011. "From Pioneer Days to Implementation: Lessons to Be Learnt." *European Journal of Palliative Care* 18 (5): 223–227. www.researchgate.net/publicat ion/287740749_From_pioneer_days_to_implementation_Lessons_to_be_learnt

Banerjee, Subhabrata. 2006. "Live and Let Die: Colonial Sovereignties and the Death Worlds of Necrocapitalism." *Borderlands* 5 (1).

Barnett, Joshua Trey. 2022. *Mourning in the Anthropocene. Ecological Grief and Earthly Coexistence.* East Lansing: Michigan State University Press.

Barry, Colette. 2019. "'You Can't Tell Anyone How You Really Feel': Exploring Emotion Management and Performance among Prison Staff Who Have Experienced the Death of a Prisoner." *International Journal of Law, Crime and Justice*, 61(November): 100364. https://doi.org/10.1016/j.ijlcj.2019.100364

Baugher, John Eric. 2008. "Facing Death: Buddhist and Western Hospice Approaches." *Symbolic Interaction* 31 (3): 259–284. https://doi.org/10.1525/SI.2008.31.3.259

Bayer, Achim. 2013. "From Transference to Transformation: Levels of Understanding in Tibetan 'Ars Moriendi.'" *The Eastern Buddhist* 44 (1): 77–96. www.jstor.org/stable/ 44362527

Beaunoyer, Elisabeth, and Matthieu J. Guitton. 2021. "Cyberthanathology: Death and beyond in the Digital Age." *Computers in Human Behavior* 122 (September): 106849. https://doi.org/10.1016/J.CHB.2021.106849

Beauthier, Jean-Pol, Eddy De Valck, Philippe Lefevre, and Joan De Winne. 2009. "Mass Disaster Victim Identification: The Tsunami Experience." *The Open Forensic Science Journal* 2: 54–62.

Bell, Jo, Nicky Stanley, Sharon Mallon, and Jill Manthorpe. 2012. "Life Will Never Be the Same Again: Examining Grief in Survivors Bereaved by Young Suicide." *Illness Crisis and Loss* 20 (1): 49–68. https://doi.org/10.2190/IL.20.1.e

Benatar, David. 2011. "A Legal Right to Die: Responding to Slippery Slope and Abuse Arguments." *Current Oncology* 18 (5): 206–207.

Bennett, Amanda. 2016. "Learn About the Grief and Death Ceremonies of Torajans." *National Geographic.* March 11, 2016. www.nationalgeographic.com/magazine/article/ death-dying-grief-funeral-ceremony-corpse

Berger, Stefan, and Holger Nehring. n.d. "The History of Social Movements." Accessed January 27, 2024. www.palgrave.com/gp/campaigns/social-movements/history-of-soc ial-movements

Billings, J. Andrew. 1998. "What Is Palliative Care?" *Journal of Palliative Medicine* 1 (1): 73–81. https://doi.org/10.1089/JPM.1998.1.73

Binder, Sherri Brokopp, and Charlene K. Baker. 2017. "Culture, Local Capacity, and Outside Aid: A Community Perspective on Disaster Response after the 2009 Tsunami in American Sāmoa." *Disasters* 41 (2): 282–305. https://doi.org/10.1111/DISA.12203

Black Lives Matter. n.d.-a. "About – Black Lives Matter." Accessed January 27, 2024. https://blacklivesmatter.com/about/

———. n.d.-b. "Herstory – Black Lives Matter." Accessed January 27, 2024. https://black livesmatter.com/herstory/

Black, Peter McL. 1977. "Three Definitions of Death." *The Monist* 60 (1): 136–146. www. jstor.org/stable/27902464

BMA. 2021. "Physician Assisted Dying." 2021. www.bma.org.uk/advice-and-support/eth ics/end-of-life/physician-assisted-dying

Borgstrom, Erica. 2015a. "Planning for an (Un)Certain Future: Choice within English End-of-Life Care." *Current Sociology* 63 (5): 700–713. https://doi.org/10.1177/001139211 5590084

———. 2015b. "Social Death in End-of-Life Care Policy." *Contemporary Social Science* 10 (3): 272–283. https://doi.org/10.1080/21582041.2015.1109799

———. 2016a. "National End-of-Life Care Policy in the English Context: The Problem and Solution to Death and Dying." In *Death and Social Policy in Challenging Times*, edited by Liam Foster and Kate Woodthorpe, 35–53. Houndmills, Basingstoke: Palgrave Macmillan.

———. 2016b. "Images of Hospices on Social Media." *Medicine Anthropology Theory* 3 (3): 105–111. https://doi.org/10.17157/MAT.3.3.317

———. 2020. "What Is a Good Death? A Critical Discourse Policy Analysis." *BMJ Supportive & Palliative Care*, July. https://doi.org/10.1136/BMJSPCARE-2019-002173

Borgstrom, Erica, and Natashe Lemos Dekker. 2022. "Standardising Care of the Dying: An Ethnographic Analysis of the Liverpool Care Pathway in England and the Netherlands." *Sociology of Health & Illness* 44 (9): 1445–1460. https://doi.org/10.1111/ 1467-9566.13529

Borgstrom, Erica, and Julie Ellis. 2021. "Internalising 'Sensitivity': Vulnerability, Reflexivity and Death Research(Ers)." *International Journal of Social Research Methodology* 24 (5): 589–602. https://doi.org/10.1080/13645579.2020.1857972

Borgstrom, Erica, Joanne Jordan, and Claire Henry. 2022. *Ambitions for Palliative and End of Life Care: Mapping Examples of Use in Practice.* Milton Keynes: The Open University

Borgstrom, Erica, and Sharon Mallon. 2021. *Narratives of Covid Loss, Dying, Death and Grief during Covid-19.* Milton Keynes: The Open University.

Borgstrom, Erica, Ryann Sowden, and E. Lucy Sellman. 2024. "Reflecting Grief During a Pandemic: Online UK Newspapers' Reportage and Researchers' Experiences." In *Difficult Death, Dying and the Dead in Media and Culture*, edited by Sharon Coleclough, Beth Michael-Fox, and Renske Visser, 249–264. London: Palgrave Macmillan.

Borgstrom, Erica, and Tony Walter. 2015. "Choice and Compassion at the End of Life: A Critical Analysis of Recent English Policy Discourse." *Social Science and Medicine* 136–137 (2015): 99–105. http://dx.doi.org/10.1016/j.socscimed.2015.05.013

Bosco, Fernando J. 2006. "The Madres de Plaza de Mayo and Three Decades of Human Rights' Activism: Embeddedness, Emotions, and Social Movements." *Annals of the Association of American Geographers* 96 (2): 342–365. https://doi.org/10.1111/ J.1467-8306.2006.00481.X

Bradbury, Mary. 1999. *Representations of Death: A Social Psychological Perspective.* London: Routledge. www.routledge.com/Representations-of-Death-A-Social-Psycho logical-Perspective/Bradbury/p/book/9780415150224

Bradshaw, Ann. 1996. "The Spiritual Dimension of Hospice: The Secularization of an Ideal." *Social Science and Medicine* 43 (3): 409–419. https://doi.org/10.1016/ 0277-9536(95)00406-8

Braidotti, Rosi. 2013. *The Posthuman.* Cambridge: Polity Press.

Brassington, Iain. 2020. "What Passive Euthanasia Is." *BMC Medical Ethics* 21 (1): 1–13. https://doi.org/10.1186/s12910-020-00481-7

Breen, Lauren J., and Moira O'Connor. 2007. "The Fundamental Paradox in the Grief Literature: A Critical Reflection." *Omega: Journal of Death and Dying* 55 (3): 199–218. https://doi.org/10.2190/OM.55.3.c

Broadfield, Kirstie. 2021. "A Tale of Two Deaths: Necropolitics in the Criminal Justice System." https://demosjournal.com/article/a-tale-of-two-deaths-necropolitics-in-the-criminal-justice-system/

Bruno, Marie-Aurelie, Didier Ledoux, and Steven Laureys. 2009. "The Dying Human: A Perspective from Biomedicine." In *The Study of Dying*, edited by A. Kellehear, 51–75. Cambridge: Cambridge University Press.

Buchbinder, Mara. 2021. *Scripting Death Stories of Assisted Dying in America*. Berkley: University of California Press.

Buchbinder, Mara, and Cindy Cain. 2023. "Medical Aid in Dying: New in Medicine, Law, and Culture." *Annual Review of Law and Social Science* 19: 195–214. https://doi.org/10.1146/annurev-lawsocsci-110722

Bucur, Maria. 2009. *Heroes and Victims: Remembering War in Twentieth-Century Romania:* Bloomington: Indiana University Press. https://gender.indiana.edu/research/books/heroes-and-victims.html

Burcu, Oana, and Weixiang Wang. 2023. "The View from Beijing on Black Lives Matter: Why Do Black Lives Matter for Beijing?" *Journal of Current Chinese Affairs* 52 (3): 413–433. https://doi.org/10.1177/18681026231178560

Burles, Meridith C., Cindy A. Peternelj-Taylor, and Lorraine Holtslander. 2016. "A 'Good Death' for All?: Examining Issues for Palliative Care in Correctional Settings." *Mortality* 21 (2): 93–111. https://doi.org/10.1080/13576275.2015.1098602

Burrell, Alexander, and Lucy E. Selman. 2022. "How Do Funeral Practices Impact Bereaved Relatives' Mental Health, Grief and Bereavement? A Mixed Methods Review with Implications for COVID-19." *Omega (United States)* 85 (2): 345–383. https://doi.org/10.1177/0030222820941296/ASSET/IMAGES/LARGE/10.1177_0030222820941296-FIG1.JPEG

Busfield, Joan. 2017. "The Concept of Medicalisation Reassessed." *Sociology of Health & Illness* 39 (5): 759–774. https://doi.org/10.1111/1467-9566.12538

Butler, Judith. 2004. *Precarious Life: The Powers of Mourning and Violence*. London: Verso. https://books.google.com/books/about/Precarious_Life.html?id=iXj3rCh9zRwC

———. 2009. *Frames of War: When Is Life Grievable?* London: Verso.

Byron, Shirley, and Robert Hoskins. 2013. "Implementing the 'Verification of Expected Death' Policy in Clinical Practice." *British Journal of Community Nursing* 18 (10): 505–511. https://doi.org/10.12968/BJCN.2013.18.10.505

Calver, Kay, and Bethan Michael-Fox. 2021. "Under Pressure: Representations of Student Suicide in British Documentary Television." *Mortality* 26 (4): 376–393. https://doi.org/10.1080/13576275.2021.1987658

Can, Başak. 2022. "FIVE / The Necropolitics of Documents and the Slow Death of Prisoners in Turkey." *Turkey's Necropolitical Laboratory*, March, 97–117. https://doi.org/10.1515/9781474450287-007/HTML

Cann, Candi. 2018. "Buying an Afterlife. Mapping Religious Beliefs through Consumer Death Goods." In *The Routledge Handbook of Death and the Afterlife*, edited by Candi Cann, 377–392. London and New York: Routledge .

Cann, Candi K. 2020. "Black Deaths Matter Earning the Right to Live: Death and the African-American Funeral Home." *Religions* 11 (8): 1–15. https://doi.org/10.3390/REL11080390

Cardona, Magnolia, and Sally Greenaway. 2019. "The Medicalisation of Dying from Natural Causes: Unacceptable to Patients, Low-Value for the Health System." *The Health Advocate*, 54: 34–36. https://research.bond.edu.au/en/publications/the-medical isation-of-dying-from-natural-causes-unacceptable-to-p

Castañeda, Heide. 2022. *Migration and Health*. London: Routledge. https://doi.org/10.4324/9781003307532

Castree, Noel, Rob Kitchin, and Alisdair Rogers. 2013. "A Dictionary of Human Geography." In *Oxford Paperback Reference*, 573–577. https://books.google.co.uk/books?hl=en&lr=&id=eYWcAQAAQBAJ&oi=fnd&pg=PP2&dq=castree+et+al,+2013+&ots=kE91PCBegD&sig=musltEQQq7rxvtFaSSlW3AYJpNc#v=onepage&q=castree et al%2C 2013&f=false

"Cause of Death." n.d. Accessed January 27, 2024. www.who.int/standards/classifications/classification-of-diseases/cause-of-death

Celikates, Robin, and Jeffrey Flynn. 2023. "Critical Theory (Frankfurt School)." The Stanford Encyclopedia of Philosophy. https://Plato.Stanford.Edu/Archives/Win2023/Entries/Critical-Theory/.

Chang, Harrison, Kehao Chang, and Elliott Fan. 2020. "The Intended and Unintended Effects of Drunk Driving Policies." *Oxford Bulletin of Economics and Statistics* 82 (1): 23–49. https://doi.org/10.1111/OBES.12326

Chase, Garrett. 2018. "The Early History of the Black Lives Matter Movement, and the Implications Thereof." *Nevada Law Journal* 18, 1091–1112. https://perma.cc/BP4W-Q7ZS]

Chatelain, Marcia, and Kaavya Asoka. 2015. "Women and Black Lives Matter: An Interview with Marcia Chatelain – Dissent Magazine." Dissent. 2015. www.dissentmagazine.org/article/women-black-lives-matter-interview-marcia-chatelain/

Chirico, Andrea, Pierluigi Diotaiuti, Elisa Cavicchiolo, Lauren Sillis, Laurence Claes, and Karl Andriessen. 2022. "Association between Grief and Somatic Complaints in Bereaved University and College Students." *International Journal of Environmental Research and Public Health* 19 (19): 12108. https://doi.org/10.3390/IJERPH191912108

Clark, Davide. 2004. "Religion, Medicine, and Community in the Early Origins of St. Christopher's Hospice." *Journal of Palliative Medicine* 4 (3): 353–360. https://doi.org/10.1089/109662101753123977

Clark, David. 1998. "Originating a Movement: Cicely Saunders and the Development of St Christopher's Hospice, 1957–1967." *Mortality* 3 (1): 43–63. https://doi.org/10.1080/713685885

———. 2002. "Between Hope and Acceptance: The Medicalisation of Dying." *BMJ: British Medical Journal* 324 (7342): 905. https://doi.org/10.1136/BMJ.324.7342.905

———. 2014. "'Total Pain': The Work of Cicely Saunders and the Maturing of a Concept | End of Life Studies." 2014. http://endoflifestudies.academicblogs.co.uk/total-pain-the-work-of-cicely-saunders-and-the-maturing-of-a-concept/

———. 2022. *Cicely Saunders: Founder of the Hospice Movement: Selected Letters 1959–1999*. Oxford: Oxford University Press. https://books.google.co.uk/books?hl=en&lr=&id=cMLADwAAQBAJ&oi=fnd&pg=PR11&dq=david+clark+hospice+&ots=8emSQ20Mcy&sig=9i-HgWOs3s5sv3jmWv-X_gIQobk#v=onepage&q=david%20clark%20hospice&f=false

Clark, David, Nicole Baur, David Clelland, Eduardo Garralda, Jesús López-Fidalgo, Stephen Connor, and Carlos Centeno. 2020. "Mapping Levels of Palliative Care Development in

198 Countries: The Situation in 2017." *Journal of Pain and Symptom Management* 59 (4): 794. https://doi.org/10.1016/J.JPAINSYMMAN.2019.11.009

Clark, Joseph, Lucia Crowther, Miriam J. Johnson, Christina Ramsenthaler, and David C. Currow. 2022. "Calculating Worldwide Needs for Morphine for Pain in Advanced Cancer and Proportions Feasibly Met by Country Estimates of Requirements and Consumption. Retrospective, Time-Series Analysis (1997–2017)." *PLOS Global Public Health* 2 (7): e0000533. https://doi.org/10.1371/JOURNAL.PGPH.0000533

Clarke, Juanne N., and Michelle M. Everest. 2006. "Cancer in the Mass Print Media: Fear, Uncertainty and the Medical Model." *Social Science & Medicine* 62 (10): 2591–2600. https://doi.org/10.1016/J.SOCSCIMED.2005.11.021

Close, Eliana, Ben P. White, Lindy Willmott, Cindy Gallois, Malcolm Parker, Nicholas Graves, and Sarah Winch. 2019. "Doctors' Perceptions of How Resource Limitations Relate to Futility in End-of-Life Decision Making: A Qualitative Analysis." *Journal of Medical Ethics* 45 (6): 373–379. https://doi.org/10.1136/MEDETHICS-2018-105199

Connisbee, Molly. 2020. "The Southwark Way of Death — University of Bristol." Bristol: University of Bristol. https://research-information.bris.ac.uk/en/studentTheses/the-southwark-way-of-death

Connolly, Amanda, Elizabeth L. Sampson, and Nitin Purandare. 2012. "End-of-Life Care for People with Dementia from Ethnic Minority Groups: A Systematic Review." *Journal of the American Geriatrics Society* 60 (2): 351–360. https://doi.org/10.1111/J.1532-5415.2011.03754.X

Connor, Stephen R. 1998. *Hospice: Practice, Pitfalls and Promise*. Washington DC: Taylor and Francis.

Conrad, Paul. 2009. "'Interview with Peter Conrad, Author of The Medicalization of Society: On the Transformation of Human Conditions into Treatable Disorders." *Blue Cross Blue Shield of Massachusetts Foundation*.

Coppens, Pieter. 2023. "Islamic Ars Moriendi and Ambiguous Deathbed Emotions." In *End-of-Life Care, Dying and Death in the Islamic Moral Tradition*, 152–171. BRILL. https://doi.org/10.1163/9789004459410_008

Cornelius, W.A. 2001. "Death at the Border: Efficacy and Unintended Consequences of US Immigration Control Policy." *Population and Development Review* 27: 661–685. https://doi.org/10.1111/j.1728-4457.2001.00661.x

Cornelius, Wayne A. 2004. "Death at the Border: Efficacy and Unintended Consequences of US Immigration Control Policy." *Population and Development Review* 27 (4): 661–685. https://doi.org/10.1111/J.1728-4457.2001.00661.X

Coward, Harold, and Kelli I. Stajduhar. 2012. *Religious Understandings of a Good Death in Hospice Palliative Care*. Albany, NY: State of New York Press. https://books.google.co.uk/books/about/Religious_Understandings_of_a_Good_Death.html?id=_oPeWqdoqJQC&redir_esc=y

Crear-Perry, Joia, Rosaly Correa-De-Araujo, Tamara Lewis Johnson, Monica R. Mclemore, Elizabeth Neilson, and Maeve Wallace. 2021. "Social and Structural Determinants of Health Inequities in Maternal Health." *Journal of Women's Health* 30 (2): 230–235. https://doi.org/10.1089/jwh.2020.8882

Crowcroft, Natasha, and Azeem Majeed. 2001. "Improving the Certification of Death and the Usefulness of Routine Mortality Statistics." *Clinical Medicine JRCPL* 1 (1): 22–25.

Daher-Nashif, Suhad. 2020. "Colonial Management of Death: To Be or Not to Be Dead in Palestine." 69 (7): 945–962. https://doi.org/10.1177/0011392120948923

Davies, Douglas. 2017. *Death, Ritual and Belief The Rhetoric of Funerary Rites*. London: Bloomsbury.

Davies, Douglas, and Hannah Rumble. 2012. *Natural Burial: Traditional-Secular Spiritualities and Funeral Innovation.* https://durham-repository.worktribe.com/output/1124439/natural-burial-traditional-secular-spiritualities-and-funeral-innovation

Davis, Sara L., C. Miles Harmon, Brady Baker Urquhart, Bridget Moore, and Rene Sprague. 2020. "Women and Infants in the Deep South Receiving Perinatal and Neonatal Palliative and Supportive Care Services." *Advances in Neonatal Care: Official Journal of the National Association of Neonatal Nurses* 20 (3): 216–222. https://doi.org/10.1097/ANC.0000000000000706

DeBoom, Meredith J. 2022. "Climate Coloniality as Atmospheric Violence: From Necropolitics toward Planetary Mutuality." *Political Geography* 99 (November): 102786. https://doi.org/10.1016/J.POLGEO.2022.102786

Department of Health. 2000. "The NHS Cancer Plan A Plan for Investment A Plan for Reform."

———. 2008. "End of Life Care Strategy. Promoting High Quality Care for All Adults at the End of Life." London.

Devich-Cyril, Malkia. 2021. "Grief Belongs in Social Movements. Can We Embrace It?" *In These Times.* July 28, 2021. https://inthesetimes.com/article/freedom-grief-healing-death-liberation-movements

Dewedar, Farah. 2022. "Exploring the Absence of a Black Lives Matter Movement in Egypt." *The Undergraduate Research Journal* 8 (1). https://fount.aucegypt.edu/urje/vol8/iss1/4

Diani, Mario. 1992. "The Concept of Social Movement." *The Sociological Review* 40 (1): 1–25. https://doi.org/10.1111/J.1467-954X.1992.TB02943.X

Doka, Kenneth J. 2014. "Disenfranchised Grief in Historical and Cultural Perspective." In *Handbook of Bereavement Research and Practice: Advances in Theory and Intervention*, edited by M. S. Stroebe, R. O. Hansson, H. Schut, and W. Stroebe. July, 223–240. American Psychological Association. https://doi.org/10.1037/14498-011

Doka, Kenneth J., and Terry L. Martin. 2011. "Grieving Styles: Gender and Grief." *Grief Matters* 14 (2): 42–45. https://search.informit.org/doi/10.3316/informit.339916590087229

Downe, Emily, and Kathryn Mannix. 2023. "Dying for Beginners ." Theos Think Tank. October 2023. www.theosthinktank.co.uk/comment/2023/10/25/dying-for-beginners

Downie, Jocelyn, Mona Gupta, Stefano Cavalli, and Samuel Blouin. 2022. "Assistance in Dying: A Comparative Look at Legal Definitions." *Death Studies* 46 (7): 1547–1556. https://doi.org/10.1080/07481187.2021.1926631

Downs, Jim. 2021. *Maladies of Empire How Slavery, Imperialism, and War Transformed Medicine*. Kittredge Hall: The Belknap Press of Harvard University Press. www.hup.harvard.edu/books/9780674971721

Driessen, Annelieke, Erica Borgstrom, and Simon Cohn. 2021a. "Placing Death and Dying: Making Place at the End of Life." *Social Science & Medicine* 291: 113974. https://doi.org/10.1016/j.socscimed.2021.113974

———. 2021b. "Ways of 'Being with' Caring for Dying Patients at the Height of the COVID-19 Pandemic." *Anthropology in Action* 28 (1): 16–20. https://doi.org/10.3167/AIA.2021.280103

Driftmier, Peter, and Jessica Shaw. 2021. "Medical Assistance in Dying (MAiD) for Canadian Prisoners: A Case Series of Barriers to Care in Completed MAiD Deaths." *Health Equity* 5 (1): 847–853. https://doi.org/10.1089/HEQ.2021.0117

Duncan, Sallyanne, and Ann Luce. 2022. "Using the Responsible Suicide Reporting Model to Increase Adherence to Global Media Reporting Guidelines." *Journalism* 23 (5): 1132–1148. https://doi.org/10.1177/1464884920952685

Easthope, Lucy. 2019. "The Meaning of 'Things': The Evolution of an Ethic of Care in the Return of Personal Effects after Disaster 2001–2019." *Bereavement Care* 38 (2–3): 122–128. https://doi.org/10.1080/02682621.2019.1679465

———. 2022. *When the Dust Settles: Stories of Love, Loss and Hope from an Expert in Disaster*. London: Hodder and Stoughton.

Economist Intelligence Unit. 2010. "The Quality of Death Ranking End-of-Life Care across the World Commissioned by The Quality of Death Ranking End-of-Life Care across the World." www.eiu.com/sponsor/lienfoundation/qualityofdeath

Economist Intelligence Unit. (2015). *The 2015 Quality of Death Index*. Economist Intelligence Unit.

Edouard, Mathieu, Hannah Ritchie, Lucas Rodés-Guirao, Cameron Appel, Charlie Giattano, Joe Hassel, Bobbie MacDonald, et al. 2020. "Coronavirus Pandemic (COVID-19)." OurWorldinData.Org. 2020.

Edwards, Nigel, Helen Crump, and Mark Dayan. 2015. "Rationing the NHS." https://medievalbookshop.co.uk/tdpdf/Rationing.pdf

Ellershaw, J. 2024. "The Human Rights Act 1998 Imposes an Obligation to Facilitate a 'Good Death'." *BMJ* 326 (7379): 30–34. https://doi.org/10.1136/BMJ.326.7379.30

Elnakib, Mohamed M., and Monique Turner. 2023. "The Power of Activism as Self-Care: An Autoethnography of the Arrest of Activists in the Wake of the George Floyd Protests." *Women & Therapy* 46 (4): 391–406. https://doi.org/10.1080/02703149.2023.2286056

Engelhardt, H. Tristram. 1999. "Redefining Death: The Mirage of Consensus." In *The Definition of Death*, edited by S.J. Younger, R.M. Arnold, and R. Schapiro. Baltimore: The John Hopkins University Press.

Erazo-Munoz, Marcela, Diana Borda-Restrepo, and Johana Benavides-Cruz. 2023. "Euthanasia in Colombia: Experience in a Palliative Care Program and Bioethical Reflections." *Developing World Bioethics*, 1–7. https://doi.org/10.1111/dewb.12430

Evans, Ruth, Jane Ribbens McCarthy, Fatou Kébé, Sophie Bowlby, and Joséphine Wouango. 2017. "Interpreting 'Grief' in Senegal: Language, Emotions and Cross-Cultural Translation in a Francophone African Context." *Mortality* 22 (2): 118–135. https://doi.org/10.1080/13576275.2017.1291602

Evans-Pritchard, E.E. 1976. *Witchcraft, Oracles, and Magic among the Azande*. Oxford: Clarendon Press.

Everts Mykytyn, Courtney. 2010. "A History of the Future: The Emergence of Contemporary Anti-Ageing Medicine." *Sociology of Health and Illness* 32 (2): 181–196. https://doi.org/10.1111/J.1467-9566.2009.01217.X

Fairhead, James. 2016. "Understanding Social Resistance to the Ebola Response in the Forest Region of the Republic of Guinea: An Anthropological Perspective." *African Studies Review* 59 (3): 7–31. https://doi.org/10.1017/ASR.2016.87

Fair, Helen and Roy Walmsley. 2021. *World Prison Population List. 13th Edition*. London: Institute for Crime & Justice Policy Research. www.prisonstudies.org/sites/default/files/resources/downloads/world_prison_population_list_13th_edition.pdf

Feror Ruyes, Juanita. 2014. "Dying 101: Emotion, Experience, and Learning How to Die in the Late Medieval 'Artes Moriendi.'" *Parergon* 31 (2): 55–79. https://search.informit.org/doi/abs/10.3316/ielapa.960409053701607

Few, Stephen. 2007. *Data Visualization – Past, Present, and Future*. Cognos Innovation center for Perfomance Management.

Fisman, Raymond, and Yongxiang Wang. 2017. "The Distortionary Effects of Incentives in Government: Evidence from China's 'Death Ceiling' Program." *American Economic Journal: Applied Economics* 9 (2): 202–218. https://doi.org/10.1257/app.20160008

Flaherty, Adele, and Anna Meurer. 2021. "Unbefriended, Uninvited: How End-of-Life Doulas Can Address Ethical and Procedural Gaps for Unrepresented Patients and Ensure Equal Access to the 'Good Death.'" *Clinical Ethics* 18 (1): 55–61. https://doi.org/10.1177/14777509211057250

Flaskerud, Jacquelyn H. 2017. "Non-Western Perspectives of a Good Death." *Issues in Mental Health Nursing* 38 (9): 763–766. https://doi.org/10.1080/01612840.2017.1303857

Fletcher, Kami. 2023a. "Are Enslaved African Americans Buried at Mount Harmon Plantation? Space and Reflection for National Mourning and Memorialising." *Mortality* 28 (3): 510–525. https://doi.org/10.1080/13576275.2022.2080541

———. 2023b. "Black Women Undertakers of the Early Twentieth Century Were Hidden in Plain Sight." *Meridians* 22 (2): 478–502. https://doi.org/10.1215/15366936-10637582

Fontana, Andrea and Jennifer Reid Keene. 2009. *Death and Dying in America*. Edited by Jennifer Reid Keene. Cambridge: Cambridge: Polity.

Foucault, Michel. 1978. *The History of Sexuality, Vol. 1: The Will to Knowledge*. Vol. 1. London: Penguin.

———. 2003. "The Birth of Biopolitics." In *The Essential Foucault: Selections from Essential Works of Foucault 1954–1984*, edited by Paul Rabinow and Nikolas Rose, 202–207. London: The New Press.

Fox, Stefanie. 2023. "Jewish Grief Must Not Be Used as a Weapon of War." The Nation. October 13, 2023. www.thenation.com/article/world/jews-gaza-response/

Freeman, Michael. 2022. *Human Rights. 4th Edition*. Hoboken: Wiley . www.wiley.com/en-ie/Human+Rights%2C+4th+Edition-p-9781509546053

Frontiers. 2018. "Why Don't We Understand Statistics? Fixed Mindsets May Be to Blame." Science Daily. October 12, 2018. www.sciencedaily.com/releases/2018/10/181012082713.htm

Furuya, Sugio, Odgerel Chimed-Ochir, Ken Takahashi, Annette David, and Jukka Takala. 2018. "Global Asbestos Disaster." *International Journal of Environmental Research and Public Health* 15 (5): 1–11. https://doi.org/10.3390/IJERPH15051000

Geest, Sjaak van der, and Priya Satalkar. 2021. "Autonomy and Dying: Notes about Decision-Making and 'Completed Life' Euthanasia in the Netherlands." *Death Studies* 45 (8): 613–622. https://doi.org/10.1080/07481187.2019.1671543

Gennep, Arnold van. 2019. *The Rites of Passage*. Chicago: University of Chicago Press. https://books.google.fi/books?hl=nl&lr=&id=tTqUDwAAQBAJ&oi=fnd&pg=PR5&dq=arnold+van+gennep+rites+of+passage&ots=XzfjN_IrCX&sig=m7NOrScbo7hWucF9GB3-PTylLcg&redir_esc=y#v=onepage&q=arnold%20van%20gennep%20rites%20of%20passage&f=false

Gieseler, Carly. 2022. *Milestone Celebrations in the Age of Social Media: Performativity, Ritual, and Representation*. https://rowman.com/ISBN/9781666902501/Milestone-Celebrations-in-the-Age-of-Social-Media-Performativity-Ritual-and-Representation

Girling, Evi, and Lizzie Seal. 2016. "Encountering Death In Punishment: The Deathscapes of Incarceration (Introduction)." *The Howard Journal of Criminal Justice* 55 (3): 267–277. https://doi.org/10.1111/HOJO.12169

Goldin, Grace. 1981. "A Protohospice at the Turn of the Century: St. Luke's House, London, from 1893 to 1921." *Journal of the History of Medicine and Allied Sciences* XXXVI (4): 383–415. https://doi.org/10.1093/JHMAS/XXXVI.4.383

Gomes, Mireille, Rehana Begum, Prabha Sati, Rajesh Dikshit, Prakash C. Gupta, Rajesh Kumar, Jay Sheth, Asad Habib, and Prabhat Jha. 2017. "Nationwide Mortality Studies to Quantify Causes of Death: Relevant Lessons from India's Million Death Study." *Health Affairs* 36 (11): 1887–1895. https://doi.org/10.1377/HLTHAFF.2017.0635

Goodfellow, Maya. 2019. *Hostile Environment: How Immigrants Became Scapegoats*. London: Verso. www.versobooks.com/en-gb/products/777-hostile-environment

Gould, Hannah, Michael Arnold, Tony Dupleix, and Tamara Kohn. 2023. "'Stood to Rest': Reorientating Necrogeographies for the 21st Century." *Mortality* 28 (1): 54–72. https://doi.org/10.1080/13576275.2021.1878120

Graven, Vibeke, Anders Petersen, and Helle Timm. 2021. "Hospice Care: Between Existential and Medical Hope." *Mortality* 26 (3): 326–342. https://doi.org/10.1080/13576275.2020.1803249

Greenwood, Ian Mark. 2023. *The Politics of Road Death: Critical Discourse Analysis of Road Safety Policy in Britain between 1987–2021*. Leeds: University of Leeds.

Gudmundsdottir, Maria. 2009. "Embodied Grief: Bereaved Parents' Narratives of Their Suffering Body." *OMEGA-Journal of Death and Dying* 59 (3): 253–269. https://doi.org/10.2190/OM.59.3.E

Guither, Harold D. 1998. *Animal Rights: History and Scope of a Radical Social Movement*. Carbondale and Edwardsville: Southern Illinois University Press. https://books.google.com/books/about/Animal_Rights.html?id=231b9jGgqN4C

Gunew, Sneja Marina. 2013. *Feminist Knowledge: Critique and Construct*. Routledge. www.routledge.com/Feminist-Knowledge-RLE-Feminist-Theory-Critique-and-Construct/Gunew/p/book/9780415754132

Gysels, Marjolein, Christopher Pell, Lianne Straus, and Robert Pool. 2011. "End of Life Care in Sub-Saharan Africa: A Systematic Review of the Qualitative Literature." *BMC Palliative Care* 10 (1): 1–10. https://doi.org/10.1186/1472-684X-10-6/TABLES/4

Haines, Herb. 1992. "Flawed Executions, the Anti-Death Penalty Movement, and the Politics of Capital Punishment." *Social Problems* 39 (2): 125–138. https://doi.org/10.2307/3097033

Haines, Krista L., Hee Soo Jung, Tiffany Zens, Scott Turner, Charles Warner-Hillard, and Suresh Agarwal. 2018. "Barriers to Hospice Care in Trauma Patients: The Disparities in End-of-Life Care." *The American Journal of Hospice & Palliative Care* 35 (8): 1081–1084. https://doi.org/10.1177/1049909117753377

Hale, Lilly. 2018. "Death Positive: An Analysis of an Authenticity Movement." San Marcos: Texas State University . https://hdl.handle.net/10877/7813

Hamilton, Sukhbinder, Berenice Golding, and Jane Ribbens McCarthy. 2022. "Do We Need to Decolonise Bereavement Studies?" *Bereavement* 1 (January). https://doi.org/10.54210/BJ.2022.20

Hannig, Anita. 2022. *The Day I Die: The Untold Story of Assisted Dying in America*. Naperville: Sourcebooks.

Haritaworn, Jin, Adi Kuntsman, and Silvia Posocco, eds. 2014. *Queer Necropolitics*. Oxfordshire, England: Routledge. https://doi.org/10.4324/9780203798300

Harper, Sheila. 2010. "The Social Agency of Dead Bodies." *Mortality* 15 (4): 308–322. https://doi.org/10.1080/13576275.2010.513163

Harris, Darcy. 2010. "Oppression of the Bereaved: A Critical Analysis of Grief in Western Society." *Omega: Journal of Death and Dying* 60 (3): 241–253. https://doi.org/10.2190/OM.60.3.c

Harrison, James E., Stefanie Weber, Robert Jakob, and Christopher G. Chute. 2021. "ICD-11: An International Classification of Diseases for the Twenty-First Century." *BMC Medical Informatics and Decision Making* 21 (November): 1–10. https://doi.org/10.1186/S12911-021-01534-6

Health and Care Act 2022. n.d. King's Printer of Acts of Parliament. Accessed January 27, 2024.

Health Council of the Netherlands. 2020. "Executive Summary The Admissibility of New Techniques of Disposing of the Dead."

Heath, Jessica. n.d. "Exploring Counter Memorials: The UK AIDS Memorial Quilt | Living With Dying." Accessed January 27, 2024. https://livingwithdying.leeds.ac.uk/2019/08/16/exploring-counter-memorials-the-uk-aids-memorial-quilt/

Heffernan, Amanda. 2023. "Pregnancy in United States Immigration Detention: The Gendered Necropolitics of Reproductive Oppression." *International Feminist Journal of Politics* 25 (1): 30–53. https://doi.org/10.1080/14616742.2022.2078393

Hennemann, Severin, Clare Killikelly, Philip Hyland, Andreas Maercker, and Michael Witthöft. 2023. "Somatic Symptom Distress and ICD-11 Prolonged Grief in a Large Intercultural Sample." *European Journal of Psychotraumatology* 14 (2). https://doi.org/10.1080/20008066.2023.2254584

Herek, Gregory M., and Eric K. Glunt. 1988. "An Epidemic of Stigma: Public Reactions to AIDS." *American Psychologist* 43 (11): 886–891. https://doi.org/10.1037/0003-066X.43.11.886

Hernandez, Viviana M. Abreu. 2002. "The Mothers of La Plaza de Mayo: A Peace Movement." *Peace & Change* 27 (3): 385–411. https://doi.org/10.1111/0149-0508.00235

Herrera, Esther Ayuso, & Carlos, Alonso Mayo, & Santiago, and Garcia-Tizon Larroca. 2019. "Maternal Mortality Among Immigrant Women in Europe and the USA: A Systematic Review." *SN Comprehensive Clinical Medicine 2019 2:1* 2 (1): 16–24. https://doi.org/10.1007/S42399-019-00190-2

Higginson, Irene. 1993. "Palliative Care: A Review of Past Changes and Future Trends." *Journal of Public Health* 15 (1): 3–8. https://doi.org/10.1093/OXFORDJOURNALS.PUBMED.A042817

Hilhorst, Dorothea. 2005. "Dead Letter or Living Document? Ten Years of the Code of Conduct for Disaster Relief." *Disasters* 29 (4): 351–369. https://doi.org/10.1111/j.0361-3666.2005.00297.x

Hoare, Sarah, Zoe Slote Morris, Michael P. Kelly, Isla Kuhn, and Stephen Barclay. 2015. "Do Patients Want to Die at Home? A Systematic Review of the UK Literature, Focused on Missing Preferences for Place of Death." *PLOS ONE* 10 (11): 1–17. https://doi.org/10.1371/journal.pone.0142723

Hooker, Juliet. 2023. *Black Grief/ White Grievance: The Politics of Loss*. Princeton: Princeton University Press.

Hope, Valerie Margaret. 2018. "'Dulce et Decorum Est pro Patria Mori': The Practical and Symbolic Treatment of the Roman War Dead." *Mortality* 23 (1): 35–49. https://doi.org/10.1080/13576275.2017.1282943

Hospice UK. n.d. "Hospice UK Calls for Action over Rising Costs." Accessed January 28, 2024. www.hospiceuk.org/latest-from-hospice-uk/hospice-uk-calls-action-over-rising-costs

Howarth, Glennys. 2009. "The Demography of Dying." In *The Study of Dying: From Autonomy to Transformation. 1st Edition*, edited by Allan Kellehear, 99–122. Cambdrige: Cambridge University Press .

Hui, Tan Boon, and Brenda S A Yeoh. 2002. "The 'Remains of the Dead': Spatial Politics of Nation-Building in Post-War Singapore." *Source: Human Ecology Review* 9 (1): 1–13.

Human Rights Watch. 2021. "Sri Lanka: Covid-19 Forced Cremation of Muslims Discriminatory." Human Rights Watch. 2021. www.hrw.org/news/2021/01/18/sri-lanka-covid-19-forced-cremation-muslims-discriminatory

Hurtado, Joshua. 2023. "Exploited in Immortality: Techno-Capitalism and Immortality Imaginaries in the Twenty-First Century." *Mortality*, October. https://doi.org/10.1080/13576275.2023.2266373

Iles, Jennifer. 2008. "In Remembrance: The Flanders Poppy." *Mortality* 13 (3): 201–221. https://doi.org/10.1080/13576270802181640

Iliadou, Evgenia. 2023. "Necroharms: The Normalisation and Routinisation of Social Death in Refugee Camps on the Greek Island of Lesvos." *Mortality* 28 (2): 299–313. https://doi.org/10.1080/13576275.2023.2185128

Illich, Ivan. 1975. "The Medicalization of Life." *Journal of Medical Ethics* 1 (2): 73. https://doi.org/10.1136/JME.1.2.73

Incorvaia, Aubrey De Veny. 2022. "Death Positivity in America: The Movement—Its History and Literature." *Omega (United States)* 2022 (0): 1–20. https://doi.org/10.1177/00302228221085176/FORMAT/EPUB

Incorvaia, A. D. 2023. "Inside American End-of-Life Doula Trainings through Analytic Autoethnography: A Social Movement for Death Positivity Manifests in a New Profession." *Journal of Contemporary Ethnography* 52(5): 691–720. https://doi.org/10.1177/08912416231169501

IOM. 2015. "GMDAC Briefing Series: Towards Safer Migration in Africa: Migration and Data in Northern and Western Africa CALCULATING 'DEATH RATES' IN THE CONTEXT OF MIGRATION JOURNEYS: Focus on the Central Mediterranean." http://gmdac.iom.int

Islam, Nazrul, Dmitri A. Jdanov, Vladimir M. Shkolnikov, Kamlesh Khunti, Ichiro Kawachi, Martin White, Sarah Lewington, and Ben Lacey. 2021. "Effects of Covid-19 Pandemic on Life Expectancy and Premature Mortality in 2020: Time Series Analysis in 37 Countries." *BMJ* 375 (November): 1–14. https://doi.org/10.1136/BMJ-2021-066768

Jackson, Beth E. 2003. "Situating Epidemiology." In *Gender Perspectives on Health and Medicine (Advances in Gender Research*, edited by Marcia Texler Segal, Vasilikie Demos, and Jennie J. Kronenfeld, 7: 11–58. Leeds: Emerald. https://doi.org/10.1016/S1529-2126(03)07002-4

Jacobs, R.K., and M. Hendricks. 2018. "Medical Students' Perspectives on Euthanasia and Physician-Assisted Suicide and Their Views on Legalising These Practices in South Africa." *South African Medical Journal* 108 (6): 484–489. https://doi.org/10.7196/SAMJ.2018.v108i6.13089

Jaja, Ishmael Festus, Madubuike Umunna Anyanwu, and Chinwe Juliana Iwu Jaja. 2020. "Social Distancing: How Religion, Culture and Burial Ceremony Undermine the Effort to Curb COVID-19 in South Africa." *Emerging Microbes & Infections* 9 (1): 1077–1079. https://doi.org/10.1080/22221751.2020.1769501

Jaramillo, Ceydy. 2023. "Love, Memory, and Resistance. The Respectability Politics of the AIDS Memorial Quilt and the AIDS Social Movement." *CONCEPT* 46 (May). https://concept.journals.villanova.edu/index.php/concept/article/view/2768

Jasper, James M. 2010. "Social Movement Theory Today: Toward a Theory of Action?" *Sociology Compass* 4 (11): 965–976. https://doi.org/10.1111/J.1751-9020.2010.00329.X

Javanparast, Sara, Julia Anaf, and Jennifer Tieman. 2022. "Equity Consideration in Palliative Care Policies, Programs, and Evaluation: An Analysis of Selected Federal and South Australian Documents." *BMC Palliative Care* 21 (1): 1–14. https://doi.org/10.1186/S12904-022-00997-2/TABLES/3

Jaye, Chrystal, Jessica Young, Isabelle Lomax-Sawyers, and Richard Egan. 2021. "Assisted Dying in New Zealand: What Is Known about the Values Underpinning Citizens' Positions?" *Mortality* 26 (1): 66–82. https://doi.org/10.1080/13576275.2020.1771295

Jimenez, Geronimo, Woan Shin Tan, Amrit K. Virk, Chan Kee Low, Josip Car, and Andy Hau Yan Ho. 2018. "Overview of Systematic Reviews of Advance Care Planning: Summary of Evidence and Global Lessons." *Journal of Pain and Symptom Management* 56 (3): 436–459.e25. https://doi.org/10.1016/J.JPAINSYMMAN.2018.05.016

Jones, Kerry, Katy Schnitzler, and Erica Borgstrom. 2022. "The Implications of COVID-19 on Health and Social Care Personnel in Long-Term Care Facilities for Older People: An International Scoping Review." *Health and Social Care in the Community* 30(6): e3493–3506. https://doi.org/10.1111/hsc.13969

Joyce, Kelly, and Meika Loe. 2010. "A Sociological Approach to Ageing, Technology and Health." *Sociology of Health and Illness* 32 (2): 171–180. https://doi.org/10.1111/J.1467-9566.2009.01219.X

Jupp, Peter C. 2005. *From Dust to Ashes: Cremation and the British Way of Death. From Dust to Ashes: Cremation and the British Way of Death.* London: Palgrave Macmillan. https://doi.org/10.1057/9780230511088/COVER

Kalanzi, Dorothy J.N. 2013. "The Controversy over Euthanasia in Uganda: A Case of the Baganda." *International Journal of Sociology and Social Policy* 33 (3): 203–217. https://doi.org/10.1108/01443331311308249

Kastenbaum, Robert 2013. "Good Death." In *Macmillan Encyclopedia of Death and Dying*, edited by Robert Kastenbaum, 337–343. New York: Macmillan.

Kaufman, Sharon. 2005. *...And a Time to Die. How American Hospitals Shape the End of Life*. New York: Scribner.

Kaufman, Sharon. 2010. "Time, Clinic Technologies, and the Making of Reflexive Longevity: The Cultural Work of Time Left in an Ageing Society." *Sociology of Health and Illness* 32 (2): 225–237. https://doi.org/10.1111/J.1467-9566.2009.01200.X

Kaufman, Sharon. 2015. *Ordinary Medicine. Extraordinary Treatments, Longer Lives and Where to Draw the Line*. Durham and London: Duke University Press.

Kellehear, Allan. 2007. *A Social History of Dying*. Cambridge: Cambridge University Press.

———. 2008. "Dying as a Social Relationship: A Sociological Review of Debates on the Determination of Death." *Social Science and Medicine* 66 (7): 1533–1544. https://doi.org/10.1016/j.socscimed.2007.12.023

Keller, Emily R. 2023. "Our Bodies: Holders of Unspoken Grief." In *Disenfranchised Grief: Examining Social, Cultural, and Relational Impacts*, edited by Renee Blocker Turner and Sarah D. Stauffer, 42–58. Oxfordshire, England: Taylor & Francis. https://doi.org/10.4324/9781003292890-4/BODIES-EMILY-KELLER

Keller, Richard C. 2022. "Memorializing Death in an Age of Mass Mortality: Keywords of Covid-19 – Somatosphere." Somatosphere. 2022. https://somatosphere.com/2022/memorializing-death-mass-mortality-covid-keller.html/

Kemp, Hellen R., Nicky Jacobs, and Sandra Stewart. 2016. "The Lived Experience of Companion-Animal Loss: A Systematic Review of Qualitative Studies." *Anthrozoös* 29 (4): 533–557. https://doi.org/10.1080/08927936.2016.1228772

Kennedy, Helen, and Rosemary Lucy Hill. 2018. "The Feeling of Numbers: Emotions in Everyday Engagements with Data and Their Visualisation." *Sociology* 52 (4): 830–848. https://doi.org/10.1177/0038038516674675/ASSET/IMAGES/LARGE/10.1177_00380 38516674675-FIG7.JPEG

Kenney, Fiona L. 2024. "'A Prison for the Dead': Hart Island and Spatial Histories of Marginalization." In *Difficult Death, Dying and the Dead in Media and Culture*, edited by Sharon Coleclough, Bethan Michael-Fox, and Renske Visser, 149–159. Cham: Palgrave Macmillan. https://doi.org/10.1007/978-3-031-40732-1_10

Kinney, Mary V., David Roger Walugembe, Phillip Wanduru, Peter Waiswa, and Asha George. 2021. "Maternal and Perinatal Death Surveillance and Response in Low- and Middle-Income Countries: A Scoping Review of Implementation Factors." *Health Policy and Planning* 36 (6): 955–973. https://doi.org/10.1093/HEAPOL/CZAB011

Kirby, Emma, Erica Borgstrom, and John MacArtney. 2020. "Tallies and Tolls: What Counting the Dead Can Tell Us about Death and Dying amidst the COVID-19 Pandemic | Discover Society." Discover Society. 2020. https://archive.discoversociety.org/2020/06/09/tallies-and-tolls-what-counting-the-dead-can-tell-us-about-death-and-dying-ami dst-the-covid-19-pandemic/

Klass, Dennis. 2006. "Continuing Conversation about Continuing Bonds." *Death Studies* 30 (9): 843–858. https://doi.org/10.1080/07481180600886959

———. 2014. "Grief, Consolation, and Religions: A Conceptual Framework." *Omega (United States)* 69 (1): 1–18. https://doi.org/10.2190/OM.69.1.a

———. 2023. "Continuing Bonds in the Existential, Phenomenological, and Cultural Study of Grief: Prolegomena." *Omega (United States)*. https://doi.org/10.1177/0030222823 1205766

Klass, Dennis, Phyllis R. Silverman, and Steven L. Nickman. 1996. *Continuing Bonds: New Understandings of Grief.* Oxfordshire, England: Taylor & Francis. www.routledge.com/Continuing-Bonds-New-Understandings-of-Grief/Klass-Silverman-Nickman/p/book/9781560323396

Klass, Dennis, and Edith Maria Steffen. 2018. "Introduction: Continuing Bonds—20 Years On." In *Continuing Bonds in Bereavement: New Directions for Research and Practice*, edited by Dennis Klass and Edith Maria Steffen, 1–14. Series in Death, Dying, and Bereavement. New York: Routledge/Taylor & Francis Group. https://doi.org/10.4324/9781315202396-1

Knettel, Brandon A., Armstrong Obale, Hamza Iqbal, Mela C. Fotabong, Ngaha N. Philippe, Margaret Graton, and Leila Ledbetter. 2024. "A Profound Absence of Counseling Interventions for Suicide Prevention among Youth in Africa: A Call to Action Based on an Empty Scoping Review." *Suicide and Life-Threatening Behavior*. https://doi.org/10.1111/SLTB.13041

Knight, Lucia, and Alicia Ely Yamin. 2015. "Without a Mother: Caregivers and Community Members' Views about the Impacts of Maternal Mortality on Families in KwaZulu-Natal, South Africa." *Reproductive Health* 12 (1): 1–11. https://doi.org/10.1186/1742-4755-12-S1-S5/METRICS

Knight, Marian, Kathryn Bunch, Nicola Vousden, Anita Banerjee, Philippa Cox, Fiona Cross-Sudworth, Mandish K Dhanjal, et al. 2021. "A National Cohort Study and Confidential Enquiry to Investigate Ethnic Disparities in Maternal Mortality." *The Lancet*, 1–15. https://doi.org/10.1016/j

Knox, Crissy, and John A. Vereb. 2005. "Allow Natural Death: A More Humane Approach to Discussing End-of-Life Directives." *Journal of Emergency Nursing* 31 (6): 560–561. https://doi.org/10.1016/j.jen.2005.06.020

Knudsen, S.K. 2009. "The Dying Animal: A Perspective from Veterinary Medicine." In *The Study of Dying*, edited by Allan Kellehear, 27–50. Cambridge: Cambridge University Press.

Koffman, Jonathan. 2023. "Researching Minoritised Communities in Palliative Care: An Agenda for Change." In *EAPC 2023*.

Koffman, Jonathan, Sabrina Bajwah, Joanna M. Davies, and Jamilla Akhter Hussain. 2023. "Researching Minoritised Communities in Palliative Care: An Agenda for Change." *Palliative Medicine* 37 (4): 530–542. https://doi.org/10.1177/02692163221132091

Koksvik, Gitte H. 2020. "Neoliberalism, Individual Responsibilization and the Death Positivity Movement." *International Journal of Cultural Studies* 23 (6): 951–967. https://doi.org/10.1177/1367877920924426

Koksvik, Gitte H., and Naomi Richards. 2023. "Death Café, Bauman and Striving for Human Connection in 'Liquid Times.'" *Mortality* 28 (3): 349–366. https://doi.org/10.1080/13576275.2021.1918655

Konadu, Kwasi, and Bright Gyamfi. 2018. "Black Lives Matter: How Far Has the Movement Come?" The Conversation. September 8, 2018. https://theconversation.com/black-lives-matter-how-far-has-the-movement-come-165492

Krawczyk, Marian, Emma Clare, Erin Collins, Elizabeth Johnson, Jennifer Mallmes, Annetta Mallon, Sarah Farr, Kelly Oberle, and Jennifer Rigal. 2022. "The International End-of-Life Doula Symposium Report." https://doi.org/10.36399/GLA.PUBS.281490

Krawczyk, Marian, Joseph Wood, and David Clark. 2018. "Total Pain: Origins, Current Practice, Future Directions." *Omsorg: The Norwegian Journal of Palliative Care*.

Kurbasic, Izeta, Haris Pandza, Izet Masic, Senad Huseinagic, Salih Tandir, Fredi Alicajic, and Selim Toromanovic. 2008. "The Advantages and Limitations of International Classification of Diseases, Injuries and Causes of Death from Aspect of Existing Health Care System of Bosnia and Herzegovina." *Acta Informatica Medica* 16 (3): 159–161. https://doi.org/10.5455/AIM.2008.16.159-161

Kutner, Luis. 1969. "Due Process of Euthanasia: The Living Will, A Proposal." *44 Indiana Law Journal 539 (1969)* 44 (4). www.repository.law.indiana.edu/ilj/vol44/iss4/2

Lai, W. S., W. P. Yang, Y. L. Shih and & H. C. Liu. 2011. "ACP Is a National Social Movement – The Effectiveness of Life Education Programs for School Children: A Preliminary Study." *BMJ Supportive & Palliative Care* 1(1), 104–105. https://doi.org/10.1136/bmjspcare-2011-000053.135

Lancaster, H.O. 1990. *Expectations of Life. A Study in the Demography, Statistics, and History of World Mortality. Expectations of Life*. New York: Springer. https://doi.org/10.1007/978-1-4612-1003-0

Landau, Mark J., Sheldon Solomon, Jeff Greenberg, Florette Cohen, Tom Pyszczynski, Jamie Arndt, Claude H. Miller, Daniel M. Ogilvie, and Alison Cook. 2004. "Deliver Us from Evil: The Effects of Mortality Salience and Reminders of 9/11 on Support for President George W. Bush." *Personality and Social Psychology Bulletin* 30 (9): 1136–1150. https://doi.org/10.1177/0146167204267988

Laqueur, Thomas W. 2015. *The Work of the Dead: A Cultural History of Mortal Remains.* Princeton: Princeton University Press. https://doi.org/10.2307/j.ctvc77h3r

Lau, Christine, Christopher Meaney, Matthew Morgan, Rose Cook, Camilla Zimmermann, and Kirsten Wentlandt. 2021. "Disparities in Access to Palliative Care Facilities for Patients with and without Cancer: A Retrospective Review." *Palliative Medicine* 35 (6): 1191. https://doi.org/10.1177/02692163211007387

Lebron, Christopher J. 2023. *The Making of Black Lives Matter: A Brief History of an Idea.* Oxford: Oxford University Press.

Lee, Yung-Jin. 2015. "Postwar Japan and the Politics of Mourning: The Meaning and the Limits of War Experiences." *Seoul Journal of Japanese Studies* 1 (1): 89–113.

Leget, Carlo. 2007. "Retrieving the Ars Moriendi Tradition." *Medicine, Health Care and Philosophy* 10 (3): 313–319. https://doi.org/10.1007/S11019-006-9045-Z/METRICS

Lemos Dekker, Natashe. 2017. "Moral Frames for Lives Worth Living: Managing the End of Life with Dementia." *Death Studies* 42 (5): 1–7. https://doi.org/10.1080/07481187.2017.1396644

———. 2021. "Anticipating an Unwanted Future: Euthanasia and Dementia in the Netherlands." *Journal of the Royal Anthropological Institute* 27 (4): 815–831. https://doi.org/10.1111/1467-9655.13429

Lerum, Kari A. 2023. "Teaching Death Ritual during States of Emergency: Centering Death Positivity, Anti-Racism, Grief, & Ritual." *Journal of Curriculum and Pedagogy* 20 (1): 40–62. https://doi.org/10.1080/15505170.2021.1964114

"Lesson 3: Measures of Risk | CDC Archive." n.d. Accessed January 27, 2024. https://archive.cdc.gov/#/details?url=https://www.cdc.gov/csels/dsepd/ss1978/lesson3/section3.html

Leyh, Brianne Mc Gonigle. 2020. "Imperatives of the Present: Black Lives Matter and the Politics of Memory and Memorialization." *Netherlands Quarterly of Human Rights* 38 (4): 239–245. https://doi.org/10.1177/0924051920967541

Liebling, Alison. 2017. "The Meaning of Ending Life in Prison." *Journal of Correctional Health Care* 23 (1): 20–31. https://doi.org/10.1177/1078345816685070

"Life Expectancy – Our World in Data." n.d. Accessed January 27, 2024. https://ourworldindata.org/life-expectancy

Lillie, Kate. 2018. "Loss at the End of Life: Palliative Care in Prisons." In *Loss, Dying and Bereavement in the Criminal Justice System*, edited by Sue Read, Sotirios Santatzoglou, and Anthony Wrigley, 43–53. London: Routledge. https://doi.org/10.4324/9781315270166-5

Lipman, Arthur G., Kenneth C. Jackson, and Linda S. Tyler. 2000. *Evidence Based Symptom Control in Palliative Care: Systematic Reviews and Validated Clinical Practice Guidelines for 15 Common Problems in Patients with Life Limiting Disease.* Pharmaceutical Products Press. www.routledge.com/Evidence-Based-Symptom-Control-in-Palliative-Care-Systemic-Reviews-and/Lipman-Jackson-II-Tyler/p/book/9780789010148

Liu, Fannie, Denae Ford, Chris Parnin, and Laura Dabbish. 2017. "Selfies as Social Movements." *Proceedings of the ACM on Human-Computer Interaction* 1 (CSCW): 1–21. https://doi.org/10.1145/3134707

Lloyd, Caroline A. 2018. *Grief Demystified: An Introduction.* https://uk.jkp.com/products/grief-demystified

Lofland, Lyn H. 1985. "The Social Shaping of Emotion: The Case of Grief." *Symbolic Interaction* 8 (2): 171–190. https://doi.org/10.1525/si.1985.8.2.171

———. 2019. *The Craft of Dying*. Boston, MA: MIT Press. https://mitpress.mit.edu/978026 2537346/the-craft-of-dying/

Lowe, Lindsey. 2016. "Crying Wolf: An Analysis of the Use of Sensational Content within the Media and the Desensitizing Effects It Has on Audiences." San Jose: San Jose State University .

Lukes, Steven. 2005. *Power, Second Edition: A Radical View*. London: Palgrave Macmillan. http://books.google.com/books?id=XxpwQgAACAAJ&pgis=1

Lykke, Nina. 2022. *Vibrant Death: A Posthuman Phenomenology of Mourning*. London: Bloomsbury.

Lynch, T., S. Connor, and D. Clark. 2013. "Mapping Levels of Palliative Care Development: A Global Update." *Journal of Pain and Symptom Management* 45 (6):1094–1106. doi: 10.1016/j.jpainsymman.2012.05.011

Lyons, Anna, and Louise (Funeral director) Winter. 2021. *We All Know How This Ends: Lessons about Life and Living from Working with Death and Dying*.

MacDonald, Susan M., Leonie M. Herx, and Anne B. Boyle. 2021. *Palliative Medicine: A Case-Based Manual*. Oxford: Oxford Academic.

Mada din, Mohammed, Houria S. Al Sahwan, Khadijah K. Altarouti, Sarraa A. Altarouti, Zahra S. Al Eswaikt, and Ritesh G. Menezes. 2020. "The Islamic Perspective on Physician-Assisted Suicide and Euthanasia." *Medicine, Science and the Law* 60 (4): 278–286. https://doi.org/10.1177/0025802420934241

Malkowski, Jennifer. 2017. *Dying in Full Detail. Mortality and Digital Documentary*. Durham: Duke University Press. https://doi.org/10.1215/9780822373414

Mallon, Sharon, Karen Galway, Lynette Hughes, Janeet Rondón-Sulbarán, and Gerard Leavey. 2016. "An Exploration of Integrated Data on the Social Dynamics of Suicide among Women." *Sociology of Health and Illness* 38 (4): 662–675. https://doi.org/ 10.1111/1467-9566.12399

Manguvo, Angellar, and Benford Mafuvadze. 2015. "The Impact of Traditional and Religious Practices on the Spread of Ebola in West Africa: Time for a Strategic Shift." *The Pan African Medical Journal* 22 (Suppl 1): 9. https://doi.org/10.11694/PAMJ. SUPP.2015.22.1.6190

Marriott, Kim, Bongshin Lee, Microsoft Research, Matthew Butler, Ed Cutrell, Kirsten Ellis, Cagatay Goncu, et al. 2021. "Inclusive Data Visualization for People with Disabilities: A Call to Action." *Interactions*, 47–51. https://doi.org/10.1145/3457875.

Marsh, Ian. 2010. *Suicide, Foucault, History and Truth. .* Cambridge: Cambridge University Press.

———. 2015. "Critiquing Contemporary Suicidology." In *Critical Suicidology: Transforming Suicide Research and Prevention for the 21st Century*, edited by Jennifer White, Michael Kral, Jonathan Morris, and Ian Marsh, 15–30. Vancouver: Vancouver UCB Press.

Martí, Jordi Bonet, and Barbara Biglia. 2014. "Social Movements." In *Encyclopedia of Critical Psychology*, 1788–1794. New York, NY: Springer, New York, NY. https://doi. org/10.1007/978-1-4614-5583-7_290

Martin, Emily. 1994. *Flexible Bodies: Tracking Immunity in American Culture from the Days of Polio to the Age of AIDS*. Boston: Beacon Press.

Marzetti, Hazel, Lisa McDaid, and Rory O'Connor. 2022. "'Am I Really Alive?': Understanding the Role of Homophobia, Biphobia and Transphobia in Young LGBT+ People's Suicidal Distress." *Social Science and Medicine* 298 (April): 114860. https://doi.org/10.1016/j.socscimed.2022.114860

Masson, John D. 2002. "Non-Professional Perceptions of 'Good Death': A Study of the Views of Hospice Care Patients and Relatives of Deceased Hospice Care Patients." *Mortality* 7 (2): 191–209. https://doi.org/10.1080/13576270220136294

"Maternal Mortality Ratio (per 100 000 Live Births)." n.d. Accessed January 27, 2024. www.who.int/data/gho/indicator-metadata-registry/imr-details/26

Mathers, Colin, and Ties Boerma. 2010. "Mortality Measurement Matters: Improving Data Collection and Estimation Methods for Child and Adult Mortality." *PLoS Medicine* 7 (4). https://doi.org/10.1371/JOURNAL.PMED.1000265

Mathijssen, Brenda. 2017. "Transforming Bonds: Ritualising Post-Mortem Relationships in the Netherlands." *Mortality* 6275 (December): 1–16. https://doi.org/10.1080/13576275.2017.1364228

Mbembe, Achille. 2019. *Necropolitics*. Durham: Duke University Press .

MBRRACE-UK. 2023. "Maternal Mortality 2019–2021." National Perinatal Epidemiology Unit. October 2023. www.npeu.ox.ac.uk/mbrrace-uk/data-brief/maternal-mortality-2019-2021

McCarthy, Jane Ribbens, Kate Woodthorpe, and Kathryn Almack. 2023. "The Aftermath of Death in the Continuing Lives of the Living: Extending 'Bereavement' Paradigms through Family and Relational Perspectives." *Sociology* 57 (6): 1356–1374. https://doi.org/10.1177/00380385221142490

McConville, Alex, Tim McCreanor, Margaret Wetherell, and Helen Moewaka Barnes. 2016. "Imagining an Emotional Nation: The Print Media and Anzac Day Commemorations in Aotearoa New Zealand." *Media, Culture & Society* 39 (1): 94–110. https://doi.org/10.1177/0163443716672300

McCreanor, Tim, Margaret Wetherell, Alex McConville, Helen Moewaka Barnes, and Angela Moewaka Barnes. 2019. "New Light; Friendly Soil: Affective–Discursive Dimensions of Anzac Day Commemorations in Aotearoa New Zealand." *Nations and Nationalism* 25 (3): 974–996. https://doi.org/10.1111/NANA.12474

McDermott, Ella, and Lucy Ellen Selman. 2018. "Cultural Factors Influencing Advance Care Planning in Progressive, Incurable Disease: A Systematic Review With Narrative Synthesis." *Journal of Pain and Symptom Management* 56 (4): 613–636. https://doi.org/10.1016/J.JPAINSYMMAN.2018.07.006

McEntire, David A. 2007. *Disaster Response and Recovery: Strategies and Tactics for Resilience*. University of North Texas, Hoboken: John Wiley & Son.

Mckee, Kim. 2009. "Post-Foucauldian Governmentality: What Does It Offer Critical Social Policy Analysis?" *Critical Social Policy* 29 (3): 465–486.

McKnight, John. 1995. *The Careless Society: Community and Its Counterfeits*. New York: Basic Books.

McLeod, Kari S. 2000. "Our Sense of Snow: The Myth of John Snow in Medical Geography." *Social Science & Medicine* 50 (7–8): 923–935. https://doi.org/10.1016/S0277-9536(99)00345-7

McManus, Ruth. 2023. "Examining Sustainability and Death." In *The Sustainable Dead: Searching for the Intolerable*, edited by Ruth McManus, 1–9. Newcastle upon Tyrne: Cambridge Scholars Publishing .

McNamara, Beverley. 2004. "Good Enough Death: Autonomy and Choice in Australian Palliative Care." *Social Science and Medicine* 58 (5): 929–938. https://doi.org/10.1016/j.socscimed.2003.10.042

McNamara, Beverley, Charles Waddell, and Margaret Colvin. 1994. "The Institutionalization of the Good Death." *Social Science & Medicine (1982)* 39 (11): 1501–1508. https://doi.org/10.1016/0277-9536(94)90002-7

———. 1995. "Threats to the Good Death: The Cultural Context of Stress and Coping among Hospice Nurses." *Sociology of Health & Illness* 17 (2): 222–241. https://doi.org/10.1111/1467-9566.EP10933398

Meier, Emily A., Jarred V. Gallegos, Lori P. Montross-Thomas, Colin A. Depp, Scott A. Irwin, and Dilip V. Jeste. 2016. "Defining a Good Death (Successful Dying): Literature Review and a Call for Research and Public Dialogue." *The American Journal of Geriatric Psychiatry: Official Journal of the American Association for Geriatric Psychiatry* 24 (4): 261. https://doi.org/10.1016/J.JAGP.2016.01.135

Meloni, Maurizio. 2023. "An Unproblematized Truth: Foucault, Biopolitics, and the Making of a Sociological Canon." *Social Theory and Health* 21 (2): 99–118. https://doi.org/10.1057/S41285-022-00177-5/METRICS

Michel, Janet. 2020. "Towards Universal Health Coverage (UHC) Policy Roll-out Experience in South Africa: How and Why Policy-Practice Gaps Come about in a UHC Context." https://doi.org/10.5451/UNIBAS-007211852

Miladinov, Goran. 2020. "Socioeconomic Development and Life Expectancy Relationship: Evidence from the EU Accession Candidate Countries." *Genus* 76 (1): 1–20. https://doi.org/10.1186/S41118-019-0071-0/FIGURES/4

Millner, Alexander J., Donald J. Robinaugh, and Matthew K. Nock. 2020. "Advancing the Understanding of Suicide: The Need for Formal Theory and Rigorous Descriptive Research." *Trends in Cognitive Sciences* 24 (9): 704–716. https://doi.org/10.1016/j.tics.2020.06.007

Ministry of Health. 2019. "End of Life Choice Act 2019." 2019. www.legislation.govt.nz/act/public/2019/0067/latest/DLM7285950.html?search=sw_096be8ed81b7485f_waiting+period_25_se&p=1

Morabia, Alfredo. 2013. "Epidemiology's 350th Anniversary: 1662–2012." *Epidemiology (Cambridge, Massachusetts)* 24 (2): 179. https://doi.org/10.1097/EDE.0B013E31827B5359

Moreno-Betancur, Margarita, Hamza Sadaoui, Clara Piffaretti, and Grégoire Rey. 2017. "Survival Analysis with Multiple Causes of Death." *Epidemiology* 28 (1): 12 19. https://doi.org/10.1097/EDE.0000000000000531

Morgan, Oliver W., Pongruk Sribanditmongkol, Clifford Perera, Yeddi Sulasmi, Dana Van Alphen, and Egbert Sondorp. 2006. "Mass Fatality Management Following the South Asian Tsunami Disaster: Case Studies in Thailand, Indonesia, and Sri Lanka." *PLOS Medicine* 3 (6): e195. https://doi.org/10.1371/JOURNAL.PMED.0030195

Morris-Suzuki, Tessa. 1998. "Unquiet Graves: Katō Norihiro and the Politics of Mourning." *Japanese Studies* 18 (1): 21–30. https://doi.org/10.1080/10371399808727639

Moutogiannis, Panagiota P., Jason Thrift, J. Keais Pope, Matthew H.E.M. Browning, Olivia McAnirlin, and Tracy Fasolino. 2023. "A Rapid Review of the Role of Virtual Reality in Care Delivery of Palliative Care and Hospice." *Journal of Hospice and Palliative Nursing* 25 (6): 300–308. https://doi.org/10.1097/NJH.0000000000000983

Mroz, Sarah, Sigrid Dierickx, Luc Deliens, Joachim Cohen, and Kenneth Chambaere. 2021. "Assisted Dying around the World: A Status Quaestionis." *Annals of Palliative Medicine* 10 (3): 3540–3553. https://doi.org/10.21037/APM-20-637

Mullings, Leith. 2021. "The Necropolitics of Reproduction: Racism, Resistance, and the Sojourner Syndrome in the Age of the Movement for Black Lives." In *The Routledge*

Handbook of Anthropology and Reproduction, edited by Sallie Han and Cecilia Tomori, 106–122. New York: Routlegde.

Muposhi, Asphat, Fainos Chokera, and Edward Mudzimba. 2023. "Green Burial Conundrum: Constructing the Intersection between Stakeholder Perceptions and Sustainable Land Use in a Multi-Cultural Society." *Mortality*, 1–16. https://doi.org/10.1080/13576275.2023.2231864

Murie, Jill. 2006. "Palliative Medicine." *BMJ* 333 (7571): s136–137. https://doi.org/10.1136/BMJ.333.7571.S136

Murray, Scott A., and Aziz Sheikh. 2008. "Palliative Care Beyond Cancer: Care for All at the End of Life." *BMJ: British Medical Journal* 336 (7650): 958. https://doi.org/10.1136/BMJ.39535.491238.94

National Palliative and End of Life Care Partnership. 2021. "Ambitions for Palliative and End of Life Care: A National Framework for Local Action 2021–2026."

Negri, Stefania. 2013. "Universal Human Rights and End-of-Life Care." In *Advance Care Decision Making in Germany and Italy. A Comparative, European and International Law Perspective*, edited by Stefania Negri, J. Taupitz, A Salkić, and A. Zwick, 1–37. Springer. https://doi.org/10.1007/978-3-642-40555-6_1

Neimeyer, Robert A, and Joseph M Currier. 2009. "Grief Therapy Evidence of Efficacy and Emerging Directions." *Current Directions in Psychological Science* 18 (6): 352–356.

Neimeyer, Robert A., Dennis Klass, and Michael Robert Dennis. 2014. "A Social Constructionist Account of Grief: Loss and the Narration of Meaning." *Death Studies* 38 (8): 485–498. https://doi.org/10.1080/07481187.2014.913454

Neimeyer, Robert, Lauren Breen, and Evginia Milman. 2023. "The Effectiveness of Grief Therapy: A Meta-Analytic Perspective." In *The Handbook of Grief Therapies*, edited by Edith Maria Steffen, Evgenia Milman, and Robert Neimeyer, 29–41. London: SAGE.

NHS. 2022. "What End of Life Care Involves ." 2022. zww.nhs.uk/conditions/end-of-life-care/what-it-involves-and-when-it-starts/

Nicolucci, Viola. 2019. "A Death-Positive Video Game for Death Education of Adolescents." *Italian Journal of Educational Technology* 27 (2): 186–197. https://doi.org/10.17471/2499-4324/1071

Nielsen, Emma, Prianka Padmanathan, and Duleeka Knipe. 2016. "Commit* to Change? A Call to End the Publication of the Phrase 'Commit* Suicide.'" *Wellcome Open Research* 1 (21). https://doi.org/10.12688/wellcomeopenres.10333.1

Nkechi, Gloria Onah, and Tyavkase Gudaku Benjamin. 2023. "Personhood and the Importance of Name and Naming in Africa: An Expository Discourse." *AKU: An African Journal of Contemporary Research* 4 (4): 305–321. https://acjol.org/index.php/aku/article/view/4098

Norwood, Frances. 2007. "Nothing More to Do: Euthanasia, General Practice, and End-of-Life Discourse in the Netherlands." *Medical Anthropology: Cross Cultural Studies in Health and Illness* 26 (2): 139–174. https://doi.org/10.1080/01459740701283165

———. 2009. *The Maintenance of Life Preventing Social Death through Euthanasia Talk and End-of-Life Care--Lessons from The Netherlands*. Durham, North Carolina: Carolina Academic Press.

O'Keefe, Victoria M., Raymond P. Tucker, Ashley B. Cole, David W. Hollingsworth, and La Ricka R. Wingate. 2018. "Understanding Indigenous Suicide Through a Theoretical Lens: A Review of General, Culturally-Based, and Indigenous Frameworks." 55 (6): 775–799. https://doi.org/10.1177/1363461518778937

Olenja, Joyce M. 1999. "Assessing Community Attitude towards Home-Based Care for People with AIDS (PWAs) in Kenya." *Journal of Community Health* 24 (3): 187–199. https://doi.org/10.1023/A:1018709314503

Osterholm, Michael T., Kristine A. Moore, Nicholas S. Kelley, Lisa M. Brosseau, Gary Wong, Frederick A. Murphy, Clarence J. Peters, et al. 2015. "Transmission of Ebola Viruses: What We Know and What We Do Not Know." *MBio* 6 (2). https://doi.org/10.1128/MBIO.00137-15/FORMAT/EPUB

Padmanathan, Prianka, Lucy Biddle, Katherine Hall, Elizabeth Scowcroft, Emma Nielsen, and Duleeka Knipe. 2019. "Language Use and Suicide: An Online Crosssectional Survey." *PLOS ONE* 14 (6): 1–15. https://doi.org/10.1371/journal.pone.0217473.

Palgi, Phyllis, and Henry Abramovitch. 1984. "Death: A Cross-Cultural Perspective." *Annual Review of Anthropology* 13 (1): 385–417. https://doi.org/10.1146/ANNUREV. AN.13.100184.002125

Park, Chulwoo. 2020. "Traditional Funeral and Burial Rituals and Ebola Outbreaks in West Africa: A Narrative Review of Causes and Strategy Interventions Africa." *Journal of Health and Social Sciences*. https://doi.org/10.19204/2020/trdt8

Payne, Sheila A., Alison Langley-Evans, and Richards Hillier. 1996. "Perceptions of a 'good' Death: A Comparative Study of the Views of Hospice Staff and Patients." *Palliative Medicine* 10 (4): 307–312. https://doi.org/10.1177/026921639601000406

Paynter, Martha Jane, Emily K. Drake, Christine Cassidy, and Erna Snelgrove-Clarke. 2019. "Maternal Health Outcomes for Incarcerated Women: A Scoping Review." *Journal of Clinical Nursing* 28 (11–12): 2046–2060. https://doi.org/10.1111/JOCN.14837

Pearce, Caroline. 2019. *The Public and Private Management of Grief. The Public and Private Management of Grief.* Springer International Publishing. https://doi.org/10.1007/978-3-030-17662-4

Pearce, Caroline, and Carol Komaromy. 2022. "Recovering the Body in Grief: Physical Absence and Embodied Presence." *Health (United Kingdom)* 26 (4): 393–410. https://doi.org/10.1177/1363459320931914

Pedersen, Grete Skøtt, Anders Grøntved, Laust Hvas Mortensen, Anne Marie Nybo Andersen, and Janet Rich-Edwards. 2014. "Maternal Mortality among Migrants in Western Europe: A Meta-Analysis." *Maternal and Child Health Journal* 18 (7): 1628–1638. https://doi.org/10.1007/S10995-013-1403-X/FIGURES/5

Penal Reform International. 2022. "Deaths in Prison Examining Causes, Responses, and Prevention of Deaths in Prison Worldwide." www.nottingham.ac.uk

Perkins, Henry S. 2007. "Controlling Death: The False Promise of Advance Directives." *Annals of Internal Medicine* 147 (1): 51–57. https://doi.org/10.7326/0003-4819-147-1-200707030-00008

Pernick, Martin S. 1999. "Brain Death in a Cultural Context: The Reconstruction of Death." In *The Definition of Death*, edited by Stuart R. Youngner, Robert M. Arnold, and Renie Schapiro, 3–33. Baltimore: The John Hopkins University Press.

Peskin, Harvey. 2019. "Who Has the Right to Mourn?: Relational Deference and the Ranking of Grief." *Psychoanalytic Dialogues* 29 (4): 477–492. https://doi.org/10.1080/10481885.2019.1632655

Petersen, Emily E., Nicole L. Davis, David Goodman, Shanna Cox, Carla Syverson, Kristi Seed, Carrie Shapiro-Mendoza, William M. Callaghan, and Wanda Barfield. 2019. "Racial/Ethnic Disparities in Pregnancy-Related Deaths — United States, 2007–2016." *Morbidity and Mortality Weekly Report* 68 (35): 762. https://doi.org/10.15585/MMWR. MM6835A3

Petju, M., A. Suteerayongprasert, R. Thongpud, and K. Hassiri. 2007. "Importance of Dental Records for Victim Identification Following the Indian Ocean Tsunami Disaster in Thailand." *Public Health* 121 (4): 251–257. https://doi.org/10.1016/J.PUHE.2006.12.003

Pilar, Meagan R., Amy A. Eyler, Sarah Moreland-Russell, and Ross C. Brownson. 2020. "Actual Causes of Death in Relation to Media, Policy, and Funding Attention: Examining Public Health Priorities." *Frontiers in Public Health* 8 (July): 545333. https://doi.org/10.3389/FPUBH.2020.00279/BIBTEX

Pillay, Suntosh Rathanam. 2022. "Where Do Black Lives Matter? Coloniality, Police Violence, and Epistemic Injustices During the COVID-19 Pandemic in South Africa and the U.S." *Psychology of Violence* 12 (4): 293–303. https://doi.org/10.1037/VIO0000419

Pitsillides, Stacey, Claire Nally, Anita Luby, Rhonda, Brooks, Fiona Hill, Joanne, Ghee, Katherine, Ingram, and Judith Robinson. 2023. "The Death Positive Library." In *The Routledge Handbook of Museums, Heritage, and Death*, edited by Trish Biers and Katie Stringer Clary, 389–401. London: Routledge.

Pollock, Nathaniel J., Kiyuri Naicker, Alex Loro, Shree Mulay, and Ian Colman. 2018. "Global Incidence of Suicide among Indigenous Peoples: A Systematic Review." *BMC Medicine* 16 (1): 1–17. https://doi.org/10.1186/S12916-018-1115-6/FIGURES/2

PPO. 2023. "Learning Lessons Bulletin – Post-Release Death Investigations Issue 17." www.ppo.gov.uk/document/learning-lessons-reports/

Prozorov, Sergei. 2013. "Powers of Life and Death: Biopolitics beyond Foucault." *Alternatives* 38 (3): 191–193. https://doi.org/10.1177/0304375413497841

———. 2022. "When Did Biopolitics Begin? Actuality and Potentiality in Historical Events." *European Journal of Social Theory* 25 (4): 539–558. https://doi.org/10.1177/13684310221077198

Quah, Elaine Li Ying, Keith Zi Yuan Chua, Jun Kiat Lua, Darius Wei Jun Wan, Chi Sum Chong, Yun Xue Lim, and Lalit Krishna. 2023. "A Systematic Review of Stakeholder Perspectives of Dignity and Assisted Dying." *Journal of Pain and Symptom Management* 65 (2): e123–136. https://doi.org/10.1016/J.JPAINSYMMAN.2022.10.004

Quinan, Christine, and Kathrin Thiele. 2020. "Biopolitics, Necropolitics, Cosmopolitics–Feminist and Queer Interventions: An Introduction." *Journal of Gender Studies*. Routledge. https://doi.org/10.1080/09589236.2020.1693173

Rabinow, Paul, and Nikolas Rose. 2006. "Biopower Today." *BioSocieties* 1 (2): 195–217. https://doi.org/10.1017/S1745855206040014/METRICS

Radbruch, Lukas, Liliana De Lima, Felicia Knaul, Roberto Wenk, Zipporah Ali, Sushma Bhatnaghar, Charmaine Blanchard, et al. 2020a. "Redefining Palliative Care—A New Consensus-Based Definition." *Journal of Pain and Symptom Management* 60 (4): 754. https://doi.org/10.1016/J.JPAINSYMMAN.2020.04.027

———. 2020b. "Redefining Palliative Care—A New Consensus-Based Definition." *Journal of Pain and Symptom Management* 60 (4): 754–764. https://doi.org/10.1016/J.JPAINSYMMAN.2020.04.027.

"Radiolab Presents: Border Trilogy." 2018. https://radiolab.org/series/border-trilogy.

Rao, Seema Rajesh, Naveen Salins, Udita Joshi, Jatin Patel, Bader Nael Remawi, Srinagesh Simha, Nancy Preston, and Catherine Walshe. 2022. "Palliative and End-of-Life Care in Intensive Care Units in Low- and Middle-Income Countries: A Systematically Constructed Scoping Review." *Journal of Critical Care* 71 (October): 154115. https://doi.org/10.1016/J.JCRC.2022.154115.

Ratcliffe, Matthew. 2022. *Grief Worlds: A Study of Emotional Experience*.

Rau, Roland, Christina Bohk-Ewald, Magdalena M. Muszyńska, and James W. Vaupel. 2018. "Visualizing Mortality Dynamics in the Lexis Diagram." *Springer Series on Demographic Methods and Population Analysis* 44: 1–169. https://doi.org/10.1007/978-3-319-64820-0_1

Rawlings, Deb, Caroline Litster, Lauren Miller-Lewis, Jennifer Tieman, and Kate Swetenham. 2021. "End-of-Life Doulas: A Qualitative Analysis of Interviews with Australian and International Death Doulas on Their Role." *Health & Social Care in the Community* 29 (2): 574–587. https://doi.org/10.1111/HSC.13120

Rawlings, Deb, Jennifer Tieman, Lauren Miller-Lewis, and Kate Swetenham. 2019. "What Role Do Death Doulas Play in End-of-Life Care? A Systematic Review." *Health & Social Care in the Community* 27 (3): e82–94. https://doi.org/10.1111/HSC.12660

Recuber, Timothy. 2023. *The Digital Departed*. New York: New York University Press. https://doi.org/10.18574/NYU/9781479814985.001.000.

Reuters. 2023. "Dutch to Widen 'right-to-Die' to Include Terminally Ill Children." April 14, 2023. www.reuters.com/world/europe/dutch-widen-right-to-die-include-terminally-ill-children-2023-04-14/

Richards, Naomi. 2016. "Euthanasia and Policy — Choosing When to Die." In *Death and Social Policy in Challenging Times*, edited by Liam Foster and Kate Woodthorpe, 53–70. London: Palgrave Macmillan. https://doi.org/10.1057/9781137484901_4

———. 2017. "Assisted Suicide as a Remedy for Suffering? The End-of-Life Preferences of British 'Suicide Tourists.'" *Medical Anthropology: Cross Cultural Studies in Health and Illness* 36 (4): 348–362. https://doi.org/10.1080/01459740.2016.1255610

———. 2022. "The Equity Turn in Palliative and End of Life Care Research: Lessons from the Poverty Literature." *Sociology Compass* 16 (5): e12969. https://doi.org/10.1111/SOC4.12969

Richards, N., G.H. Koksvik, S.M. Gerson, and D. Clark. 2020. "The Global Spread of Death Café: A Cultural Intervention Relevant to Policy?" *Social Policy and Society* 19(4):553–572. doi:10.1017/S1474746420000081

Richards, Naomi, and Marian Krawczyk. 2021. "What Is the Cultural Value of Dying in an Era of Assisted Dying?" *Medical Humanities* 47 (1): 61–67. https://doi.org/10.1136/medhum-2018-011621

Ridge, Damien, Hannah Smith, Alison Fixsen, Alex Broom, and John Oliffe. 2021. "How Men Step Back – and Recover – from Suicide Attempts: A Relational and Gendered Account." *Sociology of Health and Illness* 43 (1): 238–252. https://doi.org/10.1111/1467-9566.13216

Riley, Jennifer, Vikki Entwistle, Arnar Arnason, Louise Locock, Paolo Maccagno, Abi Pattenden, and Rebecca Crozier. 2023. "Hybrid Funerals: How Online Attendance Facilitates and Impedes Participation." *Mortality*, April. https://doi.org/10.1080/13576275.2023.2201421

Riley Snorton, C., and Jin Haritaworn. 2022. *Trans Necropolitics: A Transnational Reflection on Violence, Death, and the Trans of Color Afterlife. The Transgender Studies Reader Remix*. London: Routledge. https://doi.org/10.4324/9781003206255-33/TRANS-NECROPOLITICS-RILEY-SNORTON-JIN-HARITAWORN

Risat, Ilias Karmal. 2024. "Understanding the Notions of 'Good Death' in Bangladesh: A Critical Exploration." University of Brighton and University of Sussex.

Roberts, Alice. 2022. *Ancestors: A Prehistory of Britain in Seven Burials*. London: Simon & Schuster.

Robinson, Georgina M. 2021. "Dying to Go Green: The Introduction of Resomation in the United Kingdom." *Religions* 12 (2): 1–21. https://doi.org/10.3390/rel12020097

Robson, Patricia, and Tony Walter. 2013. "Hierarchies of Loss: A Critique of Disenfranchised Grief." *OMEGA-Journal of Death and Dying* 66 (2): 97–119. https://doi.org/10.2190/OM.66.2.A

Rosa, Gabriel Santana da, Gustavo Santos Andrades, Arthur Caye, Maria Paz Hidalgo, Melissa Alves Braga de Oliveira, and Luísa K. Pilz. 2019. "Thirteen Reasons Why: The Impact of Suicide Portrayal on Adolescents' Mental Health." *Journal of Psychiatric Research* 108 (January): 2–6. https://doi.org/10.1016/J.JPSYCHIRES.2018.10.018

Rosbrow, Thomas. 2019. "On Grief, Guilt, Shame, and Nostalgia. Discussion of 'Who Has the Right to Mourn?: Relational Deference and the Ranking of Grief.'" *Psychoanalytic Dialogues* 29 (4): 501–506. https://doi.org/10.1080/10481885.2019.1632656

Rosen, Dennis. 2012. "Helping Certain Patients End Their Lives." *CMAJ: Canadian Medical Association Journal* 184 (18): E983. https://doi.org/10.1503/CMAJ.120089

Rosenwax, Lorna K., and Beverley A. McNamara. 2006. "Who Receives Specialist Palliative Care in Western Australia--and Who Misses Out." *Palliative Medicine* 20 (4): 439–445. https://doi.org/10.1191/0269216306PM1146OA

Rotar, Marius. 2018. "The Romanian Orthodox Church and Issues of Cremation." In *The Routledge Handbook of Death and the Afterlife*, edited by Candi Cann, 60–72. New York and London: Routledge.

Routen, Ash, Natalie Darko, Andrew Willis, Joanne Miksza, and Kamlesh Khunti. 2021. "'It's so Tough for Us Now' – COVID-19 Has Negatively Impacted Religious Practices Relating to Death among Minority Ethnic Groups." *Public Health* 194 (May): 146–148. https://doi.org/10.1016/J.PUHE.2021.03.007

Rugg, Julie. 2000. "Defining the Place of Burial: What Makes a Cemetery a Cemetery?" *Mortality* 5 (3): 259–275.

Rukmini, S. 2021. "Deaths By 'Unknown Causes' On National Health Mission Portal 2X Official Covid Toll." IndiaSpend. 2021. www.indiaspend.com/covid-19/deaths-unkn own-causes-national-health-mission-portal-covid-toll-760219

Rumble, Hannah, John Troyer, Tony Walter, and Kate Woodthorpe. 2014. "Disposal or Dispersal? Environmentalism and Final Treatment of the British Dead." *Mortality* 19 (3): 243–260. https://doi.org/10.1080/13576275.2014.920315

Ryan, Suzanne, Joanne Wong, Ronald Chow, and Camilla Zimmermann. 2020. "Evolving Definitions of Palliative Care: Upstream Migration or Confusion?" *Current Treatment Options in Oncology* 21 (3): 1–17. https://doi.org/10.1007/S11864-020-0716-4/TABLES/3

Sallnow, Libby, Richard Smith, Sam H. Ahmedzai, Afsan Bhadelia, Charlotte Chamberlain, Yali Cong, Brett Doble, et al. 2022. "Report of the Lancet Commission on the Value of Death: Bringing Death Back into Life." *The Lancet*. 399 (10327): 837–84. https://doi.org/10.1016/S0140-6736(21)02314-X

Sarbey, Ben. 2016. "Definitions of Death: Brain Death and What Matters in a Person." *Journal of Law and the Biosciences* 3 (3): 743–752. https://doi.org/10.1093/JLB/LSW054

Saunders, Cicely. 1961. "A Patient." *Nursing Times* 57 (March): 394–397. https://doi.org/10.1093/acprof:oso/9780198570530.003.0006

———. 1967. *The Management of Terminal Illness*. London: Hospital Medicine Publications Ltd.

———. 1996. "Hospice." *Mortality* 1 (3): 317–321. https://doi.org/10.1080/1357627960 9696251

Savitz, David A., Charles Poole, and William C. Miller. 1999. "Reassessing the Role of Epidemiology in Public Health." *American Journal of Public Health* 89 (8): 1158–1161. https://doi.org/10.2105/AJPH.89.8.1158

Sawyer, Jeremy, and Anup Gampa. 2018. "Implicit and Explicit Racial Attitudes Changed During Black Lives Matter." *Personality and Social Psychology Bulletin* 44 (7): 1039–1059. https://doi.org/10.1177/0146167218757454/ASSET/IMAGES/LARGE/10.1177_0146167218757454-FIG3.JPEG

Scanlon, Joseph. 2008. "Identifying the Tsunami Dead in Thailand and Sri Lanka: Multi-National Emergent Organizations." *International Journal of Mass Emergencies & Disasters* 26 (1): 1–18. https://doi.org/10.1177/028072700802600101

Scheideler, Jennifer K., Jennifer M. Taber, Rebecca A. Ferrer, Emily G. Grenen, and William M.P. Klein. 2017. "Heart Disease versus Cancer: Understanding Perceptions of Population Prevalence and Personal Risk." *Journal of Behavioral Medicine* 40 (5): 839–845. https://doi.org/10.1007/S10865-017-9860-0/METRICS

Schüttengruber, Gerhilde, Franziska Großschädl, and Christa Lohrmann. 2022. "A Consensus Definition of End of Life from an International and Interdisciplinary Perspective: A Delphi Panel Study." *Https://Home.Liebertpub.Com/Jpm* 25 (11): 1677–1685. https://doi.org/10.1089/JPM.2022.0030

Seale, Clive. 1998. *Constructing Death: The Sociology of Dying and Bereavement.* Cambridge: Cambridge University Press.

———. 2004. "Media Constructions of Dying Alone: A Form of 'Bad Death.'" *Social Science & Medicine* 58 (5): 967–974. https://doi.org/10.1016/j.socscimed.2003.10.038

Selman, Lucy E., Ryann Sowden, and Erica Borgstrom. 2021. "'Saying Goodbye' during the COVID-19 Pandemic: A Document Analysis of Online Newspapers with Implications for End of Life Care." *Palliative Medicine* 35 (7): 1277–1287. https://doi.org/10.1177/02692163211017023

Seuc, Armando H., Lisbeth Fernández, Mayelin Mirabal, Armando Rodríguez, and Carlos A. Rodríguez. 2018. "Cuban Application of Two Methods for Analyzing Multiple Causes of Death." *MEDICC Review* 20 (3): 30–35.

Seymour, Jane Elizabeth. 1999. "Revisiting Medicalisation and 'Natural' Death." *Social Science and Medicine* 49 (5): 691–704. https://doi.org/10.1016/S0277-9536(99)00170-7

———. 2000. "Negotiating Natural Death in Intensive Care." *Social Science and Medicine* 51 (8): 1241–1252. https://doi.org/10.1016/S0277-9536(00)00042-3

Seymour, Jane E. 2012. "Looking Back, Looking Forward: The Evolution of Palliative and End-of-Life Care in England." *Mortality* 17 (1): 1–17. https://doi.org/10.1080/13576 275.2012.651843.

Sheehan, Mark, and Martyn Davison. 2017. "'We Need to Remember They Died for Us': How Young People in New Zealand Make Meaning of War Remembrance and Commemoration of the First World War." *London Review of Education* 15 (2): 259–271. https://doi.org/10.18546/LRE.15.2.09

Sikka, Tina. 2021. "Barriers to Access: A Feminist Analysis of Medically Assisted Dying and the Experience of Marginalized Groups." *Omega (United States)* 84 (1): 4–27. https://doi.org/10.1177/0030222819873770

Singer, Jonathan, Courtney Daum, Megan J. Shen, Gabrielle Zecha, Louise Kaplan, Kathy Plakovic, Meagan Blazey, et al. 2022. "Assessment of Oncology Advanced Practice

Professional Willingness to Participate in Medical Aid in Dying." *JAMA Network Open* 5 (10): E2239068. https://doi.org/10.1001/JAMANETWORKOPEN.2022.39068

Singh, Om P. 2022. "Startling Suicide Statistics in India: Time for Urgent Action." *Indian Journal of Psychiatry* 64 (5). https://journals.lww.com/indianjpsychiatry/fulltext/2022/64100/startling_suicide_statistics_in_india__time_for.1.aspx

Sjoblom, Erynne, Winta Ghidei, Marya Leslie, Ashton James, Reagan Bartel, Sandra Campbell, and Stephanie Montesanti. 2022. "Centering Indigenous Knowledge in Suicide Prevention: A Critical Scoping Review." *BMC Public Health* 22 (1): 1–17. https://doi.org/10.1186/S12889-022-14580-0/TABLES/1

Skakum Jorgensen, Danika Vilene. 2018. "Death Positivity and Death Justice in the Anthropocene." University of Alberta.

"Smoking Facts and Figures – HSE.Ie." n.d. Accessed January 27, 2024. www2.hse.ie/living-well/quit-smoking/reasons-to-quit/facts-and-figures/

Souza, João Paulo, Louise Tina Day, Ana Clara Rezende-Gomes, Jun Zhang, Rintaro Mori, Adama Baguiya, Kapila Jayaratne, et al. 2023. "A Global Analysis of the Determinants of Maternal Health and Transitions in Maternal Mortality." *The Lancet Global Health*, December. https://doi.org/10.1016/s2214-109x(23)00468-0

Sowden, Ryann, Erica Borgstrom, and Lucy E. Selman. 2021. "'It's like Being in a War with an Invisible Enemy': A Document Analysis of Bereavement Due to COVID-19 in UK Newspapers." *PLOS ONE* 16 (3 March). https://doi.org/10.1371/journal.pone.0247904

St Christopher's Hospice. 2024. "About – St Christopher's Hospice." 2024. www.stchristophers.org.uk/about/

Stajduhar, K.I., A. Mollison, M. Giesbrecht, R. McNeil, B. Pauly, S. Reimer-Kirkham, N. Dosani, et al. 2019. "'Just Too Busy Living in the Moment and Surviving': Barriers to Accessing Health Care for Structurally Vulnerable Populations at End-of-Life 16 Studies in Human Society 1608 Sociology." *BMC Palliative Care* 18 (1): 1–14. https://doi.org/10.1186/S12904-019-0396-7/TABLES/3

Stanley, Daina. 2021. "Touching Life, Death, and Dis/Connection in a State Prison Infirmary." In *Sensory Penalities: Exploring the Senses in Spaces of Punishment and Social Control*, 53–68. Leeds: Emerald. https://doi.org/10.1108/978-1-83909-726-320210005/FULL/XML

Stanley, Eric A. 2021. *Atmospheres of Violence: Structuring Antagonism and the Trans/Queer Ungovernable*. Durham, NC: Duke University Press.

Statista. 2019. "United States – Fear of Death in 2019 | Statista." 2019. www.statista.com/statistics/959347/fear-of-death-in-the-us/

Steijn, Danny van, Juan José Pons Izquierdo, Eduardo Garralda Domezain, Miguel Antonio Sánchez-cárdenas, and Carlos Centeno Cortés. 2021. "Population's Potential Accessibility to Specialized Palliative Care Services: A Comparative Study in Three European Countries." *International Journal of Environmental Research and Public Health* 18 (19). https://doi.org/10.3390/IJERPH181910345

Stevens, Hannah R, Yoo Jung Oh, and Laramie D Taylor. 2021. "Desensitization to Fear-Inducing COVID-19 Health News on Twitter: Observational Study." *JMIR Infodemiology* 1 (1): e26876. https://doi.org/10.2196/26876

Storeng, Katerini T., and Dominique P. Béhague. 2014. "'Playing the Numbers Game': Evidence-Based Advocacy and the Technocratic Narrowing of the Safe Motherhood Initiative." *Medical Anthropology Quarterly* 28 (2): 260–279. https://doi.org/10.1111/MAQ.12072

———. 2017. "'Guilty until Proven Innocent': The Contested Use of Maternal Mortality Indicators in Global Health." *Critical Public Health* 27 (2): 163–176. https://doi.org/10.1080/09581596.2016.1259459

Stroebe, Margaret, and Henk Schut. 1999. "The Dual Process Model of Coping with Bereavement: Rationale and Description." *Death Studies* 23 (3): 197–224. https://doi.org/10.1080/074811899201046

Stroud, Ellen. 2018. "Law and the Dead Body: Is a Corpse a Person or a Thing?" *Annual Review of Law and Social Science* 14: 115–125. https://doi.org/10.1146/annurev-lawsocsci

Sufrin, Carolyn. 2017. *Jailcare: Finding the Safety Net for Women Behind Bars By*. Oakland: University of California Press. https://doi.org/10.1353/anq.2018.0059

Sumba, Eric Otieno. 2021. "Necropolitics at Large: Pandemic Politics and the Coloniality of the Global Access Gap." *Critical Studies on Security* 9 (1): 48–52. https://doi.org/10.1080/21624887.2021.1904354

Sunlife Direct. 2024. "Funeral Costs – Cost Of Dying Report 2024 | SunLife | SunLife." 2024. www.sunlife.co.uk/funeral-costs/

Szasz, Thomas. 1970. *The Manufacture of Madness: A Comparative Study of the Inquisition and the Mental Health Movement. The Manufacture of Madness: A Comparative Study of the Inquisition and the Mental Health Movement*. Oxford, England: Harper & Row.

———. 2007. *Coercion as Cure: A Critical History of Psychiatry. Coercion as Cure: A Critical History of Psychiatry*. Piscataway: Transaction Publishers.

Taylor, Bev. 1993. "Hospice Nurses Tell Their Stories about a Good Death: The Value of Storytelling as a Qualitative Health Research Method." *Annual Review of Health Social Science* 3 (1): 97–108. https://doi.org/10.5172/HESR.1993.3.1.97

Tenzek, Kelly E., and Rachel Depner. 2017. "Still Searching: A Meta-Synthesis of a Good Death from the Bereaved Family Member Perspective." *Behavioral Sciences* 7 (2): 25. https://doi.org/10.3390/BS7020025

The Economist. 2018. "Proper Palliative Care Makes Assisted Dying Unnecessary." August 24, 2018. www.economist.com/open-future/2018/08/24/proper-palliative-care-makes-assisted-dying-unnecessary

The Order of the Good Death. 2018. "What Death Positive Is NOT | The Order of the Good Death." January 25, 2018. www.orderofthegooddeath.com/article/what death positive-is-not/

———. n.d.-a. "Death Positive Movement ." Accessed January 27, 2024. www.orderofthegooddeath.com/death-positive-movement/

———. n.d.-b. "Our Story ." Accessed January 27, 2024. www.orderofthegooddeath.com/our-story/

Thomas, Brennan. 2024. "'To Show the Problem Inside Out': Representations of Mental Illness and Suicide in Eric Steel's *The Bridge*." In *Difficult Death, Dying and the Dead in Media and Culture,* edited by S. Coleclough, B. Michael-Fox, and R. Visser, 23–37. London: Palgrave Macmillan.

Thomas, Keri, Ben Lobo, and Karen Detering. 2018. *Advance Care Planning in End of Life Care*. Oxford: Oxford University of Press.

Thompson, Neil, and Gerry R. Cox. 2017. *Handbook of the Sociology of Death, Grief, and Bereavement*. Edited by Neil Thompson and Gerry R. Cox. 1 Edition. | New York: Routledge. https://doi.org/10.4324/9781315453859

Thornton, Katherine, and Christine B. Phillips. 2009. "Performing the Good Death: The Medieval Ars Moriendi and Contemporary Doctors." *Medical Humanities* 19 (41). https://doi.org/10.1136/jmh.2009.001693

Tidball-Binz, Morris. 2007. "Managing the Dead in Catastrophes: Guiding Principles and Practical Recommendations for First Responders." *International Review of the Red Cross* 89 (866): 421–442. https://doi.org/10.1017/S1816383107001130

Timmermans, Stefan. 2013. "Seven Warrants for Qualitative Health Sociology." *Social Science and Medicine* 77 (1): 1–8. https://doi.org/10.1016/j.socscimed.2012.10.004

Tobin, Joseph Jay, and Joan Friedman. 1983. "Spirits, Shamans, and Nightmare Death: Survivor Stress in a Hmong Refugee." *American Journal of Orthopsychiatry* 53 (3): 439–448. https://doi.org/10.1111/J.1939-0025.1983.TB03388.X

Tobin, Jake, Alice Rogers, Isaac Winterburn, Sebastian Tullie, Asanish Kalyanasundaram, Isla Kuhn, and Stephen Barclay. 2022. "Hospice Care Access Inequalities: A Systematic Review and Narrative Synthesis." *BMJ Supportive & Palliative Care* 12: 142–151. https://doi.org/10.1136/bmjspcare-2020-002719

Tomczak, Philippa, and Róisín Mulgrew. 2023. "Making Prisoner Deaths Visible: Towards a New Epistemological Approach." *Incarceration* 4 (January): 1–21. https://doi.org/10.1177/26326663231160344

Tonkin, Lois. 1996. "Growing around Grief—Another Way of Looking at Grief and Recovery." *Bereavement Care* 15 (1): 10. https://doi.org/10.1080/02682629608657376

Treharne, Gareth J., Damien W. Riggs, Sonja J. Ellis, Jayde A.M. Flett, and Clare Bartholomaeus. 2020. "Suicidality, Self-Harm, and Their Correlates among Transgender and Cisgender People Living in Aotearoa/New Zealand or Australia." *International Journal of Transgender Health* 21 (4): 440–454. https://doi.org/10.1080/26895269.2020.1795959

Troyer, John. 2020. *Technologies of the Human Corpse*. Cambridge: MIT Press. https://mitpress.mit.edu/9780262542319/technologies-of-the-human-corpse/

Tulchinsky, Theodore H. 2018. "John Snow, Cholera, the Broad Street Pump; Waterborne Diseases Then and Now." *Case Studies in Public Health*, 77. https://doi.org/10.1016/B978-0-12-804571-8.00017-2

Turner, Mary, Sheila Payne, and Zephyrine Barbarachild. 2011. "Care or Custody? An Evaluation of Palliative Care in Prisons in North West England." *Palliative Medicine* 25 (4): 370–377. https://doi.org/10.1177/0269216310393058

Turner, Mary, and Marian Peacock. 2017. "Palliative Care in UK Prisons: Practical and Emotional Challenges for Staff and Fellow Prisoners." *Journal of Correctional Health Care* 23 (1): 56–65. https://doi.org/10.1177/1078345816684847

Turner, Mary, Marian Peacock, Sheila Payne, Andrew Fletcher, and Katherine Froggatt. 2018. "Ageing and Dying in the Contemporary Neoliberal Prison System: Exploring the 'Double Burden' for Older Prisoners." *Social Science and Medicine* 212 (December 2017): 161–167. https://doi.org/10.1016/j.socscimed.2018.07.009

Tyrer, Peter. 2014. "A Comparison of DSM and ICD Classifications of Mental Disorder." *Advances in Psychiatric Treatment* 20 (4): 280–285. https://doi.org/10.1192/APT.BP.113.011296.

Tyrrell, Patrick, Seneca Harberger, Caroline Schoo, and Waquar Siddiqui. 2023. "Kubler-Ross Stages of Dying and Subsequent Models of Grief." *A Physician's Guide to Coping with Death and Dying*, February, 14–38. https://doi.org/10.1515/9780773572102-004

Ughetti, Anthony C. 2019. "A Contemporary Ars Moriendi for End-of-Life Care." *Ethics & Medics* 44 (3): 1–2. https://doi.org/10.5840/EM20194433

UK Statistics Authority. 2018. "Code of Practice for Statistics: Ensuring Official Statistics Serve the Public." London. www.statisticsauthority.gov.uk/osr/

United Nations Statistics Division. n.d. "UNSD — Partners." Accessed March 26, 2024. https://unstats.un.org/home/nso_sites/

Valls, Rosa, Carmen Elboj, Olga Serradell, Javier Díez-Palomar, Emilia Aiello, Sandra Racionero, Ana Vidu, Esther Roca, Mar Joanpere, and Ane López De Aguileta. 2022. "Promoting Admiration of Foucault Hiding His Defense of Rape and Pederasty." *International and Multidisciplinary Journal of Social Sciences* 11 (1): 1–26. https://doi.org/10.17583/RIMCIS.9560

Vaswani, Nina. 2018. "Beyond Loss of Liberty: How Loss, Bereavement and Grief Can Affect Young Men's Prison Journeys." In *Loss, Dying and Bereavement in the Criminal Justice System*, edited by Sue Read, Sotirios Sanatatzoglou, and Anthony Wrigley, 177–188. London: Routledge.

Velasquez-Potts, Michelle C. 2023. "Between Past and Future: The Slow Death of Indefinite Detention." *Catalyst: Feminism, Theory, Technoscience* 9 (1). https://doi.org/10.28968/cftt.v9i1.38477

Vernon E. Jordan Law Library. n.d. "A Brief History of Civil Rights in the United States." Accessed January 27, 2024. https://library.law.howard.edu/civilrightshistory/BLM

Vincent, Ben, Evelyn Callahan, Erica Borgstrom, Holti, and Richard. 2022. "Healthcare Professionals' Experiences of Pandemics: A Rapid Review of Qualitative Research." Milton Keynes.

Visser, R.C. 2017. "'Doing Death': Reflecting on the Researcher's Subjectivity and Emotions." *Death Studies* 41 (1): 6–13. https://doi.org/10.1080/07481187.2016.1257877

Visser, Renske C. 2018. *Unpacking Home: Ageing and Dying in the Southwest of England.* University of Bath.

Visser, Renske C. 2021. "Dying in the Margins: A Literature Review on End of Life in English Prisons." *Religions* 12 (6): 413. https://doi.org/10.3390/REL12060413

Vocabulary.com. n.d. "Hospice." Accessed January 28, 2024. www.vocabulary.com/dictionary/hospice

Walshe, Catherine, Chris Todd, Ann Caress, and Carolyn Chew-Graham. 2009. "Patterns of Access to Community Palliative Care Services: A Literature Review." *Journal of Pain and Symptom Management* 37 (5): 884–912. https://doi.org/10.1016/J.JPAINSYMMAN.2008.05.004

Walter, Tony. 1996. "A New Model of Grief: Bereavement and Biography." *Mortality* 1 (1): 7–25. https://doi.org/10.1080/713685822

———. 2020. *Death in the Modern World.* Sage.

Walter, T. 2022. "'Heading for Extinction': How the Climate and Ecological Emergency Reframes Mortality." *Mortality* 28(4): 661–679. https://doi.org/10.1080/13576275.2022.2072718

Walters, Geoffrey. 2004. "Is There Such a Thing as a Good Death?" *Palliative Medicine* 18 (5): 404–408. https://doi.org/10.1191/0269216304PM908OA

Webb, Michelle, Susan Lysaght Hurley, Jennifer Gentry, Melanie Brown, and Cynthia Ayoub. 2021. "Best Practices for Using Telehealth in Hospice and Palliative Care." *Journal of Hospice and Palliative Nursing* 23 (3): 277–285. https://doi.org/10.1097/NJH.0000000000000753

Weeramanthri, Tarun, and Clifford Plummer. 1994. "Land, Body and Spirit—Talking about Adult Mortality in an Aboriginal Community." *Australian Journal of Public Health* 18 (2): 197–200. https://doi.org/10.1111/J.1753-6405.1994.TB00225.X

Wendland, Claire. 2018. "Who Counts? What Counts? Place and the Limits of Perinatal Mortality Measures." *AMA Journal of Ethics* 20: 278–287. www.amajournalofethics.org

Westendorp, M. and H. Gould. 2021. "Re-Feminizing Death: Gender, Spirituality and Death Care in the Anthropocene." *Religions* 12: 667. https://doi.org/10.3390/rel12080667

Weston, Janet. 2021. "Aids: History Of The Epidemic That Changed Britain." History Extra. 2021. www.historyextra.com/period/20th-century/aids-hiv-epidemic-changed-britain-how/

White, Jennifer. 2012. "Youth Suicide as a 'Wild' Problem: Implications for Prevention Practice." *Suicidology Online* 3: 42–50.

———. 2017. "What Can Critical Suicidology Do?" *Death Studies* 41 (8): 472–480. https://doi.org/10.1080/07481187.2017.1332901

WHO. 2008. "Closing the Gap in a Generation Health Equity through Action on the Social Determinants of Health Commission on Social Determinants of Health."

———. 2015a. "Sierra Leone: A Traditional Healer and a Funeral." www.who.int/news/item/01-09-2015-sierra-leone-a-traditional-healer-and-a-funeral#:~:text=Mourn ers%20came%20by%20the%20hundreds,many%20as%20365%20Ebola%20deaths

———. 2015b. "Sierra Leone: A Traditional Healer and a Funeral - More Than 300 Ebola Cases Link Back to One Funeral." World Health Organization [updated 2015 Sept 01; cited 2020 Jan 06]. www.who.int/csr/disease/ebola/ebola-6-months/sierra-leone/en/ (2015).

———. 2019. *Global Health Estimates: Leading Causes of Death - Cause-specific mortality, 2000–2019* . www.who.int/data/gho/data/themes/mortality-and-global-health-estimates/ghe-leading-causes-of-death.

———. 2020. "WHO Methods and Data Sources for Country-Level Causes of Death 2000–2019." www.who.int/gho/mortality_burden_disease/en/index.html

———. 2021. "Suicide Worldwide in 2019 Global Health Estimates."

———. 2023a. "Left behind in Pain Extent and Causes of Global Variations in Access to Morphine for Medical Use and Actions to Improve Safe Access."

———. 2023b. "Suicide." 2023. www.who.int/news-room/fact-sheets/detail/suicide

Wiebe, Ellen, Jessica Shaw, Stefanie Green, Konia Trouton, and Michaela Kelly. 2018. "Reasons for Requesting Medical Assistance in Dying." *Canadian Family Physician* 64 (9): 674–679.

Wijngaarden, Els van, Carlo Leget, and Anne Goossensen. 2015. "Ready to Give up on Life: The Lived Experience of Elderly People Who Feel Life Is Completed and No Longer Worth Living." *Social Science and Medicine* 138: 257–264. https://doi.org/10.1016/j.socscimed.2015.05.015

Wijngaarden, Els Van, Carlo Leget, and Anne Goossensen. 2016. "Caught between Intending and Doing: Older People Ideating on a Self-Chosen Death." *BMJ Open* 6 (1): 1–11. https://doi.org/10.1136/bmjopen-2015-009895

Wilde, Anna. n.d. "Researching the Death Positive Movement ." Accessed January 27, 2024. www.deathpositiveresearch.com/

Wilson, Brenda K., Alexis Burnstan, Cristina Calderon, and Thomas J. Csordas. 2023. "'Letting Die' by Design: Asylum Seekers' Lived Experience of Postcolonial Necropolitics." *Social Science & Medicine* 320 (March): 115714. https://doi.org/10.1016/J.SOCSCIMED.2023.115714

Worden, J William. 1996. "Tasks and Mediators of Mourning: A Guideline for the Mental Health Practitioner." *Session: Psychotherapy in Practice* 2 (4): 73–80. https://doi.org/https://doi.org/10.1002/(SICI)1520-6572(199624)2:4<73::AID-SESS7>3.0.CO;2-9

Wrigley, Anthony. 2015. "Ethics and End of Life Care: The Liverpool Care Pathway and the Neuberger Review." *Journal of Medical Ethics* 41 (8): 639–643. https://doi.org/10.1136/MEDETHICS-2013-101780

Xiao, Jingjie, Carleen Brenneis, Nadine Ibrahim, Alyssa Bryan, and Konrad Fassbender. 2021. "Definitions of Palliative Care Terms: A Consensus-Oriented Decision-Making Process." 24 (9): 1342–1350. https://doi.org/10.1089/JPM.2020.0679

Yamin, Alicia Ely, Vanessa M. Boulanger, Kathryn L. Falb, Jane Shuma, and Jennifer Leaning. 2013. "Costs of Inaction on Maternal Mortality: Qualitative Evidence of the Impacts of Maternal Deaths on Living Children in Tanzania." *PLOS ONE* 8 (8): 1–7. https://doi.org/10.1371/JOURNAL.PONE.0071674

York, Sheona. 2018. "The 'Hostile Environment': How Home Office Immigration Policies and Practices Create and Perpetuate Illegality." *Journal of Immigration, Asylum and Nationality Law* 32 (4). www.bloomsburyprofessionalonline.com/view/journal_immi gration/b-17467632_32-4-0000891.xml?p=emailAW1UlIK5X.51Y&d=/journal_immi gration/b-17467632_32-4-0000891.xml

Zaman, Mehreen, Sara Espinal-Arango, Ashita Mohapatra, and Alejandro R. Jadad. 2021. "What Would It Take to Die Well? A Systematic Review of Systematic Reviews on the Conditions for a Good Death." *The Lancet Healthy Longevity* 2 (9): e593–600. https://doi.org/10.1016/S2666-7568(21)00097-0

Zaman, Shahaduz, Hamilton Inbadas, Alexander Whitelaw, and David Clark. 2016. "Common or Multiple Futures for End of Life Care around the World? Ideas from the 'Waiting Room of History.'" https://doi.org/10.1016/j.socscimed.2016.11.012

Zavattaro, Staci M., Rebecca Entress, Jenna Tyler, and Abdul Akeem Sadiq. 2021. "When Deaths Are Dehumanized: Deathcare during COVID-19 as a Public Value Failure." *Administration and Society* 53 (9): 1443–1462. https://doi.org/10.1177/00953997211023 185/ASSET/IMAGES/LARGE/10.1177_00953997211023185-FIG1.JPEG

Zehfuss, Maja. 2009. "Hierarchies of Grief and the Possibility of War: Remembering UK Fatalities in Iraq." *Millennium: Journal of International Studies* 38 (2): 419–440. https://doi.org/10.1177/0305829809347540

Zengin, Aslı. 2022. "Caring for the Dead Corpse Washers, Touch, and Mourning in Contemporary Turkey." *Meridians* 21 (2): 350–370. https://doi.org/10.1215/15366936-9882086

Zer-Aviv, Mushon. 2015. "DataViz—The UnEmpathetic Art – Responsible Data." 2015. https://responsibledata.io/2015/10/19/dataviz-the-unempathetic-art/

Zibaite, Solveiga. 2020. "The Jovial Aesthetics of the Death-Positivity Movement: Notes on the Appeal of Playfulness in Activism." In *Death, Culture & Leisure: Playing Dead*, edited by Matt Coward-Gibbs, 157–172. Leeds: merald. https://doi.org/10.1108/978-1-83909-037-020201018

Zolala, Farzaneh and Ali Akbar Haghdoost, -Alavi Highway, and Associate Professor of Epidemiology. 2011. "A Gap Between Policy and Practice: A Case Study on Maternal Mortality Reports, Kerman, Iran." *International Journal of Preventive Medicine* 2 (2): 88. www.ncbi.nlm.nih.gov/pmc/articles/PMC3093778/

INDEX